THE PHILOSOPHERS' GIFT

The Philosophers' Gift

Reexamining Reciprocity

Marcel Hénaff

Translated by Jean-Louis Morhange

FORDHAM UNIVERSITY PRESS

New York 2020

This book was first published in French as *Le don des
philosophes: Repenser la réciprocité*, by Marcel Hénaff
© Éditions du Seuil, 2012.

Fordham University Press has no responsibility for the
persistence or accuracy of URLs for external or third-party
Internet websites referred to in this publication and does
not guarantee that any content on such websites is, or will
remain, accurate or appropriate.

Fordham University Press also publishes its books in a
variety of electronic formats. Some content that appears in
print may not be available in electronic books.

Visit us online at www.fordhampress.com.

Library of Congress Cataloging-in-Publication Data
available online at https://catalog.loc.gov.

Printed in the United States of America
22 21 20   5 4 3 2 1
First edition

CONTENTS

The Philosophers' Gift is a precise and in-depth critical examination of the way various French philosophers and entire traditions of thought, in France and elsewhere, have understood—and misunderstood—the concept and practice of the gift.

Marcel Hénaff was a keen reader of Marcel Mauss and Claude Lévi-Strauss, and the gift is one of the central questions in his entire work. He meant to clarify the many confusions associated with this concept, which he felt resulted mostly from a lack of awareness that the term and concept of gift actually stand for several profoundly different types of giving, one of which is the ceremonial reciprocal gift found in every traditional society.

In Continental Europe, the privileged type of giving is a different one—unilateral gracious giving—and most continental philosophers have inappropriately viewed other types of giving as primitive or morally faulty versions of that type.

English-speaking countries, on the contrary, tend to focus on trade, commodities, and the economy in general. This often leads English speakers to interpret gift exchanges as primitive or peculiar forms of trade. Contributing to that misunderstanding is the fact that the English term "gift," the literal and accepted translation of the French term *don*, is not its exact equivalent. There is such a thing as a gift shop, but there is no such thing as a *boutique de dons*. The term *don* can designate a donation or a donated good, but it cannot designate a commodity. Most often, it designates not the thing given, but the gesture or act of giving.

For Marcel Hénaff, the reciprocity implied by ceremonial gift exchange —a practice unique to humans among all living beings—is the basis and guarantor of the public recognition of the other, which was the foundation of the social bond in every human society until the advent of larger societies, writing, states, the political realm, and ultimately our Modernity.

More generally, of the three types of gifts that Marcel Hénaff analyzes, none amounts or can be equated to a commercial relationship. What matters here is never the thing given, but the giver, the receiver, the gesture by which the one gives to the other, the bond that can be established between them through the mediation of the gift, and the community that this mediation can bring into being.

Drawing on a wealth of philosophical, linguistic, and anthropological sources, Marcel Hénaff develops an original and profound theory of the relationship between the self and the other—as the individual other human being, the collective other of the community and the institution, and the impersonal other of the world.

Marcel died on June 11, 2018. His body is no longer with us, but his thought is—in the memory of those who knew him, and in his writings, which are available to all. It is an important thought, among the few that have the power to help us understand the world and ourselves. It is up to us to welcome it and make it ours, if we wish.

Jean-Louis Morhange

THE PHILOSOPHERS' GIFT

Preliminary Directions

The man who, when he gives, has any thought
of repayment, deserves to be deceived.

SENECA, *De beneficiis*

Do to Others as you would have them do to you.

Golden Rule

Ontologically, the gift is gratuitous, not motivated, and disinterested.

SARTRE, *Notebooks for an Ethics*

It is not philosophers who know men best. They see
them only through the prejudices of philosophy, and
I know of no station where one has so many.

ROUSSEAU, *Emile*

First Questions

When it comes to the gift, philosophers love to be the most generous. For them the only true gift is the unreciprocated gift. According to them, to expect that Others return a gift, to call on reciprocity, amounts to pulling back the movement of giving toward oneself, thus canceling the disinterested intent that alone gives meaning to the gesture of offering. This view, however, is not shared by all philosophers; neither does it inform all of their actions. Stated in those terms, this very demanding requirement of generosity might remain out of the reach of the very thinkers who express it.

This radical claim, however, is not pure bravado. Its primary purpose is to activate critical awareness. By denying the donor any expectation of a return, it aims to proclaim that the gift as a gesture can never be identified with a commercial transaction. This requirement thus amounts to resisting giving in to self-interested considerations and to reject the domination of an economy directed almost exclusively toward maximum profit and return on investment—in other words, everything philosophers tend to call *exchange*, without realizing that this word also carries a wealth of noneconomic meanings. In the context of discussions on the gift, exchange is assumed to be a gesture of compensation expected and performed as a reply to a generous gesture. Some believe that the exchange originates in the giver's expectation of a symbolic compensation, if only in the form of gratitude expressed by the beneficiary and sometimes inseparable from the obscure sense of a debt to be repaid. For them any form of reciprocity, even in intent, cancels the gift. Any expectation of a reply, even a non-tangible one, is suspicious; it must be so because that expectation presupposes a self-interested aim through which the movement that originated in the self returns to the self. The giver is assumed to be imprisoned within the circle of sameness. This is why on this question most philosophers adamantly support the principle of gracious generosity: They categorically reject any compensatory logic. Skeptics might say that philosophers have no reason to accept such logic since doing so might make them appear petty, whereas *on the conceptual level* their position, while incurring no costs, brings them the admiration we tend to grant to any form of intransigence viewed as resistance to mediocrity. This skeptical position is overly ironic: The greatest moral traditions have always deemed the affirmation of the highest requirements inseparable from the fact that only a few wise beings are capable of practicing them.

We can also ask—the list of the thinkers discussed is basis enough for this—whether the questions we have raised are in fact recent ones. Clearly, they are not. A few ancient writings come to mind, such as the Gospels or Seneca's *De beneficiis*, where a praise of disinterested generosity appears fundamental. Is the aim of those traditions to point to one of the fundamental features of all morality? Is its purpose to understand the nature of the bond that unites all humans? Without attempting a genealogy that would require an exacting inquiry involving philology and historical anthropology, it is worth noting that no explicit praise of gracious giving such as proposed by Seneca is found in Plato or Aristotle. Instead, the founder of the Academy expresses this rejection of self-interest mostly indirectly, through a violent condemnation of the Sophists he denounces as "merchants of knowledge." He contrasts them with Socrates, who talks with whoever wishes to listen, without any expectation of a financial compensation. This rejection is also found in a long passage from *Laws* that calls for the complete exclusion of merchants from the city, to spare the citizens from the risks of contamination involved in practices of self-interested exchange, which Plato declares immoral.[1] More moderate, Aristotle tolerates merchants in the city, but he relegates them to a separate neighborhood. In his search for the "fair middle-ground" he defines the situations where, in our relationships to

Others, generous liberality is worthy of esteem. Liberality can cease to be so if it turns into irresponsible squandering, concession to flatterers, or means of domination. This takes us far from Homer's world, where, just like relationships of alliance among lineages and chiefdoms or cities, relationships of friendship were expressed primarily through often-sumptuous reciprocal presents, and hospitality itself was ruled by a ritual giving and reciprocating of gifts.[2]

It is interesting that the time of Socrates in Greece was situated within a few decades of the emergence of several great figures of wisdom in Asia—the Buddha in India, Confucius and Lao-Tse in China, the establishment of Zoroastrianism in Persia, and the renewal of prophetism in Israel—in what Karl Jaspers calls the "axial age,"[3] characterized by specific features: suspicion about the validity of ancient rituals, trend toward monotheistic beliefs, and development of personal moral views. This is a major turning point that valorizes the internalization of norms, sincerity in relationships, and purity in intentions. The ceremonial reciprocity of gifts and services largely loses its legitimacy in favor of personal moral choices that grant priority to unilateral generosity. This spiritual watershed, however, has left apparently intact a crucial principle known as the Golden Rule: Do unto Others what you would have done unto you. This is the very statement of the requirement of reciprocity. Is this the vestige of an ancient time, not yet sufficiently refined by an uncompromising morality that favors unselfish attitudes? If it is, how can we understand that a few centuries later the Gospels still celebrate this commandment on which "hang all the law and the prophets"?

At the time when Christianity was born, a very different configuration was taking shape, both at the center and at the periphery of the Roman Empire. The "axial age" witnessed the emergence of an as-yet-unknown inner freedom. In this new age, communities entered a crisis, and inequalities of status and income came into question. This crisis had many aspects. Jesus spoke in a context of social divisions and acute religious conflicts within the Jewish world. In Rome itself, Seneca, Paul's contemporary, observed and deplored the selfishness prevalent in privileged classes. Hearts were closing down and groups shutting themselves off. Reciprocal generosity had no hold on those frozen worlds. What prevailed instead was the negative reciprocity of jealousy, denunciations, and bloody settlements within the context of the large-scale exploitation of a subjugated and most often foreign population. There was only one way out: upward, offered from On High. This is the situation in which we must read Seneca's *De beneficiis* and understand its theology: "Not even the immortal gods are deterred from showing lavish and unceasing kindness to those who are sacrilegious and indifferent to them" (1, 1, 9). This is also the background against which we must hear the Gospels' message, "If anyone strikes you on the cheek, offer the other" (Luke 6:27–29). Those are very daring statements. A major watershed was unquestionably under way.

The monotheistic idea, at first a local and sometimes ephemeral experience, found a new opportunity in the crossing of borders. In the already cosmopolitan Roman Empire, the love of a single God, indifferent to nations as well as social status, who favored the poor and the downtrodden, was bound to generate an increasingly unanimous and passionate response in metropolises where cultures blended with one another and rituals had become empty of substance. The message of Paul, who introduced himself as a witness to the Resurrection, proclaimed above all the existence of a shared world, a single god, and an eternal life offered to all: "There is no longer Jew or Greek, There is no longer slave or free, there is no longer male or female; for all of you are one in Christ Jesus" (Gal. 3:28). No local religion was capable of matching such a full and generous offer of salvation. Furthermore, it can be said that from the moment when religious faith was associated with a promise of salvation, the monotheistic idea was on the march. Those monotheistic beliefs were opening the first breaches for a triumphant universalism. Stoic philosophies had already pointed to that path, but without the logistics of symbols and rituals that a religion can provide. This is why they remained incapable of reaching the masses on an emotional level, incapable above all of creating the associations between representations and everyday-life practices that persist through time and form the accumulated layers of a culture. A dual generosity could now be affirmed: the deity's offer of salvation through a gesture of incommensurable grace, together with the believers' mutual support understood as a religious calling.

From the Gospels' and Paul's message to the philosophies that emphasize selflessness, through two thousand years of religious, moral, and intellectual history the West has lived on that heritage. This is of course a complex story that has involved considerable variations, from the emergence of Islam in the Middle East and the incorporation of Greek thought in medieval theology to the new direction brought to Christianity by the Reformation. But this is not the place to develop those considerations.

The historical outline just presented should provide a framework for today's questioning of the ethics of the relationship with Others, particularly with respect to the gift relationship. Let us now return to our own age and the tendency shown by many philosophers to understand reciprocity exclusively as self-interested exchange, as opposed to the requirement of unconditional giving that entails—at least implicitly—a rejection of self-interest. The purpose of this essay is not to provide a history of those ideas. In fact its title encompasses much more than the materials it considers—merely the writings of a half-dozen French philosophers who have approached the problem of the gift in association with the problem of reciprocity. Despite their divergent modalities and their own unique styles those approaches can be divided into two main directions: first, phenomenology and its legacy (Ricoeur, Levinas, Derrida, Marion); second, the philosophies whose object is society, considered either through political reflection (Claude Lefort) or through an epistemology of the relationship with Others based on the social sciences (Vincent Descombes). In this book, examinations of those thinkers will alternate with propositions on the anthropology of the gift, social recognition, the concepts of reciprocity and mutuality, and the question of the third party. Before considering why this concern has been particularly significant for contemporary French thought, let us return to the authors selected for this debate on the question of the gift.

Around Phenomenology

At least with respect to a significant part of their work, the authors listed in the first group claim an association with phenomenology, which is to say primarily Edmund Husserl, but also, in a different way, Martin Heidegger. In both of those thinkers the question of the "givenness"—of the phenomenon of being—is at the core of both the method and the theory. This is confirmed by the formulations chosen by the French authors who have taken up this problematic. It is worth asking why a few of the major heirs of phenomenology, such as Jean-Paul Sartre[4] and Maurice Merleau-Ponty, do not show a concern for this question in their phenomenological works, or if so only incidentally.

Despite an obvious family likeness there are clear differences within that first group. In Derrida the question of givenness in its Husserlian sense of welcoming the given (*Gegebenheit*), but above all its Heideggerian sense—which, instead, involves giving (*Geben*)—is a crucial element of the argument of *Giving Time*. The entire enterprise of deconstruction of Mauss's *The Gift*, which is at the core of Derrida's book, hangs on a few pages dedicated to the concept of *Es gibt*—It is given/there is—taken from *Being and Time*, which allows Derrida to state the aporia of the gift as follows:

the gift as *the* impossible thing. Levinas's thought on the question of the gift, on the contrary, has little to do with the phenomenological motif of givenness, which he ignores almost entirely, except in passages where it appears that to understand the world as *given*—intentional object—amounts above all to the world's capacity to be taken (the etymological meaning of the French term *concept* and the German term *Begriff*). As for giving in the literal sense, it involves no aporia: According to Levinas the generous gesture is not only possible, but also inescapable when we face the suffering and destitution of Others. From this perspective Marion is closer to Derrida, with whom he shares a steadfast suspicion of the idea of exchange. More precisely, in Marion the question of givenness becomes the phenomenological question par excellence (as in *Reduction and Givenness*, and above all *Being Given*), summarized by the statement, "So much reduction, as much givenness." It remains to be determined whether the shift is legitimate from the givenness of the phenomenon to the gift as a gesture among persons, which illuminates this donation while being subsumed into it. As we will see, this is doubtful.

Things are different with Ricoeur, who in *À l'école de la phénoménologie* discusses givenness as part of an examination of Husserl's method. He rarely approached the question of giving as generous gesture until his last books (*Memory, History, Forgetting*, and especially *The Course of Recognition*), where he discusses explicitly the ritual form of the gift that Mauss analyzes. A crucial feature, however, separates Ricoeur from the three authors we have considered: He never views the idea of reciprocity with suspicion; he even grants reciprocity a consistently positive status associated with the tradition of the Golden Rule, although in the end he confers an axiological preeminence on the different notion of mutuality, which he views as more properly ethical. Not only does Ricoeur take care not to let his own religious positions[5] interfere with his philosophical reflection, but he also rejects Derrida and Levinas's aporetic or paroxysmal positions. Ricoeur's quest for a *capable man* leads him to a view of interpersonal relationships that he summarizes as follows in *Oneself as Another*: "*Aiming at the 'good life' with and for others, in just institutions*."[6]

AROUND POLITICAL AND SOCIAL SCIENCE

Besides those associated with phenomenology, few philosophers have approached the question of the gift; for those who have, it was neither the main topic of a book nor the recurrent theme in a problematic. Yet it could have constituted a very significant contribution in the context of a reflection on the social bond or on the way interpersonal relationships are formalized within a group. For example, not only does the discussion of the ritual gift that Lefort presents, based on his reading of Mauss, allow him to examine the distance between traditional and modern societies from the perspective of the exchange of goods, but it also allows him to identify the defining element of the historicity of those societies. In many ways his reading is in the wake of Hegel and Marx, and therefore of a specific conception of humans' relationship with the natural world. It remains to determine whether what Lefort discusses actually is the ritual form of the gift theorized by Mauss, and whether the theoretical legacy within which Lefort is situated might not carry as many prejudices as critical breakthroughs.

In an important chapter of *The Institutions of Meaning* Descombes proposes an entirely different perspective on Mauss's *The Gift*. Descombes's questions are not focused on the production or exchange of goods or on their economic status. More formally, their purpose is to identify the nature of the relationship instituted between oneself and Others and, more precisely, to define the criteria that make it possible to distinguish intersubjective from specifically social relationships. In the first case the gift relationship sheds light on the specificity of triadic relationships (in Peirce's sense, where two agents are connected through a good exchanged)—irreducible to dyadic relationships—and in the second case it legitimizes in a rigorous manner the relevance of holistic positions (in which the nature of the whole belongs to a different order than does the sum of its parts). For reasons entirely different from those relevant to Lefort, we can question whether the form of gift discussed in Descombes's book, where reciprocity appears so unimportant that it is barely mentioned, really is the type of gift considered by Mauss in *The Gift*, where this reciprocity, expressed by the term *exchange*, constitutes the core of the problem.

Clearly, unlike some of the heirs of phenomenology, Lefort and Descombes do not view oblative generosity as a crucial feature. Neither Lefort nor Descombes raises any principled objection with respect to the requirement of reciprocity, but nor do they question it explicitly. In Lefort this requirement shares in the self-evident character of exchanges among groups; in Descombes it is not crucial to the definition of the triadic relationship. In addition (and for very different reasons), neither of those authors proposes to subject the question of the gift to an ethical approach that leads most others to view the relationship of reciprocity with suspicion—or, more rarely, with approval. We will consider what lessons the differences or divergences among those various approaches can teach us—in other words, what the stakes of our inquiry are.

A French Story?

A final interrogation remains with respect to this discussion about gift and reciprocity. Is there any reason—other than circumstantial—why the authors presented here are all French? This is a difficult question to answer, given the degree of uncertainty involved in any attempt to identify the causalities in this field. Yet the following observation is inescapable: No such phenomenon can be found in other national traditions in twentieth-century Europe, even if this debate has now begun to develop outside France. From the outset an objection can be presented: Isn't the source of phenomenology primarily German? Isn't this question a legacy of the concepts of givenness (*Gegebenheit*) or giving (*Geben*)—terms endowed with a precise status in Husserl and Heidegger? That is unquestionably the case. It is striking, however, that in neither of those authors can we observe this highly problematic—or even unacceptable—derivation from the givenness of the phenomenon to the gift as a gesture among persons or groups. Should we interpret the presence of that derivation in their French disciples as an aspect of the "theological turn" of phenomenology suspected by Dominique Janicaud?[7] We will not engage in this debate, or only marginally. Although it is probably legitimate, it does not shed light on the approaches of the other authors, who do not belong to the phenomenological trend. Above all it does not provide us with the elements of the intellectual context where this shift occurred.

It is worth noting the presence in France, since the 1930s and throughout the latter half of the twentieth century, of an intellectual movement at the same time widespread and devoid of a specific doctrine, whose primary feature is a spirit of contestation of the economic order—a movement that the very name of Mauss, put forth as an emblem, is almost enough to characterize. The aim of this movement becomes clearer if we consider the work of Georges Bataille—while keeping in mind its specificity. This involves a complex and in some ways unusual story. This essay is not the place to trace its origins and ramifications.[8] Let us only remember that Mauss was an heir to a tradition of social philosophy with deep roots in the nineteenth century in the writings of such thinkers as Joseph Proudhon, Louis Blanc, and Georges Leroux. That tradition was eclipsed and sometimes mocked by the tradition embodied by Marx and his followers. By taking it up again, Mauss gave it the new legitimacy of an anthropological knowledge then in full ascent. Not only did the study of societies called at the time archaic or primitive make it possible to relativize the forms of production and exchange dominant in our own societies, but above all it provided models of life in common and social bond, so utterly lacking in the capitalistic world. This most likely explains the unusual reception of *The Gift* (as compared to other no less important writings by Mauss on sacrifice, bodily techniques, magic, personhood, or prayer). This reception was granted not only to his bringing to the fore the triple ritual obligation—to give, receive, and reciprocate—but also to the discussion at the end of *The Gift* titled, "Conclusion Regarding General Sociology and Morality." There Mauss suggests that in the practices of the societies whose gift exchanges he analyzes, a model of generous relationships can be found, capable of counteracting the mechanisms of the market, or at least of correcting their abuses. Gift exchange thus appears as a kind of solidarity-based socialism capable of prevailing through the activity of associations (a suggestion that, although interesting in and of itself, is highly debatable since ceremonial exchanges have little to do with social mechanisms of mutual assistance or social justice).

The intervention of Bataille in the field of reflection opened by Mauss's *The Gift* is entirely different in kind and tone. What fascinates him, and what he puts forth in *The Notion of Expenditure* and *The Accursed Share*, is not generous solidarity, but almost exclusively—through a reference to the section from *The Gift* about the potlatch of the northwest coast of North America—the munificence of gifts among groups, the wasteful or even paroxysmal offer of presents that can go as far as to involve their spectacular destruction; to sum up, the potlatch constitutes a sumptuary, glorious, and occasionally violent act of destruction.[9] Bataille's insistence on this agonistic form of the gift and this logic of excess opened the way to a radical reexamination of the economic order—a reexamination that, through ways entirely different from those opened by Marx and socialist theorists, undermined the logic of the market, its narrow-mindedness, selfish calculus, and inability to institute any form of community. Those were the views shared during the twenties and thirties by the members of the Collège de Sociologie.[10]

Those are the outlines of this specifically French story. It would be difficult to determine with any rigor who among those postwar philosophers were or remain its heirs. At most it can be said that in France an original intellectual atmosphere has prevailed. It would be a mistake, however, to reduce Mauss's work to the paradoxically dual legacy of a theory of solidarity and a concept of expense. We can even wonder if the conclusion of *The Gift*, with its call for that solidarity, might not amount to an unwarranted extrapolation of the demonstration conducted in the rest of the essay. As for the practice of potlatch, whose presentation takes up only about thirty

pages of *The Gift*, in no way is it sufficient support for a theory of gift practices as embodying wasteful liberality (as claimed by so many commentators, from the most intelligent to the most naïve). What runs through the
entire text and constitutes its central element is instead the requirement of
reciprocity—which for Mauss is the primary meaning of the term *exchange*.[11]
We still need to understand that this reciprocity can be reduced neither to
an ethic of sharing nor to a posture of excess, so we can be freed from the
approximations that often brilliant and inspired philosophies have deemed
fit to resort to when commenting on ethnographic facts. It was important
to consider those facts in the same rigorous manner that those thinkers
expect their colleagues from the natural sciences to exercise in terms of
epistemological requirements. The fact that the social or human sciences
remain to a large extent sciences of interpretation—and will probably remain so in the future—does not mean that they are a pure matter of opinion, even philosophical opinion. Interpretation must develop based on the
best-established facts consistent with the current state of knowledge, and
discussed with the precision required by any inquiry worthy of its name.

Finally, we will consider whether the unusual interest of so many contemporary philosophers in the question of the gift might not be the expression of a paradoxical and perhaps untenable expectation, by which this
concept is to represent at the same time several requirements that belong
to very different orders: to define the nature of our relationship to being; provide the foundation for an ethic of generosity; legitimize forms
of solidarity; satisfy the requirement to recognize the Other; redefine the
specificity of the social bond; conceptualize the obligation of reciprocity;
and move beyond the utilitarian view of production and exchange. It is
a constant source of puzzlement that those various and sometimes contradictory demands converge on the same word, as if that word always
involved the same question. One could consider that the only thing needed
is to explore its wealth of meanings. It seems to us, however, that the true
task of thought is to clarify incompatible positions and identify orders of
problems that should not be confused with one another. But it is a sign of
our time that this debate has coalesced precisely around this question. At
the end of our journey we will need to understand why.

CHAPTER I

Derrida:
The Gift, the Impossible,
and the Exclusion of Reciprocity

The impossible has *already* occurred.

JACQUES DERRIDA, *Writing and Difference*

For there to be a gift, there must be no reciprocity.

JACQUES DERRIDA, *Given Time*

What is hateful to you, do not to your neighbor: that
is the whole Torah; the rest is commentary.

Babylonian Talmud

In *Given Time* Derrida presents an aporia of the gift that has made its mark, and has occasioned many commentaries and a few refutations. Even when those reactions—the most noteworthy of which is Jean-Luc Marion's in *Being Given*—propose alternative arguments and conclusions, they accept the terms of the problem and the lexicon chosen by Derrida. But it is on the level of its presuppositions that this problem must be reconsidered. The aporia of the gift according to Derrida can be summed up as follows: Giving is always understood as a relationship between a giver and a receiver, an exchange that generates a debt and in the final analysis remains within the confines of economic reciprocity; in this, the gift becomes the opposite of what it claims to be. To escape this logic, for the gift to be truly a gift, Derrida claims, the giver would have to be unaware that he is giving, and the receiver unaware of the giver's identity: "For there to be gift, it is necessary that the gift not even appear, that it not be perceived or received as gift."[1] Starting with those requirements Derrida proposes a critical reading of Mauss's *The Gift*,[2] a writing where the *obligation to give, receive,* and *reciprocate* established by ethnographic inquiries is understood as the core of the gift relationship. Derrida's purpose is not to reject those data, but to dispute the validity of the term "gift" as designating a gesture that presupposes or even mandates the requirement of reciprocity. I find this criticism highly debatable for many reasons, first of which is the way Derrida, along with an entire tradition, carelessly applies certain concepts to "the gift" as a gesture without discussing either its origin or its relevance, and above all without considering whether it is even possible to talk of the gift in general, and whether there might be types of gifts so profoundly different from others that they require a separate examination. Derrida intends to apply to Mauss a deconstructive approach, but he does so without subjecting to this critical test the very concepts to which he resorts. His entire presentation takes place within the space of this blind spot.

This is the problem I propose to reexamine here. My analysis may seem stern, and from a certain standpoint it will be so. Yet it will make it possible to better appreciate Derrida's approach from a more restricted perspective and from that perspective only. This remains for us to demonstrate by considering the diversity of perspectives required by an examination of the concept of the gift. Let us return to the arguments presented in *Given Time*.

The Gift—The Impossible: Questioning Mauss

From the outset the questioning on giving that Derrida proposes is situated in aporia and aims for aporia; but what kind of aporia is this? Contrary to what has often been claimed, Derrida does not proclaim that "The gift is impossible." This would be absurd, given the readily observable fact that things are offered and other things often given in return. What Derrida states is the following: "Not impossible but *the* impossible. The very figure of the impossible. It announces itself, gives itself to be thought as the impossible."[3] This statement remains enigmatic for two reasons:

First, the logical difference introduced between adjective and noun is not immediately clear. While the adjective appears as a feature among others within the table of modalities (possible vs. impossible; necessary vs. contingent; existent vs. nonexistent), the noun amounts to a definition, in which case it can be identified with the *thinkable*. The adjective involves the affirmation of existence (i.e., this either takes place or does not), whereas the noun involves the statement of what is logically acceptable (and therefore thinkable), but then the gift "gives itself to be thought" as what is eminently contradictory according to this inconceivable equation: $A = non\text{-}A$. The statement "gives itself to be thought" is posited without any commentary, yet it is clear enough that it does not arise here without aiming to point to a certain performative ability of the very concept of the gift. It can also refer to the Kantian distinction between thinking and knowing. It thus appears as something thinkable that transgresses the boundaries of intuition. Discussing in one of his first writings the possibility of death confronting the idea of an indefinite possibility of time, Derrida speaks of "bring[ing] together the impossibility of the possible with the possibility of the impossible."[4]

Second, if the gift is "the very figure of the impossible," then as a concept it constitutes the exemplary form of aporia: not just any aporia, but the very figure of aporia, and therefore absolute aporia. This exceptional status may appear odd, since it amounts to a claim that the act designated by the verb "to give" has the unique property of never occurring. It must be capable to be conceived of, but not actualized. Yet we know (according to our first point, above), that it does occur. There is only one way out: This act is not what we think it is. This is in fact the explanation Derrida proposes: Those who believe that, through the gift as a gesture, they are giving are in fact conducting an *exchange*, thus remaining within the economic order. Giving does take place—giving is possible—but as an empirical gesture it never amounts to a *gift*, since it is never what we claim it to be. "Never," in the very moment when it takes place: In this it is *the* impossible. This is the first aspect of the aporia, from a temporal perspective. But where does this privilege of excellence in aporia, which the gift is claimed to have, proceed from? Why is it not one aporia among others? Precisely because the gift relationship involves time, and does so in a unique way. Not only does it make simultaneous what is irreconcilable—gift and exchange—but it occurs only within and according to the form of a preexisting gift: the gift of time itself. The aporia of the gift is therefore not one case among others; it involves the ontological structure of any aporetic statement. We are situated within time, we receive time; this "a priori intuition"—according to Kant's resolved oxymoron—is understood by Edmund Husserl as a primeval givenness of perceptual experience, and on a more essential level by Heidegger as the foundational experience of *Dasein*, "this being whose very being is about being." *Dasein* is Being's internal distance to oneself that is time. Hence this implicit syllogism: *Time given* opens the possibility of relationship; any relationship involves the *gift of time*; the *gift relationship* is the exemplary expression of this gift of time. This explains why Derrida can claim that *to give is always to give time*: "The gift is not a gift, the gift only gives to the extent it gives time."[5]

For a gift to be truly a gift, Derrida explains, the giver would have to forget the gift as a gesture while he gives. To be aware that we are giving, or even receiving, already amounts to canceling the truth of the gift. This forgetting cannot be equated to an erasure of memory or to repression. It can be nothing else than "absolute forgetting,"[6] comparable only to what Heidegger calls "forgetting of Being," which is "the condition of Being and of the truth of Being"[7]—a formulation that can be understood only based on the difference between Being (*Sein*) and what is (*Seiendes*). The latter is what appears in the observable world—that is, in the currently present, in a time that can be grasped; in this, Being evades us. It is a quality of what is, but it does not belong to the same category; in this, Being *is* not; it remains within *forgetting*—a forgetting that does not amount to the loss of any memory.

This rereading of Heidegger makes it possible for Derrida to articulate the approach that probably constitutes the core of his reflection on the gift and time. This reflection involves a German formulation that in a way determines its interpretation: *Es gibt*—literally, "it gives," whose English counterpart is "there is." Heidegger does not fail to make use of this resource of the German language to develop an original conception of givenness. "There is Being" can become "It gives Being." Thus, Derrida comments, "The enigma is concentrated both in the 'it' or rather the '*es*,' the 'it' of 'it gives,' which is not a thing, and in this gift that gives but without giving anything and without anyone giving anything—nothing but Being and time (which are nothing)."[8] In the same way that the Beingness of what is, is not (as a thing), the temporality of time *is* not. But it can be said that *Es gibt Sein* (It gives beingness). Yet this giving gives nothing in the absence of Being. "The gift *itself* [. . .] will never be confused with the presence of its phenomenon."[9] This is why Derrida can proclaim that "the gift is another name of Being," as Maurice Blanchot said of forgetting.

Clearly, the proclamation of this giving-as-forgetting, this gift that is not a being, is what Derrida intends to reiterate whenever he questions the gestures of giving, precisely those that Mauss discusses in *The Gift*. Faced with this *gift that is not*, any talk of reciprocity, of the return of the thing given or the prestige granted to givers, appears as a mere attempt to fold forgetting into the present moment, focused only on the things given, taken, and circulated. This is the core of the question: giving time. Everything is decided in those few pages on Heidegger's *Es gibt*. The aporia is becoming clearer: If any gift—as a *gesture*—must be understood based on this "it gives," which gives no Being, *then it is true that it is impossible to give anything*: "As the condition for a gift to be given, this forgetting must be radical not only on the part of the donee but first of all, if one can say here first of all, on the part of the donor."[10] We now better understand the reference to Blanchot's formulation: "Forgetting is another name of Being."

This is the categorical requirement Derrida never ceases to put forth in his reading of Mauss's *The Gift*. Derrida's endeavor, however, is highly problematic, if not deficient, for two reasons. First, it is entirely based on granting priority to a version of *giving* promoted by Heidegger and derived from this *es gibt* (it gives), specific to the German language. It is this *es gibt* that opens Derrida's questioning on *Geben*. Nothing in the French *il y a*, the English "There is," the Italian *c'è*, or the Spanish *hay*, for example, invites this shift toward the gift. The "there" in "there is" is a marker of location; it anchors the statement in contingence, introducing the mere observation that something exists—so much so that we can wonder if the German "it gives," does not belong also, or even primarily, to this semantic neutrality expressed by "there is." What is given by *es gibt* in its ordinary use is the datum of any empirical observation. The answer to this question, however, remains undecidable, because it rests on the choice of an interpretation. Heidegger deliberately focuses on the idea of *giving*, and Derrida confirms this choice. But it is just as possible to keep to the formulation "there is Being" or "there is time,"[11] avoiding all talk of a gift, and to talk instead of "givenness" in Husserl's sense, which remains close to the most ordinary datum.

But the real problem *Given Time* raises is that it extends in a particular way the connection established between *es gibt* and the gift of Being, since it involves the extension of this articulation to gift practices among persons. A subreption has occurred: a shift from a thesis about Being to a thesis about action. Unlike the ritual gift, in no way is the gift of the givenness of Being the gesture of an agent. Whereas the idea of givenness belongs to a speculative thesis about the world, the concept of ritual gift belongs to an analysis of practices among agents and of the constitution of relationships within specific groups. To subject those practices (which involve the formation of the social bond, matrimonial exchanges, and alliances) to the requirements of an ontology of givenness, amounts to an illegitimate shift between fields that have no commensurable objects, and that do not and cannot involve the same questions; this amounts to taking advantage of a lexical kinship to presuppose the continuity of a conceptual field, and it can lead only to paralogisms; *Given Time* seems rife with those.

Yet one cannot but admire the subtle logic by which Derrida refines and deploys the aporia he formulated from the outset: "The gift is *the* impossible." But it is clear that a number of terms in his argument are put forth

without considering their polysemy—which is not a purely formal polysemy, since the different senses of those terms refer to different data. The
logical articulation becomes fragile, if not shaky, since it presupposes that
one particular meaning—and this one only—can be conferred on concepts that have not been defined and discussed. The entire line of reasoning risks collapsing if certain equivalences presupposed to be self-evident
are shown to be unfounded or to have only limited relevance. Let us briefly
point out those suspicions before taking up the main points of Derrida's
analysis and presenting a more substantial analysis of a different and partly
conflicting argument.

The first problematic element is the very concept of *gift*. From the outset
we must ask the following question: Is it even possible to talk of *gift* in general without incurring a considerable risk? Derrida himself chides Mauss
for his failure to question the polysemy of the very term *gift*: "Mauss seems
to be quite unaware of what he is naming and whether one can still call one
thing by the name of gift and another thing by the name of exchange."[12]
Derrida quotes the following excerpt from Mauss: "The terms that we
have used—present and gift—are not themselves entirely exact. We shall,
however, find no others."[13] Mauss is clearly aware that sumptuary offerings
are inseparable from an obligation of reciprocity, and that this obligation is
incompatible with the ordinary idea that the gift is by essence purely oblative and unconditional. He therefore suggests that we need different terms
to designate those two forms of gift (in fact the best solution is to establish
a distinction between heterogeneous orders of gift). Mauss is right to express his misgivings and to raise those critical questions. His questioning
does not amount to a hesitation between the terms "gift" and "exchange"
(since in *The Gift* "exchange" does not designate trade, but agonistic reciprocity). His implicit aim is to resolve the paradox by which oblativity can
coexist with reciprocity. Derrida is unaware of this contradiction, since
from the outset he has reduced reciprocity to commercial exchange; in
Mauss's term "exchange" he sees only "the circle of the economy," which,
as we will see, amounts to a regrettable misunderstanding.

It is difficult for anyone who has taken the trouble to study practices
of—festive, reciprocal, and prodigal—ceremonial exchanges among parties in traditional societies to place them on the same level as practices
of—utilitarian and unilateral—gifts meant to support those in distress
or in need. Nor can either of those two social practices be compared to
the—symbolic and unconditional—gift of oneself between lovers or by
a mystic to his deity. Those practices involve different orders. Even more
heterogeneous is "givenness" in the sense of the phenomenological tradi-

tion. A concept that refers to practices or theories whose fields of application, procedures, and goals are radically divergent cannot be used *in general* without a constant risk of confusion. One is led to staking one meaning against another without realizing that the entire field has shifted. The raising of objections thus risks becoming a sophistic game of substitutions; a general term—such as *gift*—becomes a single mask behind which different and discordant voices alternate, and are concealed. Those different voices are then assessed by the standard of the only voice recognizable and recognized by our entire religious and moral tradition: the purely oblative gift. From this perspective it can be claimed, in a Derridian way and with a critical rather than aporetic purpose, that there is no such thing as "the gift"; there are only various gift practices whose relevant categories must be defined based on epistemologically convincing criteria (we will try to do so below in "Propositions I").

The same kind of misgiving applies to the concept of *exchange*. To handle it as if it had the same meaning in the ritual exchange of presents, the contractual exchange of goods, the functional exchange of messages, the exchange of blows in a fight, the alternation of turns in a game, and the exchange of arguments in a debate, is to risk oscillating among meanings that belong to heterogeneous semantic fields as if they were all situated on the same level. Not only is this inaccurate, but from one field to another, meanings diverge and are often reversed. It then becomes possible to produce aporias galore. Furthermore, the cumulated indeterminacies of the concepts of *gift* and *exchange* lead to the trivial and arbitrary presupposition that gift practices—whether ritual or not—are primarily exchanges, whose ultimate purpose is economic. Derrida implicitly and firmly shares in this presupposition; this is why, when he proposes and opposes a model of the gift that is in fact absolute *oblativity*—so much so that its character as a gift disappears—in every form of reciprocity he finds an *interest* sought by the giver. This amounts to an unacceptable reduction, and even a serious confusion. While it is obvious that every gift *practice* constitutes a relationship (there is no giver without recipient, even if the latter is unknown), this relationship is not necessarily an *exchange* if we accept that every exchange presupposes a dual movement, and therefore reciprocity. As for reciprocity itself, while it can be symmetrical and equivalent (as in contracts), it can also be conflictual and in constant disequilibrium (as in games or fights), and lacking any profit aspect. Whereas for Mauss the meaning of exchange is primarily generous reciprocity, Derrida presupposes that every form of reciprocity is a "selfish" return to the self, and thus a canceling of time— since time is that which pulls us away from any acquired or set position, throwing us into what is yet to be. But to define reciprocity as a merely circular movement closed on itself is to reduce it to its most impoverished figure: symmetry, or back-and-forth. To reduce reciprocity to this "circle" amounts to ignoring its agonistic dimension as *alternating dissymmetry*, as in the ceremonial gift, the love joust, or generous rivalry. To reply—or countergive—does not amount to canceling the offer—or gift—or to extinguishing the debt, but to continually reopen the time of the relationship in the interplay of call and reply.

The Four Faces of Aporia, or the Misunderstanding

"The gift is *the* impossible," Derrida claims. Before making a judgment on the acceptability of this pronouncement, we must examine in more detail the steps of the argument he puts forth. They involve the four major aspects of the empirical procedure of the gift: (1) the gesture itself; (2) the beneficiary or recipient of the gift; (3) the giver or originator of the gift; (4) the thing given.[14]

(1) *The Gift as a Gesture.* From the outset Derrida disqualifies Mauss's approach by underlining the complicity he believes to exist between the concepts of exchange (mentioned in the subtitle of *The Gift*), economy, and circularity:

> If the gift is annulled in the economic odyssey of the circle as soon as it appears as gift or signifies *itself* as gift, there is no longer any "logic of the gift," and one may safely say that a consistent discourse on the gift becomes impossible: It misses its object and always speaks, finally, of something else. One could go as far as to say that a work monumental as *The Gift*[15] speaks of everything but the gift: It deals with economy, exchange, contract (*do ut des*), it speak of raising the stakes, sacrifice, gift *and* counter-gift—in short everything that in the thing itself impels the gift *and* the annulment of the gifts.[16]

The claim that when Mauss describes the ritual gift he deals only with the economy, exchange, and contracts will come as a surprise to any reader of *The Gift* who is also an observer or familiar of societies of the type Mauss considers. What those exchanges involve is not the economy, but sumptuary provisions, generous and often extravagant gestures. As for the *do ut des* contract (called synallagmatic),[17] it is the legal form of a reciprocity meant to be symmetrical, and the opposite of the *potlatch*, which requires gifts of ever-increasing value. Furthermore, this raising of stakes is not situated in the market, but in the realm of generous challenge. As for sacrifice, which

Mauss mentions in a note, it belongs to the complex relationships between gift and deities. Derrida includes sacrifice in his list as if it were an obvious aspect of the economic logic—that is, self-interested exchange. This is a trivial and reductionist thesis that Derrida appears to share, without realizing it, with the strictest and most consistent functionalist trends, which propose to explain sacrifice through utilitarian arguments. Whereas in *The Gift* Mauss continually attempts to show that the gifts he discusses are public expressions of generous expense, prestige, honor, the granting of trust, the promise of fidelity, and the creation and reinforcement of bonds, Derrida interprets Mauss's entire language of the gift as a language of trade and profit. This arbitrary reduction of *exchange* in general to trade allows Derrida to write: "Mauss does not worry enough about this incompatibility between gift and exchange or about the fact that an exchanged gift is only a tit for tat."[18] But for Mauss or any careful observer of the societies that practice ritual exchanges of gifts, those exchanges are none of those things. They *never* amount to lending[19] or bartering, but to venturing oneself toward the other through the thing given, and to cause a reply. Why? To understand this we will have to propose an entirely different interpretation of the ceremonial gift.

"The truth of the gift is equivalent to the non-gift or to the non-truth of the gift," Derrida claims.[20] If the reciprocal gift were nothing else than a profitable exchange, this proclamation would be legitimate. But to assume a relation between the kind of gift to which Derrida's statement refers and the form Mauss discusses is in fact a gross misunderstanding. It could be that Derrida's "non-truth" is really his own interpretation, which confuses the ritual gift with commercial exchange and, based on this inaccurate equivalence, implicitly judges the ritual gift by the standard of an entirely different kind: the gracious and unilateral gift, which in the West every moral and religious tradition valorizes. This is confirmed by the following statement, held to be self-evident: "And a gift must not be *bound*, in its purity, nor even binding, obligatory or obliging."[21] This is true—but only if we specify that it applies to the *gracious* gift, an entirely respectable and legitimate thing *within its own realm*: It calls on the entire field of grace (*gratia, kharis*) with its rich and complex philosophical as well as theological history. But there is no justification for implicitly constituting it as the exclusive norm and obligatory reference for the other modalities of the gift, in particular the ritual gift, which, to have any meaning, must be reciprocal. Why? This is what we will have to show.

(2) *The Recipient.* How can we understand the attitude of the beneficiary of a gift? Once again this all depends on the type of gift involved. Derrida

writes, "For there to be a gift, it is necessary that the donee not give back, amortize, reimburse, acquit himself, enter into a contract, and that he never have contracted a debt."[22] This too could be said of the gracious gift, but not of the ceremonial gift, on which Derrida's unwarranted assumption confers the attributes and requirements of trade and contractual exchange in general (amortization, reimbursement, settlement, and indebtedness). This prior distortion makes it possible to discuss a *debt* in the financial sense, while conferring on the notion the metaphorical status of a symbolic debt, and vice versa. While Derrida continually shifts from one semantic field to another, he writes as if in spite of those shifts the concepts he discusses kept the same relevance. It is easy to show that this is not tenable. For example, he uses the term "reimbursement" in a broad sense, although there is no commonality between the reimbursement of a bank loan and the "reimbursement" or "settlement"—questionable metaphors—of a generous gesture of mutual aid. This is why to consider the ritual gift a mere generator of debt—whether financial or symbolic—because it is inherently reciprocal, amounts to reducing it to an alienating gesture: a bond of dependence with respect to a dominant giver. But ritual reciprocity presupposes alternation, and it commits the future: Today's recipient will be tomorrow's giver. What this involves is not a debt of dependence, but a debt of reply,[23] which reverses the statuses of the parties through the interplay of agonistic replies. This *alternating dissymmetry* is at the core of the relationship. True, in some cases the ceremonial gift manifests a statutory inequality, but this occurs when a different process has intervened (such as the unilateral enrichment of an individual or group, or military conquest). What creates the debt is not the agonistic gift, but economic and/or political inequality—a situation of dependence—that distorts the reciprocal gift, turning it into an instrument of indebtedness.

The implicit dilemma Derrida formulates, casting suspicion on every form of reciprocity, is a dual dead end: If the recipient returns the gift, then he turns the gift into a commercial exchange; if he does not, then he contracts a debt. It may well be that this is a false dilemma that results from a misunderstanding of the ritual gift.

(3) *The Giver*. Just as the recipient should not "return" the gift, the giver should not claim he is giving, Derrida tells us. As we saw, he calls on the category of oblivion, in the sense that "forgetting is another name of Being."[24] If Being is not a being, then it *is* not, in the sense of a present thing. Being is thus absent, and in a radical sense, moves into oblivion. It cannot be given; there is *nothing* to be given, and therefore nothing to return:

It is also on the part of the donor "subject" that the gift not only must be not repaid but must not be kept in memory, retained as symbol of a sacrifice, as symbolic in general. For the symbol immediately engages in restitution.[25]

This disqualification is once again legitimized through the suspicion of a self-interested exchange—*pay back*—that weighs down the gift as a gesture (here the payment metaphor should be taken literally). But, in a more essential way, what Derrida questions is the *memory* of the relationship between the parties involved in the gift—even though this memory is crucial to the establishment of a lasting social bond. Instead of being viewed as the preserver of time, memory is assumed to be time's accountant; it is viewed as miserly: It *retains* and records what is due. This is true of commercial relationships, with their precise records that—rightly—ensure the proper functioning of justice in the contractual exchange of goods. But does it adequately describe, for example, the memory of the celebrations the parties involved in the *kula ring* of Melanesia's Trobriand Islands[26] give one another during their sailing expeditions? The bracelets and necklaces they exchange are precious because they carry the memory of their circulation; they testify to the respect the parties grant one another, and to the prestige they associate with it.

But, beyond this memory, Derrida also questions symbolism understood as a simple conventional and static order within which positions shift back and forth: "The symbolic opens and constitutes the order of exchange and of debt, the law or the order of circulation in which the gift gets annulled."[27] This idea returns persistently in *Giving Time*, to point to the closed and normative character of this carousel of gifts along a closure from which nothing seems capable of escaping. Let us mention that Mauss never talks of the symbolic—a concept created by Lacan—but of symbolism as an open process of relationships thanks to which society is affirmed not merely as something ruled by a functional order, but as constituting a system of values that defines it as culture and that is constantly in the process of being formed: the movement of the instituting within the instituted. This symbolic order must be understood primarily as an *alliance* among the parties connected by the thing offered as a guarantee on both sides: the *symbolon*—literally, what is put together. Derrida discusses the symbolic as order and law, founded on a commitment of a contractual type that calls for *restitution*. But the alliance is not the same thing as a contract; it is even the opposite. It is a risky decision to unite the Self with the

Other, to venture one's own familiar world into the unknown of the other's world, to bind one otherness to another in the uncertainty of their becoming. This is why the alliance gives itself a symbol of this commitment in the form of the thing offered, unquestionable witness for each party to the *promise* given to the other and the choice to be united. This witness to the alliance represents the bringing together of what is different; this gesture of reciprocity clearly proclaims the opposite of what is at stake in any operation of an economic type.

The same can be said of *sacrifice*, which Derrida incriminates as a self-interested negotiation with the deity, or reduces to the late-emerging figure of *renouncement*. It is therefore not surprising that, based on those various presuppositions and misinterpretations, Derrida claims:

> To tell the truth, the gift must not even appear or signify, consciously or unconsciously, *as* gift for the donors, whether individual or collective subjects. From the moment the gift would appear as gift, as such, as what it is, in its phenomenon, its sense and its essence, it would be engaged in a symbolic, sacrificial or economic structure that would annul the gift in the ritual circle of the debt.[28]

This claim locks in the aporia, since it amounts to saying that from the moment when the gift appears (*appearance* must be understood here in its phenomenological rigor), it *disappears* (as a purely oblative gesture), since as a phenomenon it appears only within this mode called *symbolic, sacrificial,* or *economic* and through the figures of the calculating reciprocity Derrida sees in it; in this sense, the gift is indeed "*the* impossible." As Derrida rightly notes after many other authors, in French the term "gift" has a dual meaning: It designates both the gesture and the thing. Both of them should thus be situated at the very core of the giving subject, but is this possible? The continuation of Derrida's argument excludes this possibility: "A subject as such never gives or receives a gift."[29] Why? Because by doing so a subject would be reduced to being the correlate of an object, one of the two poles involved in an exchange of goods. In his earliest writings Derrida was able to crack open in an original and inspiring way the carapace of the old certainties as to the identity of the subject. From this perspective *Writing and Difference* and *Grammatology* have preserved intact their ability to rejuvenate the reading of philosophical writings; we should keep this in mind when, with respect to the exchange of gifts, Derrida questions the status of the "subject identical to itself and conscious of its identity, or even seeking through the gesture of the gift to constitute its own unity and, precisely, to get its own identity recognized so that identity comes back to it, so that it can reappropriate its identity: as its property." Just before this passage he specifies that, just as well as an individual, this subject can be "a group, a community, a nation, a clan, a tribe;"[30] thus calling on the fraught notion of collective subject. We cannot debate this question here; let us just ask whether it is relevant to presuppose that the various populations Mauss discusses have the same concept of the subject as do twentieth-century European philosophers, heirs to a tradition that includes Aristotle, Descartes, Kant, Hegel, Freud, and a few others.

There is a wealth of anthropological literature on the representations of personal identity in non-European cultures (notably in Mauss's text, "The Notion of Person").[31] We cannot assume that different cultures share in the presuppositions of our own metaphysical and legal heritage about the connections between personal identity and property. This does not preclude the possibility that those aspects may be found in those cultures, but if so their presence would need to be shown, and in this case their relationship to the "thing given" should be assessed. On this point deconstructionist vigilance appears to have failed since it clearly speaks from the core of its own blind spot. On this bond between thing given and giver, Mauss provides us with indications that suggest an entirely different understanding of the relationships between persons and things, based not on a relationship between subjects and objects, but on the model of a complex continuity stated as follows: "In short, this represents an intermingling. Souls are mixed with things; things with souls. Lives are mingled together, and this is how, among persons and things so intermingled, each emerges from their own sphere and mingles."[32] Mauss's choice of the term soul deserves a discussion: While it may appear old-fashioned, it is in fact quite appropriate to express the traditional view that there is continuity between the human world and the world of other living beings or artifacts. This helps us understand that the thing given is inseparable from the being of the giver (to use a formulation that is itself another translation). Thus does Mauss write of the Maori: "A tie occurring through things, is one between souls, because the thing itself possesses a soul, is of the soul. Hence it follows that to make a gift of something to someone is to make a present of some part of oneself."[33] This bond between souls therefore significantly transgresses the model of a subject cut off from the world. This is why when Derrida writes, "If there is gift, it cannot take place between two subjects exchanging objects, things, or symbols. The question of the gift should therefore seek its place before any relation to the subject, before any conscious or unconscious relation to self of the subject,"[34] he appears to be praising rather than criticizing what Mauss has constantly sought to demonstrate.

Having reduced the *reciprocal* gift to a correlation between subject and object, Derrida can then claim:

> A subject will never give an object to another subject. But the subject and the object are arrested effects of the gift, arrests of the gift. At the zero or infinite speed of the circle.[35]
>
> If the gift is annulled in the economic odyssey of the circle as soon as it appears *as* gift or as soon as it signifies *itself as* gift, there is no longer any "logic of the gift," and one may safely say that a consistent discourse on the gift becomes impossible: It misses its object and speaks, finally, of something else.[36]

Once again, those statements hold as self-evident that the ceremonial exchanges Mauss discusses with respect to traditional societies amount to barter, operations of equivalence, or even return on investment; if this were true, then it would be legitimate to claim that Mauss's *The Gift* "speaks of everything but the gift."[37] Unless it is Derrida who talks of everything except the kind of gift Mauss discusses. Having reached this degree of radicalness in his suspicion against reciprocity, Derrida comes to question not only the actual practice of the gift (which, as a form of exchange, he suspects of negating the gift), but the very fact to *want to give*, intend to give, which he views as importing within oneself the model of self-interested exchange: "The simple intention to give, insofar as it carries the intentional meaning of the gift, suffices to make a return payment to oneself. The simple consciousness of the gift right away sends itself back the gratifying image of goodness or generosity, of the giving-being who, knowing itself to be such, recognizes itself in a circular, specular fashion, in a sort of auto-recognition, self-approval, and narcissistic gratitude."[38] The subject who intends to give is viewed as being at the same time giver and recipient, engaged in a somehow incestuous exchange with him/herself. Hence the following question: "What would be a gift that fulfills the condition of the gift, namely, that it not appear as a gift, that it not be, exist, signify, want-to-say as gift? A gift without wanting, without wanting-to-say, an insignificant gift, a gift without intention to give? Why would we still call that a gift?"[39] Why, indeed? Our own suspicion is no less intense than Derrida's (which is directed against the teleology of intention), but for opposite reasons: The existence of the problem raised here derives only from a complete misunderstanding of the very concept of the gift, or more precisely from the ignorance of the fact that there are multiple kinds of gifts—as there are multiple kinds of being, according to Aristotle. This is why it is important to avoid confusing the ceremonial gift, which must be reciprocal (all the more so because it is not a self-interested exchange), and the gracious unilateral gift, which must not expect any return (even if it does not preclude feelings or expressions of gratitude). But to make the gracious gift—without clarification or awareness—the criterion of evaluation of every modality of the gift, in particular ritual ones, is an epistemological mistake that invalidates the entire demonstration. It amounts to disqualifying the entire network of relationships generated by the ritual gift—a network whose aim is the establishment of society. It is as if Mauss was expected to recognize—in a denial of reality—that not only did no gift take place, but no bond was ever wished for or created between the parties involved in the gift.

(4) *The Thing Given.* It seems obvious that if the gift—as practiced as an observable phenomenon—is understood as self-interested exchange, then the thing given cannot be *given*; it is merely an external thing, the objective *res* defined by contract in Roman law. If the ceremonial gift relationship were nothing more than the transfer of a good from one party to another, then speaking of a gift would certainly be contradictory. But what Mauss says of the thing given is entirely different: The thing has value only because in it the giver invests *him/herself* as a part of his/her being: "By giving one is giving *oneself*, and if one gives *oneself*, it is because one 'owes' *oneself*—one's person and one's goods—to others."[40] The aim of the gift is thus to commit oneself. Furthermore, the thing given is not desirable as a good, but as a *guarantee* and *substitute* of the giver. It is the means—the symbol—of an alliance or pact; it is the sign of the value of the giver group; it carries prestige and confirms the bond established. Its highest expression is the wife who moves to the allied group, following the exogamic rule; exogamy is "the supreme rule of the gift,"[41] Lévi-Strauss writes.

This exchange and commitment of the Selves in ritual gifts has nothing to do with an offer of ownership or appropriation. Derrida's remarks on the notion of *taking* are revealing in this respect. He supports them based on Émile Benveniste's analyses:[42] The Hittite term *dâ* as well as the old Iranian term *a-dâ* (equivalent to the Latin *do*) mean both "to give" and "to receive," and even "to take" (in the same way that in modern French the term *louer* means both "to rent" and "to rent out").[43] Before returning to Derrida's use of these data, let us note that this reversibility of giving and receiving is a perfect illustration of the reversibility Mauss brings to the fore with respect to the three inseparable gestures involved in the gift: In the realm of reciprocity, to give is always also to expect to receive, and often already to return a gift. In the spiral of exchanges—an ever-shifting circular movement—the positions of giver and recipient continually alternate, thus committing time as renewal and new beginning of the relationship; Derrida, however, is not interested in this. By reducing *receiving* (discussed by Mauss) to *taking*, a mere gesture of capture or appropriation, he deepens the suspicion against the gift relationship as bordering on predation. Derrida formulates this suspicion through the following cascade of deliberately playful equivalences:

> *The Gift* complicates itself, gets taken up in its own internal complication: giving itself to be an essay on the gift, it is also in truth an essay on taking. Even though it is given *to be* an essay on the gift, it can be taken as an essay on taking. Or yet again: even though it takes itself to be an essay on the gift, it gives itself in fact, in truth, as an essay on taking. We don't know if we should take it for what it takes itself to be or as it gives itself, or for what it gives itself since what it gives one to think or to read is that giving must be equivalent to taking. Which does not mean "to take oneself for" and "to give oneself for" come down—or come back—to the same thing.[44]

It will be up to the *over-taken* reader to decide is this statement is receivable, and then to see what gives . . .

We must thus recognize—and regret—that Derrida's reading of Mauss is based on a misunderstanding. Derrida clearly begins with a shift to the givenness of Being—Heidegger's *Es gibt/It gives*—and continues by positing as a standard a form of gift that is certainly admirable: the oblative unconditional gift. Were this form of gift the only existing or unquestionably legitimate one, then Derrida's critique of Mauss would be acceptable, but this is not the case. It is therefore not acceptable to implicitly set the oblative gift as a norm of reference for gift practices of a very different kind, whose purposes are specific social effects that we must be able to assess. We will have to clarify those effects to support our—certainly stern—reading of Derrida's analyses of Mauss's *The Gift*. "His essay *The Gift* begins more and more to look like an essay not on the gift but on the word 'gift,'" Derrida claims.[45] It now seems to us that this judgment applies above all to its author.

There should be no doubt that when considering a writing such as Mauss's, which presupposes precise knowledge and highly elaborate methods of analysis, the best a philosopher could do would be to inquire into the field of competence of its author, assess the state of knowledge at the time when the text was written, and determine the extent to which the text has brought and still brings a novel approach to the questions it discusses, or even reconfigures the field itself. This is in fact the—exceptional—kind of opening of the field that *The Gift* achieves. Any objections raised must concern primarily the arguments and data presented. To keep to a critique of the author's language, without considering the substance of the demonstration, amounts to embracing the wrong discipline. True, Mauss's language is not innocent; there is no doubt that many of his formulations convey enduring prejudices, as when with respect to certain gift exchanges he talks of "noble trade," "usurious offerings," or even "contract." But when considering those faulty expressions we must keep in mind the global aim of *The Gift*, which is to show that ritual gift exchanges are not trade, but activities that commit the entire group in procedures whose purpose is to create alliances, acquire prestige, honor the parties involved—sometimes through glorious challenges—and above all to reinforce life lived in common. Derrida never discusses this, nor does he inquire into the literature presented by Mauss or the considerable anthropological research developed on the topic through the twentieth century. To claim that Mauss's *The Gift* "speaks of everything but the gift" because the form of gift he discusses is and must be reciprocal, amounts to blaming him for competently performing his scientific task of observation and description, to suggesting that he should have identified the oblative gift as the truth behind the reciprocal gift. Furthermore, this would amount to saying that the societies involved should have been other than what they were.

We could put our critique of Derrida into perspective by mentioning that he never claims to situate himself in the domain of social anthropology. He states this quite explicitly: "We are here *departing*, in a peremptory and distinct fashion, from this tradition."[46] This is a perfectly legitimate decision, but only with the obvious condition that an author cannot at the same time claim to intervene in a field of competence from which he intends to distance himself and whose concepts and data he does not command. Derrida could have applied to himself—with the relevant transposition and reversal—the warning he addressed to another ethnologist, Lévi-Strauss, with respect to the latter's remarks on writing in *Tristes tropiques*: "One can often see in the descriptive practice of the 'social sciences' the most *seductive* (in every sense of the word) confusion of empirical investigation, inductive hypothesis and intuition of essence without any precautions as to the origin and function of the propositions advanced."[47] With the proper reversal, we could come to a solid agreement on this remark.

In Conclusion: Reciprocity, Gratuity, and Hospitality

The aporia Derrida formulates as a radical objection to the ritual form of gift described by Mauss is based on a serious misunderstanding associated with a constant suspicion against the very idea of reciprocity. Derrida always reduces reciprocity to a self-interested movement of return to the self, whereas, in the case of the ceremonial gift, reciprocity belongs to a logic of glorious and generous reply. It is necessarily different from the oblative unilateral relationship; while the former does not preclude the latter, it cannot be assessed by its standard. *The gratuity requirement therefore does not disqualify the reciprocity requirement.* They are two different orders of relationships—since gratuity itself involves a relationship. In the most generous, unconditional, humble, and secret gesture, the other party is still present—and it cannot be otherwise.

It is tempting to imagine what *Giving Time* would be if rid of its awkward and irrelevant opposition to Mauss. The aporia of the pure gift could then be accepted—since there is beauty in this demand—without associating it with this false debate. It could be that Derrida understood this and was able to avoid this trap in the intense meditation he develops in 1995 in *The Gift of Death* based on writings by Jan Patočka, Emmanuel Levinas, Martin Heidegger, and Soren Kierkegaard. His aim here is to explore the riskiest and most exposed advance, the most apparently unreasonable in its bareness, required by the face of the Other, the name of alien Totality, or what is given in the death of the other, and what gives me my own death. This reflection also touches on the Mosaic prohibition on killing, the renouncement of vengeance, and finally the Gospels' prescription to reply to aggression with nonviolence, and above all this absolute and "inhumanly" radical injunction: "Love your enemies" (Matt. 5:44). Here Derrida rightly underlines against Carl Schmitt that the enemy the text refers to is not a private enemy belonging to the same ethnicity (*inimicus*), but the enemy from another nation (*hostis*).[48] In these analyses, however, Derrida reiterates his old suspicion against any form of reciprocity as "economic" resorption of the generous gesture, so much so that he borders on denial: While he comments on the passages of Matthew's Gospel that advocate absolute gratuity—"When you give alms, do not let your left hand know what your right hand is doing" (Matt. 6:3)—he carefully avoids quoting the nearby verse that recalls the old Golden Rule: "Do to Others as you would have them do to you" (Matt. 7:12). This verse is obviously unsettling for Derrida's reflection. The passages from Matthew's Gospel that call for a discrete and even secret gift also include the following statement: "Your Father who sees in secret will reward you" (Matt. 6:4); this is the reward and "wages" of the Just. Derrida is aware of this nuance, and he is forced to confront his embarrassment, which he does as follows: "We need to distinguish between two types of salary: one of retribution, equal exchange, within a circular economy, the other of absolute surplus value, heterogeneous to outlay or investment. Two seemingly heterogeneous economies therefore."[49] This dialectical bypass of a difficulty—which consists of dividing a concept into two and reversing it—is a well-known procedure, as clever as it is unconvincing. It is *costly* in every respect, notably in terms of credibility. The question should have been raised differently from the outset.

The same can be said of another form of generous gift, hospitality, which, in another radical formulation, Derrida proposes to view as "absolute hospitality":[50] beyond positive law, beyond all compensation and any possibility of identifying the stranger we welcome. Here again, an aporia emerges in this unconditional openness that he calls *the* law of hospitality, as opposed to formal or informal traditions of reciprocity called *laws* of hospitality.[51] But here the aporia turns into an antinomy: "an insoluble antinomy, a non-dialectizable antinomy"[52] between "*The* law of unlimited hospitality" and "the *laws* (in the plural), those rights and duties that are always . . . concrete, determined." The former would remain "abstract, utopian, illusory" without the latter "which however deny it, or at any rate threaten it, sometimes corrupt or pervert it."[53] This antinomy between norm and positive law is not new; it is a topos Derrida subtly dramatizes here. Reciprocity finally finds an opportunity in the empirical character of practices. Is this enough to understand the specific power of reciprocity? It would be if this empirical quality were understood in its own terms rather than as a mere function of distancing. What more does it tell us about reciprocity? Answering this question required an inquiry. Something is amiss here. The entire question is the consideration of the presence of the Other—his/her necessary reaction in the gift relationship; failing to consider this amounts to denying the relationship itself; at best this gives rise to a bachelor machine. While gratuity is not the same thing as reciprocity, neither is it its opposite, and even less its negation. Gratuity is not the standard by which reciprocity should be assessed. Understanding the legitimacy of the one takes nothing away from the legitimacy of the other. They define different requirements within different *orders*—to use Pascal's term. We can bet that Derrida would understand this, if he had a chance to *reply*.[54] Let us grant him the *last word*, which best summarizes his reservation and revives ours: For him if a gift is openly known as such, if it is meant to be recognized as a gift, then it immediately ceases to be a gift. The gift is the secret. The secret is the last word of the gift, which is the last word of the secret.[55]

CHAPTER 2

Propositions I:
The Ceremonial Gift—
Alliance and Recognition

It is generally accepted without critical discussion, as a self-evident and universal fact, that the term gift refers to the transfer of a good to another person without expectation of a similar gesture in return. Almost every study and reflection on the gift, even the most complex, seems compelled to agree on this apparently common-sense definition. We are suffused in this atmosphere of principled oblativity, and we never discuss it without displaying the admiration due to what is viewed as admirable in and of itself. There is something troubling about this compulsory praise. It is sometimes associated with preachy moralism, which can go as far as to conversely mock this presupposed gratuity and to suspect, behind every generous gesture, concealed selfishness and the shameful expectation of a return on investment, but this suspicion is not a critical advance.

Philosophers rarely approach the question of the gift without mentioning Mauss's *The Gift*. This quasi-obligatory reference has the advantage of seeming to confer on an abstract reflection the guarantee of objectivity provided by a discipline with time-tested methods. More secretly, some may wish to situate the question of the gift at a distance both spatial (because of the cultural diversity of the practices discussed) and temporal (through testimonies that come from the origins). In and of themselves such attempts are worthy of respect; less so is their sometimes cursory character. Many do not go beyond a mention of the *potlatch*; others occasionally also refer to the *kula* exchanges of the Trobriand Islands or the circulation of the Maori *hau*. A number of commenters use those three famous cases analyzed by Mauss in the old tradition of the exempla, whose only purpose is to illustrate a preexisting theory.

This practice should seem odd to us. Anthropological knowledge—or at least the form of knowledge developed based on ethnographic inquiries— requires of those who acquire or assess it the same degree of precision in documentation and rigor in method as do the natural sciences. Although the social sciences remain to a large extent interpretive sciences, they are just as incompatible with imprecision and generalizing as are the so-called exact sciences. As a consequence, in the field under consideration, philosophy cannot make use of the results and methods of anthropological knowledge without a prior effort at information on the relevant data and assessment of the approaches presented by researchers in the discipline. The first step must therefore be to assess the revolution accomplished by Mauss,[1] revisit some of his analyses and hypotheses, identify certain obstacles, and finally propose different solutions that take into account the wealth of research conducted over almost a century. Many researchers have already undertaken this task.[2] To avoid repeating here a demonstration already presented elsewhere,[3] the primary aim of this clarification will be to bring out the arguments most conducive to identifying the fundamental features of the ceremonial gift and clarifying its purpose. This effort should make it possible to return with renewed critical resources to the approaches various philosophies have proposed on the question.

Mauss: The Gift as a Total Social Phenomenon

Marcel Mauss deserves credit for constituting the epistemological *problem* of the ritual gift (which he calls "archaic") based on the ethnographic documents available at the beginning of the twentieth century, and connecting them to the testimonies of ancient Indian, Roman, Celtic, Scandinavian, and Germanic literatures. While he was not the first to consider this phenomenon, he was the first to systematically gather the relevant data and propose a model according to which gift exchanges appear as a major social fact. He even called it a "total social fact" (a claim we will have to discuss). Among the mass of data he collected through his readings, three sets emerge, each characterized by a term used by a population involved.

Those terms have become emblems of practices observable elsewhere or simply possible. Let us try to extract their main features and present a brief critical evaluation.

The Three Canonical Examples: *Kula*, *Potlatch*, and *Hau*

In the elaboration of his problematic, Mauss owes much to Bronislaw Malinowski's book, *Argonauts of the Western Pacific*,[4] which deals with the great cycles of gift exchanges (*kula*) in the Trobriand Islands, a Melanesian archipelago. Those exchanges constitute the core of indigenous social life: Weeks or even months are dedicated to preparing the boats and collecting precious goods (*waigu'a*); numerous magical ceremonies are conducted to protect those goods (because they are a part of the givers that will be given away to the recipients). The most important are the bracelets that circulate from east to west and the necklaces that circulate from west to east; the former are considered male and worn by women, the latter female and worn by men; they are said to seek and meet one another in this dual movement. When the boats reach an island the postulants in *kula* place on the beach semiprecious objects: opening gifts meant to attract *kula* partners. Those who accept them are bound to continue the exchange. Then the main exchange—bracelets and necklaces—begins, stretching over several days in a festive atmosphere. When those ceremonies are over, the travelers leave with their new gifts to engage in new exchanges on the next island. Thus an entire network of bonds is woven through the exchange of the *waigu'a*, often well-known and reputed for their great beauty, and endowed with a proper name. Their value derives not only from the fact that they are carved out of rare stones or shells, but above all from the fact that they used to belong to specific persons; it has to do with the memory of the bonds they carry. This is therefore the polar opposite of a commercial exchange (which, as we will see, is also practiced during the same peregrinations, but in a very different way); what then is the purpose of those *kula* exchanges?

The second example presented by Mauss is *potlatch*, the agonistic exchange among the native populations of the northwest coast of America described by Franz Boas at the end of the nineteenth century: A chief gives a celebration in the name of his group to honor another chief who is dealt with at the same time as a party to be treated and a rival to be challenged. The high value of the gifts offered (emblazoned copper, woven blankets, furs, food) is meant to make a reply difficult. The chief most capable of giving excessive gifts gains honor and prestige, but no additional power. The main goal of this symbolic competition appears to be acquiring a higher degree of glory. This involves an intense challenge since it goes without saying that the recipients are obligated to reply. A correction must be made to Mauss's description, as well as Boas's, on which it is based: As shown by more recent studies,[5] certain extravagant aspects of those provocations through gifts are associated with the very specific context in which those populations found themselves at the end of the nineteenth century. First, the prohibition on war by the governments of Canada and the United States transferred most of the existing rivalry to the *potlatch*. Second, the accumulation of wealth due to trade with foreign merchants made possible a considerable increase in the amounts of the goods at stake. Finally, demographic decline reduced the number of positions of prestige available for conquest, exacerbating the competition for those positions. We must therefore have a more modest view of this "mad *potlatch*," from which some authors derived exaggerated conclusions on the agonistic gift.

The mandatory character of the reply appears especially clear in Mauss's third example, the *hau*. It comes from an inquiry conducted by Elsdon Best among the Maori of New Zealand at the beginning of the twentieth century. A local elder named Ranaipiri explains that if A gives a gift to B who then offers it to C, then when B receives a gift from C he will have to offer it to A, or C will have to give a countergift directly to A as a reply to the gift he received from B. There is a clear explanation for this: When the movement of reciprocity involves transmission through several parties, it must return to its source; this constitutes the spirit of the thing given, called *hau*. The existence of a third party puzzles Mauss. Yet the intervention of this third person constitutes the crucial point of the elder's demonstration: Reciprocity is not only dual; it moves through the entire sequence of the recipients (as does the so-called "generalized" exchange in exogamic circuits).[6] What returns is not the thing itself, but the very gesture of giving and reciprocating the gift, which must be repeated along the entire chain of transmission. Why? Mauss merely observes this practice and reports native beliefs without providing a convincing reason for their existence. Yet the *hau* appears in native discourse as the very spirit of reciprocity. This is what we must better understand.

Mauss's Hypotheses

First, Mauss defines the procedures of gift exchanges as a "total social fact." What he designates is a phenomenon that includes and incorporates every element of collective life: religious, political, economic, ethical, aesthetic, etc. This is at least how we can translate this phenomenon into our own categories. But the most important element lies elsewhere: This fact must be understood as the dominant fact around which everything else is organized, providing a reason for being to the whole of society. This involves two connected dimensions: a sociological purpose of integration of the various activities of the group, and a cultural purpose of valorization of one of those activities. Hence our question: What happens to this crucial fact in modern societies? Either it has disappeared, or its aim has persisted in different forms, and if so what are those forms?

Mauss also emphasizes the fact that the procedure comprises three connected and obligatory steps: giving, receiving, and giving back. What he finds most enigmatic is this obligatory character; he mentions it without explaining it. Can we find a satisfactory interpretation for it?

Mauss realizes that this exchange is in no way commercial; with respect to the famous *kula* circuit of the Trobriand Islands he even notices, after Malinowski, the existence of a self-interested exchange that aims at strict equivalence, viewed as contrary to the *kula* and conducted with different parties: *gimwali*. Gift exchanges and commercial exchanges coexist; they belong to two different spheres. How can we understand that, while the reply to the gift received is *obligatory*, it is however not self-interested? Let us note once again that Mauss's language is sometimes awkward: He speaks of "noble trade," "payment," "credit," "contract," and "gift economy"; his view often remains evolutionistic. He nevertheless insists that what is at stake in those exchanges is not profit.[7]

Finally, he emphasizes the fact that in this public exchange of precious goods what is given is always *oneself*; it is the self of the giver that is literally given to the recipient in the good offered ("By giving one is giving *oneself*, and if one gives *oneself*, it is because one 'owes' *oneself*—one's person and one's goods—to others").[8] What are the implications of this presence of the giver in the thing given? Is it a superstition we should ignore, or an exchange that brings to the fore a unique relationship between the two parties in the gift through the third-party of the thing offered and received—a relationship absent when a thing is sold?

The Ceremonial Gift Is Neither Economic nor Moral nor Legal

What is at stake in the facts discussed by Mauss is an intense bond between parties, public prestige granted and gained, and the conclusion of an alliance. Taking up and extending his analyses we can state that the ritual gift is situated outside profitable exchange, as well as outside charitable generosity and contractual relationships.

Many observers have attempted to develop an economic interpretation of gift exchange, presenting it as barter or trade. Boas considers *potlatch* an archaic form of loan with interest.[9] The same views are found in theorists as thoughtful and well-informed as Max Weber[10] and Karl Polanyi.[11] Malinowski does not make this mistake, and he underlines the difference between *kula* and *gimwali* (Mauss notices it too). The *kula* exchange does presuppose an economy: Just like us, the Trobriand natives do not live off gifts alone. They produce food and artifacts, and they have to make the precious objects they exchange. They practice exchanges of ordinary goods needed in everyday life, as does everyone else. To speak of a *gift economy* can thus lead to misinterpretations, unless we understand that ordinary economic activity focuses on the dominant social fact, in which the life of the group is expressed and exalted: the *kula* exchange, which is not an economic exchange. Its central function is to bond the groups through the network of the parties involved in the exchange. The purpose of those festive times is not to offer and gain consumer goods, but to give guarantees of and public testimonies to the will to make life in common possible.

Those ritual exchanges are not moral exchanges, however: Their goal is not to demonstrate kindness, or even solidarity. No mutual aid is involved; ceremonial goods are not survival goods meant for needy recipients, but precious goods, symbols of alliance, and guarantees to the commitment of the givers. The alliance established or renewed involves the public life of the group (as does most crucially the exogamic alliance); as such it is a political alliance. Ceremonial gift exchanges institute a pact and sanction trust; once they have been established attitudes of compassion and solidarity in difficult times may be observed. If there is a morality to those exchanges, it involves primarily the loyalty displayed and the honor at stake in the alliance rather than any oblative intention. Contrary to those collective practices, charitable gestures are admirable in proportion to their discretion; by hypothesis they do not call for a reply, no more than does philanthropy call for compensation. Unlike them, the gesture of the ceremonial gift must be *public*, visible to all; because it commits the entire group, determines the prestige of the giver, and aims at establishing an alliance, it requires a reply: It is meant to be reciprocated, since an alliance is necessarily reciprocal. The commitment of one party implies the commitment of the other. We must therefore consider seriously the existence of several fundamentally different types of gifts.

Finally, the ceremonial gift is not a legal type of gift, in the way a contractual relationship can be. In *La Foi jurée*[12] Georges Davy, a disciple of
Mauss, proposes to consider *potlatch* as an archaic form of contract. Mauss
does not follow Davy on this point, although in *The Gift* he uses the term
"contract" in the broader sense of "pact." A strictly contractual obligation
is limited in time: It defines an accounting requirement in quantitative and
qualitative terms as to the objects exchanged, and it includes constraining
legal commitments under penalty of sanctions (fines or prison time). Contracts aim at the strict equality and mutual profit of the parties, who are
formally bound as agents subject to the law and substantially committed in
their being. The gift, on the contrary, is viewed as obligatory only because
it involves prestige, honor, and the self of the giver, and it transcends any
equalitarian calculus. Gift and contract are opposite concepts.[13]

The Three Categories of the Gift

Before going further we need to reexamine the undifferentiated use generally made of the term *gift*. We have already noted that the main reason for
those false debates was the uniform consideration of profoundly different
forms of gifts—an epistemological error whose consequences on entire
domains of social philosophy and the anthropology of exchanges might be
more serious than is generally believed.

When questions are raised about the meaning of giving, a consensus
emerges on a broad definition assumed to be applicable to every case; it
could be stated as follows: To give is to provide a good or service in a
disinterested way—that is, without any expectation or guarantee of reciprocation. This definition appears to go without saying, yet to make it a criterion of assessment of every form of gift can lead to the most serious confusions, or even outright misinterpretations, since the ritual gift includes
the imperative obligation to reciprocate gifts. We must thus recognize that
the pure oblativity generally viewed as the core of the notion of gift is
not relevant in this case and cannot be part of a general definition. Confronting this difficulty, the solution most often chosen is to relegate the
ritual gift to the margins of the standard definition as an "archaic" practice,
and the requirement of reciprocity is viewed as implying the expectation
of some advantage (or interest) that constitutes the very stain of this archaic character. This move performs an implicit discriminatory judgment
between the "true gift" (presupposed to be oblative and unconditional)
and its impure figures, identifiable by their distance from the norm. Conversely, to preserve the relevance of this "old-fashioned" form of gift, some

authors present casuistic considerations on the amphibology of the term "interest," which comes to be paradoxically associated with the term gift. They then claim that the gift remains associated at a different relationship level with the seeking of an advantage. This is a way to dodge the problem of the specific form of reciprocity embodied by the ceremonial gift. It is therefore more fruitful to consider the existence of a true heterogeneity among the models of the gift than to try to superimpose a single frame onto overly diverse practices. The approach proposed here will emulate Pascal's: Those models will be viewed as pertaining to different *orders*, each endowed with its own relevance and legitimacy. This is the method used by Michael Walzer in *Spheres of Justice*[14] and Luc Boltanski and Laurent Thévenot in *On Justification*.[15]

This approach requires that the concept of gift be clarified and that the heterogeneity of the practices encompassed by this concept be brought to the fore. It is hard to imagine how the three following cases could be placed in the same category: (1) the festivities and gifts chiefs of clans (or of any other type of group) give one another in turn in traditional societies; (2) the presents parents give their children on the occasion of their birthdays, or anyone gives loved ones to make them happy and express attachment and esteem; (3) the donations in the form of necessities provided to populations following a catastrophe. Those examples are not chosen at random: They can be considered as illustrating three major categories of the gift: (a) the *ceremonial* gift (a more appropriate term than *archaic*, which carries too many presuppositions), always *public* and *reciprocal*; (b) the *gracious* or oblative gift, which may or may not be private, but is primarily *unilateral*; (c) *mutual aid*, associated with either social *solidarity* or philanthropy—which some authors mistakenly view as the modern form of the traditional ceremonial gift.

When a single notion—in this case, the gift—involves such different practices and occasions widely divergent arguments, there is reason to believe that its definition is imprecise or even confused, and that those practices have been insufficiently described and improperly categorized. It is clear enough that the three examples above do not constitute a homogeneous class of objects.

The first case is characterized by the strict obligation to reciprocate the gifts received, as shown by ethnographic inquiries. This raises the question of a *fundamental reciprocity* that cannot be reduced to a mere exchange of good manners or the expectation of a return on investment; what this practice involves is a relationship of *reply*. Its semantic field, in Greek, for example, is *dosis/antidosis* (gift/countergift), where *anti* always designates the *action in return* called for by the original action. This is the field of *agōn*, rivalry in games or even fighting—that is, within the precise boundaries of a system of rules where action and reaction alternate according to a law.

The second case manifests on the part of the giver a spontaneous and joyful generosity toward loved ones; its primary character is psychological or moral. In Greek this is the semantic field of *kharis* (one of the original meanings of this term is "joy"); it is unilateral (there is no such thing as *anti-kharis*). This also involves the entire theoretical field of Biblical grace (*hen*—favor—translated as *kharis* in the Septuagint and again by Paul), Latin *gratia* from Seneca to Augustine, and Christian theology from the Middle Ages to the Reformation, as well as *agapē*, at least as formulated in the Christian tradition (in ancient Greek writings it designates instead the ritual of hospitality).[16]

Finally, the case of the mutual-aid gift has a much more social character of generosity than does the previous case, to the benefit of either familiars (friends or neighbors, with whom reciprocity is desirable but not compulsory) or strangers who are victims of a catastrophe (in which case reciprocation would make no sense): It is the field of *philia* or *philanthrōpia* Aristotle discusses in his *Nicomachean Ethics*. It also involves the various practices of mutual aid among loved ones, neighbors, or members of a chosen community (whether religious group, friendly association, or scholarly society), as well as everything Weber describes as coming under a "religious ethic of brotherly love" [*die religiöse Ethik der Brüderlichkeit*].[17] In that case, unlike the two others, the goods offered are not primarily precious or prestigious—symbols of a pact—but goods useful in ordinary life:[18] food, clothing, housing, employment. They can also be words or gestures of support; the context is not ritual or festive, but that of an emergency requiring efficient action.

An essential question is now inescapable: Whereas the second (gracious) and third (mutual aid) forms of gift are still common practices today, it is clear that the ceremonial gift as a specifically public form of gift exchange among established groups no longer constitutes a dominant phenomenon in modern societies. This phenomenon has even almost disappeared, barely surviving in official exchanges of presents among heads of state or institutions, and in reciprocal invitations among friends. According to some authors this quasi disappearance justifies the use of the term "archaic," and it explains why it is tempting to find traces of this phenomenon in the two other forms of gift still practiced. This is a misguided way to consider the problem; an entirely different approach is possible and even indispensable, in which ceremonial exchanges are understood as exchanges not of goods, but of symbols, and more precisely as *public procedures of reciprocal recognition among groups*.

The Ceremonial Gift as a Pact of Recognition

The ceremonial gift raises a number of specific problems that profoundly distinguish it from the other two forms of gift. Without considering in detail the now-considerable ethnographic literature that has dealt with this question for almost a century, as a critical summary it will be enough for us to draw from field investigations eight variables that make it possible to better identify the specificity of the ceremonial gift: (1) *Goods exchanged*: precious objects or beings, or festive foods; (2) *Ritual procedures*: well-established and accepted by the parties involved; (3) *Level of communication*: public; (4) *Effects generated or expected*: (a) strong bonding between givers and recipients; (b) gaining prestige and rank; (5) *degree of choice*: obligatory; (6) *Mode of relationship*: reciprocal; (7) *Attitude of exchange*: generous rivalry; (8) *Content of the gesture*: giving oneself in the thing given, which is a *guarantee* and *substitute* of the giver.

This list makes it clear that the other two types of gifts (*gracious* and *mutual aid*) share with the ceremonial gift no more than two or three of those variables, which is not much. To discuss *the gift* in general therefore entails a serious epistemological risk. For the sake of consistency, the gift should be discussed only if associated with the qualifier that determines the realm in which its practice is situated; this makes it necessary to divide into three what has been called the "paradigm of the gift,"[19] or better yet to accept that there are at least three paradigms rather than one. Pascal's concept of *orders* is relevant here, because each of those paradigms has its own system of justification. Thus reciprocity, crucial in the ceremonial gift, is not relevant in the gracious gift; in the solidarity-based gift reciprocity can be either valorized or not. In the same way, discretion—the self-effacement of the giver—often appropriate or even indispensable in the gracious or the solidarity-based gift, would make no sense in *the ceremonial gift*, which is *public by definition*, as the foundation of an official recognition that binds the parties involved through goods treated as symbols of alliance. What would be the meaning of a pact unknown to its parties and nonreciprocal? One could claim that at least one of the variables above is shared by all three types of gift: *generosity*. This is unquestionable, but it is important to note that the nature of this *generosity* is different in every case: In the ceremonial gift it is essentially a public challenge, characterized by an occasionally ostentatious visibility, whereas in the gracious gift it is discrete or secret, aimed at causing joy in the beneficiary, and in the solidarity-based gift it amounts to compassion through a gesture of support.

We thus need a different interpretation of the ceremonial gift, distinct to some extent from the one Mauss presents, while still involving the idea of an exchange of *goods*. A few elements of our hypothesis have already been mentioned above; it is now time to present its central argument: *The ceremonial gift is above all a procedure of public reciprocal recognition among groups in traditional societies*, particularly those without a state structure. It remains to be determined what this *recognition* means, and why it is granted through this procedure. The best way to understand this is to pay attention to what inquiries teach us about *first encounters*. We know through multiples testimonies that those encounters are occasions of reciprocal exchanges of presents—opening gifts. They constitute an apparently reasonable and courteous practice. What is surprising to us is that those exchanges are presented as *obligatory*—unless the groups involved choose to engage in conflict—while we are aware that, today, when groups encounter one another, salutations and friendly attitudes are sufficient; this is the core of the problem. Nothing can help us better grasp what is at stake than a brief narrative reported by a British anthropologist;[20] in the 1920s his New Guinean informer had witnessed the arrival of the first white man in his village, located in the upper valleys of Mount Hagen. According to local legends the dead could return in the form of white-skinned cannibalistic ghosts. The decision was made to test whether this potentially dangerous stranger was a human: He was offered pigs (following ordinary custom with respect to guests invited to the village). In return, the white man—a well-informed Australian administrator—offered the villagers precious shells of the kind used on the occasion of weddings and other festive exchanges. Then, the informer concluded, "We decided he was human."[21]

It seems to me that this anecdote can be viewed as a reference parable that helps us understand the most general meaning of the reciprocal public ceremonial gift and its essential relation to the phenomenon of *recognition*. The *opening gifts* ritual is a procedure of recognition in three senses of the word: *identifying*, *accepting*, and finally *honoring* the Other. Let us clarify those notions, while asking why this recognition must be granted through the exchange of *goods*. What is it that one recognizes in the Other? What does this recognition make possible?

To answer those questions let us shift to an entirely different field and ask if in nonhuman animal societies, starting with those closest to us—apes—similar behaviors can be observed. The most advanced research in that field, in particular in chimpanzees,[22] show that: (1) Mutual recognition as *identification* is conducted through sound messages, smells, and above all coordinated combinations of gestures and attitudes; (2) Recognition as *acceptance* is achieved through postures and procedures of reciprocity (such as attitudes of appeasement, mutual delousing, and the sharing of food), but never through *objects given as guarantees and kept in exchange for other objects offered either immediately or at a later point* (which has nothing to do with the hierarchical distribution of food in various mammals[23] or the wedding "rituals" of certain birds, reptiles, or insects). Adam Smith sensed this human peculiarity: "Nobody ever saw a dog make a fair and deliberate exchange of one bone for another with another dog."[24] To sum up, among animals no *convention* has ever been observed (a convention is something else entirely than behaviors that show coordination or even cooperation[25] within a group, or phenomena of spontaneous hierarchy). It seems that humans alone follow procedures by which they commit themselves by *giving to Others something of their own* as a *guarantee* and *substitute of themselves*. Let us provisionally call "Self" an agent accountable for him/herself to other agents over a period of time. That he/she does so through the mediation of a *third-party thing* that testifies to his/her person is remarkable. This reminds us of the ancient Greek and Roman procedure of the *pact* contracted through a *symbolon*, a piece of pottery broken into two and of which each party kept one half that precisely fit only the other half (*sym-ballein*, "putting together") as *future* evidence to the agreement. According to this model[26] the reciprocal gift is nothing else than the inaugurating gesture of *reciprocal recognition* among humans, a gesture unique among living beings *in that it is performed through the mediation of an object from the world*, or more precisely a *third-party thing*—but not just any thing: It must come from the *self* and stand for the Self as part of his very being and as witness to the commitment made. To conduct an alliance is to bring together the specificity of the Self and the alien-ness of the Other through a precious thing desirable by the other, as an invitation to enter a pact that guarantees mutually granted trust. The third-party element conjoins the two sides: There is no covenant without an ark of covenant. This reciprocal recognition through the exchange of something that belongs inherently to the group (or its representative) and is offered to the other party is at the core of the exogamic relationship (the wife who is given is "the supreme gift," Lévi-Strauss says,[27] and he adds that exogamy "is the supreme rule of the gift").[28] This illuminates the prohibition of incest, keystone of this relationship, as a positive imperative of reciprocity. From the outset life in its very process of reproduction is caught in this regulated exchange. We are humans to the extent that we go out of the "natural" group of consanguineous relatives

through the recognition of and alliance with *those other than ourselves*: To
be what we are, we need to recognize what we are not.

This, in a few words, is the anthropological interpretation of the ceremonial gift that we are proposing; it separates it clearly from the other
two models of the gift: the gracious unilateral and the solidarity-based
gift. We now need to understand how concepts such as symbol, convention, and alliance are articulated together. An *alliance*—and an exogamic
alliance in particular—is a *pact*, and therefore an *intentional* recognition
between "us" and "you" that goes beyond the mere social self-regulation
of the groups. The alliance brings together what is not together—performing *sym-ballein*—and involves intentionality: The encounter of two
autonomous beings involves a decision—whether explicit or implicit—to
give oneself rules. To set a convention is to accept a set of rules (which is
one of the primary functions of rituals), but also to commit oneself, to
give *oneself* in the thing that guarantees the pact. On this point Edmond
Ortigues makes an illuminating remark: "Generally, symbols are the materials through which language conventions, social pacts, and guarantees
of mutual recognition among free beings are established. Symbols are the
constitutive elements of a language, considered in relation to one another
as constituting a system of communication or alliance, a law of reciprocity
among subjects."[29] The pact offered in the *opening gifts* is extended through
time in a relationship that rituals aim at stabilizing. But this commitment is
made above all through the exogamic alliance, which binds the agreement
among groups to the reproduction of life and the movement of generations. This is especially obvious in the so-called "generalized" exogamic
exchange, where the reply occurs in the long term through extended networks, and which presupposes on the part of each group trust in the entire
society. Gift exchange as a gesture of alliance immediately makes human
groups regulated by a *convention*, no matter how implicit; in this, society is
an institution.

This fundamental relationship of *recognition* is *political* in that it is radically different from the *social bond*, which exists in every animal society and
is governed by spontaneous self-regulation. An alliance is above all the
public recognition of another group through a commitment to coexist and
collaborate. To say that it is from the outset a *convention* is to understand
it as a *politeia* in Aristotle's sense. An alliance takes up the social bond,
encompasses and transcends it into a political bond—that is, an intentional relationship of association—and it embodies in every society the
very emergence of the political. The human being is a *zōon politikon* in
that through the procedure of *recognition* that turns another group into an

ally, he/she institutes a life based on rules. The specifically human bond is political primarily because it is the bond specific to autonomous beings capable of giving themselves a law (whether explicit or not). Let us calls this a *factum humanitatis* (as Kant calls moral law a *factum rationis*). We thus realize the existence of an essential articulation among human order, reciprocal *public recognition*, and instituted order. It remains to determine how this initial requirement underwent a profound transformation through history and how it is now embodied in our Modernity.

The Enigma of the Obligation to Give, Receive, and Reciprocate

Mauss's *The Gift* opens with a question that until now has remained unanswered: Why does the ceremonial gift involve an obligation? Why must the giving of a present be reciprocated? What seems surprising is that Mauss does not ask why one must give in the first place. This is probably because for him, as for most of his contemporaries—and still for most for us—the requirement to give, and to give without expecting reciprocation, goes without saying as morally desirable. The idea of obligatory reciprocity thus seems enigmatic, or even contrary to the idea of gift. It is therefore not enough to recognize this feature in ceremonial exchanges—its reason for being must be explained; Mauss is not able to do so.

To better understand this difficulty and attempt to overcome it, let us turn to Charles Peirce's theory of triadic relationships. For him every relationship that involves two agents and an object exchanged presupposes a *norm of exchange*. The relationship therefore does not amount to the addition of two separable gestures; from the outset and by definition, the parties involved and the thing exchanged are in relation *according to a law*.[30] Vincent Descombes rightly notes[31] that—contrary to Bertrand Russell's claim, which reduces every exchange to two dyadic gestures (A gives B and C receives B)—the gift relationship is not the transfer of a good from one party to another, but, as Peirce explains, a relationship *between the parties* through the mediation of the good. To give is always to give something to someone. This relationship is inherent to every "trivalent" verb (such as to grant, provide, procure, bring, deliver, lavish, award, etc.).[32] The claim that the terms of a triad are bound according to a law means that, (1) they form an indivisible structure; (2) the relationship is intentional and as such manifests a finalized action; and (3) from the outset the relationship between the parties constitutes a convention.

But we must go further: The ceremonial gift cannot be reduced to the gift of something to someone. The offer of a good to someone according to rules also characterizes the *contractual* relationship (to "sell" is also a trivalent verb). The relationship among the parties as defined by Peirce comes down to the mere provision of a good (A brings book B to C) and constitutes an authentic triad. On the contrary, from the outset the gift as a gesture—in particular the ceremonial gift—does much more than to generate a relationship according to a law: It is a *commitment of oneself* according to a law. It is the giving of *oneself* through the mediation of something. The third-party element carries the self of the giver; it is his *guarantee* and *substitute*. With respect to the ceremonial gift a second level of triadic relationships must therefore be considered. There is a shift from the neutral phenomenon of the transfer convention—the basic triadic structure—to the *personal gesture* of commitment to the recipient. In this case, to give is to give *oneself* according to a law.

But how can we understand the *obligation to reciprocate*? To do so we must consider a third level of the relationship of commitment of the self that the ceremonial gift embodies. The ceremonial gift calls for a reply, and even requires a reciprocating gesture; it is therefore necessarily a *gesture of reciprocity according to a law*. It is this obligation to reciprocate that surprises Mauss; he observes and documents it, but he recognizes his inability to explain it. He keeps to the natives' commentaries, as in the case of the *hau*. It does involve the force of the thing given, the spirit of the gift, but how does it entail the idea of reciprocation? To account for this reciprocity other authors choose to resort to the notion of interest, a serious misunderstanding that reduces the gift as a gesture to the logic of an advantage sought for oneself, whereas this gift relationship implies above all the recognition of the otherness of the other party.

Once again, what is the meaning of this *obligation* to reply that characterizes the ceremonial gift? It is neither a physical necessity to react (as a living organism reacts to an external stimulus) nor a purely legal obligation (which provides sanctions, as in breaches of contracts) or a moral requirement (in the sense that a failure to reply would be immoral). We cannot even presuppose in the spirit of Durkheim that the agents share a representation of society as a transcendent authority figure. The answer is probably simpler: We only need to understand that what we are dealing with is the structure of a game, and an alternation principle akin to that of any game with more than one player. To enter the game is to accept as a principle the obligation to reply (as in any exchange of civilities).[33] To fail to reply is to give up the game. Mauss does not realize that one does not return the ball to be generous, moral, or courteous, or by virtue of a contractual constraint, but because one's reply is part of the game as such, or of the system of rules that must be accepted for the game to be possible; this can be called a *convention*. In a more serious mode the same is true of the rules that govern fights to the death, such as duels. In the case of the ceremonial gift the impossibility of separating the terms of the triad (according to Peirce) derives not only from the relationship between the parties through the thing given—giving and receiving—but also from their reciprocal action—reciprocating. The gift-and-countergift is a gesture of reply, akin to the blow received in a game, a fight, or revenge (in fact the same parties involved in gift exchanges are also assigned responsibility for vindicatory justice when offenses have been committed).[34] What this involves is not moral choice, altruism, or charity, but the necessity to *reply* inherent to every interaction among living beings.

But in this case the "game" is at the same time a *pact* offered and accepted through the goods exchanged; in a way this pact is an armed peace. It would be a mistake and even a misunderstanding to think that rituals of reciprocal recognition testify to a natural disposition to consensus. On the contrary, opening gifts show that the offer of recognition is made on the background of a potentiality for conflict; numerous testimonies make it clear that the margin between acceptance and confrontation is a narrow one; the gift itself can be a deception.[35] The ceremonial gift must be understood as a risky *bet*, or even a challenge; it consists of *offering* to *seduce* and ultimately bind the *other*. The risk taken by one party to initiate the relationship calls for the risk accepted by the other to reply, since the risk taken testifies at the same to trust in the *guarantee* that the thing given constitutes; to enter the relationship is to accept reciprocity. In humans the two moral sentiments—alternatively active and passive—associated with this requirement are called *respect* (granted) and *honor* (received); the relationship is agonistic from the outset. Reciprocal ceremonial giving thus confronts and resolves in a particularly elegant way the prisoner's dilemma (in which a decision must be made based on limited information or with suspicion toward the other party). The giver bets on trust and gains it through the reply of the other party guaranteed by the things given. The reciprocal ceremonial gift takes on and resorbs a latent conflict. It constitutes the alternative to war in that it turns the stranger or the potential enemy into an ally; but it is not by definition the "state of peace" that Ricoeur wishes to see in it as the precursor to *agapē*[36] (in which he once again shifts the reciprocal ceremonial gift to the side of an oblative generosity alien to it).[37] If we accept that the ceremonial gift is primarily a procedure of alliance whose purpose is the reciprocal recognition of the parties involved, and if we understand that the antagonistic element inherent to it is overcome by this very recognition, then we are immediately confronted with the following question: How is public recognition granted in our own societies, and how do they displace and transpose what is at the core of the ritual?

The Question of Public Recognition Today

The ceremonial gift as described by ethnographic investigations always involves groups, even if it is conducted through the mediation of individual figures representative of those groups; this *public* character is inherent to the ritual. Malinowski is fully aware of this, and with respect to the *kula* cycle he writes: "I shall call an action ceremonial, if it is: (1) public; (2) carried on under observance of definite formalities; (3) if it has sociological, religious or magical import, and carries with it obligations."[38]

From this perspective the reciprocal ceremonial gift is inherently institutional; it does not have to do with what has been called after Simmel "primary sociality" (which on the contrary is at the core of the gracious and the solidarity-based gift). Without entering this debate, let us note that the necessarily public character of the ceremonial gift disqualifies any interpretation that questions its necessary visibility and reciprocity in the name of an (often unstated) moral norm that valorizes discretion and the gift as absolute oblativity. The primary purpose of exchange rituals is not to give goods, but to recognize one another publicly as parties in an alliance conducted through the goods exchanged. The ceremonial gift teaches us a dual lesson: (1) As a specifically human act of public recognition— and even an act foundational of humankind—its model is found across every relationship among humans (including those that involve the other two forms of gift discussed above); every encounter or social relationship presupposes the act of reciprocal recognition, and designates every human to every other as a being that must be considered in his/her dignity and respected unconditionally; *this does not mean that the ceremonial gift is foundational of human society, but only that it reveals its foundation*; (2) As institutional procedure from one group to another, initial experience of the relationship of alliance, and accepted convention, the ceremonial gift is the locus of the very emergence of *public space*—more precisely, its emergence as a specifically political relationship, intentional expression of a living-together that transcends purely social self-regulations (which are observed in every animal society). This does not entail, however, the permanence of its historical form.

A first question arises: How does this *public* reciprocal recognition, ensured in traditional societies through ritual gift exchanges, occur in societies with a central state? The most appropriate answer appears to be the following: *This recognition is performed and guaranteed by the law and the whole of the political and legal institutions*, which proclaim the dignity of our existence as citizens, subjects in law, and producers of goods. Contrary to what is too often claimed, the direct heritage of the ceremonial gift will not be found in exchanges of goods, or on the contrary in contemporary forms of generous mutual assistance, but in instituted rights and the struggles over those rights. It is for historical anthropology to show how this transformation has occurred. Without presenting its genealogy, let us recall that those ceremonial exchanges are observed in societies where, in general, forms of authority are tightly associated with statuses conferred by kinship systems (while not identical to them).[39] Hence the importance of the matrimonial alliance as the favored expression of public relationships among groups. But once an evolution has occurred that leads to the emergence of an authority that transcends kinship groups (this shift and the crisis that it generates is conveyed in Greek tragedy, in particular Aeschylus's *Oresteia*), the individual is affirmed as belonging to a broader group—such as the city—while also remaining for a long time a member of a lineage or clan. But the new identity has priority over the old, as shown by the crisis presented in *Antigone* and insightfully identified by Hegel.[40] The law that applies to all—the nomos—is the foundation of equality—*isonomia*; it belongs to the central space—the *meson*—where, in the public and identical recognition granted to all, allegiances from chief to chief are canceled, as is the face-to-face of specific groups—lineages, *genē*. From now on the *law* prevails as arbiter among individuals who have become equal members of the city.

A diverse corpus of historical research[41] shows that the invention of the space of the *polis* began to emerge in warrior circles as early as the seventh century BCE. With the "Hoplite reform," which turned all warriors into equals by eliminating clan and social differences to keep only the equality of destiny in the face of death, the decision-making assembly was formed around the *meson*, the empty center where the booty is placed to be shared equitably, the space also where every participant must stand to present to the others, seated around a circle, what he deems to be the collective interest. This is the model of public space that will organize the formation of the city, with its agora, the common hall, temples, stadia, theaters, and above all the site of political deliberation where the laws that govern the life of the community and by which every citizen is recognized in front of every other are formulated and proclaimed: All are equal before them. The old nomos—etymologically the acreage of pasture or culture granted to each lineage—becomes the shared lot, placed in the middle, the written rule as a thing exposed to the gaze of all and that all accept to follow. At the same time the law becomes the common measure, the neutral figure of the third party, the norm of equality and freedom that all citizens give one another. With the emergence of the City that originates in this empty center where the law as arbiter is proclaimed, the heroic reciprocity of the old chiefs confronting one another in the *agōn* is disqualified. Arbitrational justice is substituted for vindicatory justice, which was the converse of ceremonial gift relationships. The Furies, deities of the old lineages, must give way to Athena, the impartial goddess of the city. Debates are ruled by the *histor*—judge, investigator, and mediator[42]—new public figure of the third party; a different history has begun. Every democratic transformation will take place under the sign of the law, the third-party arbiter, against every form of reciprocal allegiance (which the feudal relationship still was). Thus, when Achilles, furious at having been robbed by Agamemnon of his share of booty, gains its return thanks to Odysseus's intervention, he refuses to let the returning gesture originate directly from Agamemnon and demands that the goods be placed in the middle—*eis to meson*—so that they will be awarded by the assembly of the Achaeans.

Yet if it is true that the law proclaims the rights of everyone and guarantees to everyone recognition based on principle, then we may ask what happens to the reciprocity of the ceremonial gift. We can assume that it shifts to the relationship between the citizen and sovereign power, thus beginning to form the model of the pact that will from then on haunt the political relationship in the West. This is true on an institutional and formal level that is today not only political and legal, but also includes economic activity, defining the first sphere of recognition, which can be called institutional. But on the level of social relationships, life lived in common, neighborhood relationships, religious practices, workplace relationships—in short the various modes of living—more direct forms of recognition are established that generate or reinforce the bonds within the group: This defines the second sphere of recognition, which can be called social, vernacular, and cultural. Finally, in the life of the agents—relationships of love or friendship, close bonds—as in every form of affection and every ethical relationship, recognition takes the form of the respect granted and gained: This is the third sphere of recognition, which can be called personal.

Following fairly closely the terminology proposed by Axel Honneth based on Hegel's Jena writings, those three spheres could be called public, common, and private.[43] Honneth problematizes and describes the following three fundamental forms of successful recognition: self-respect in the legal order, self-esteem in ethical life, and self-confidence in relationships of love and friendship. We must extend this approach, however, to a consideration of the conception of recognition embodied by the ceremonial gift. Let us do so briefly—or as a program—through the following three points.

First, on each of the levels identified—public, common, and private—we must consider recognition primarily in terms not of demand or self-realization (that is, from a subjective perspective) but of reciprocity. It is important never to separate demand from offer of recognition.[44] Recognition can only be reciprocal, at least on a normative level. It is clear, however, that when the demand takes the form of a claim, this means that the other party has failed to offer recognition. When developing a theoretical elaboration at the normative level, however, the conditions of self-esteem cannot be separated from the conditions of the recognition of the Other, in all three of the orders mentioned above. This brings us back to the logic of the ceremonial gift: betting on trust, giving and giving oneself, so that the Other will reciprocate.

To talk of spheres as does Michael Walzer[45]—or of "cities" as do Luc Boltanski and Laurent Thévenot[46]—is to take up a Pascalian approach in which each "order" has its own mode of legitimation. Thus, being an excellent writer or a reliable friend does not confer any right to be recognized as a good citizen; conversely, being a good citizen gives no right to be recognized as a talented artist—the relevant criteria of assessment are not the same. To understand the risks of interference among the different spheres, we only need to use Walzer's critical concepts such as "dominance" (when one sphere prevails over another—for instance, the political over the religious, or vice versa) and "structure of conversion" (in a more subtle and insidious move, one sphere "translates" its values into another to control it).[47]

There is another principle, however, that can have the opposite effect; let us call it principle of subjective consolidation. Thus the recognition gained in one sphere can provide the basis of a self-esteem that can make it possible for us to succeed in another sphere. This is precisely what John Rawls states in the third part of his *Theory of Justice*[48] (professional success can encourage better civic engagement, and vice versa; a solid friendship can encourage responsible economic choices). Yet the first sphere has a foundational priority: In Rawls's terms it is the sphere where the two fundamental principles recognized by the agents "under a veil of ignorance" are affirmed. Not only do those two principles found the crucial esteem of the self as a free being claiming equal rights, but this sphere is the locus of an inextricable articulation of that which constitutes the new public space: the political, legal, and economic realms. Rawls deserves great credit for raising from the outset the question of justice in terms of equal opportunity based on economic conditions. This demand is inherent to Modernity (as it developed on an intellectual and cultural level since the Renaissance, but above all as it was configured on a political and legal level since the Industrial Revolution).

This leaves us with the second and third spheres, where the two other forms of gift, which we have clearly distinguished from the public ceremonial gift, can be practiced to their full extent.

In the sphere of *life in common*, the sphere of neighborhood relationships, civilities of every kind, contacts among communities, and life in associations, relatively informal forms of gift and reciprocal services develop. Those practices contribute to the formation of the primary sociality without which there can be no trust, respect, or mutual recognition of the dignity of the other.

In the same way, in *interpersonal* relationships forms of unilateral generosity are, as Seneca well understood,[49] the very source of bonds of trust and attachment capable of transcending social differences. More radically still, this generosity generates gestures of recognition of and respect for every human being without any distinction, which brings to mind the content of Kant's imperative, as well as the absolute call that, according to Levinas, the face of the Other addresses us—anyone, anywhere, whenever we experience our first encounter with another human being.

This clarification on the ceremonial gift forced us to break with a number of clichés about the gift in general. It demanded of us an effort to move away from the field of attraction—in the magnetic sense of the term— imposed on our representations of the generous gesture by the idea of oblativity (or gratuity). From this different orbit and thanks to this necessary decentering, and now aware that ritual gift practices lead us toward interpretations entirely unrelated to the religious and moral conceptions that have dominated our Western culture for over two thousand years, we now become capable of recognizing without any misgivings those ritual practices for what they are, and as a consequence to proclaim the beauty of the gracious and disinterested gesture that utilitarianism can never dilute in the acid of its suspicion. Beautiful gestures are impervious to commercial accounting just as well as to altruistic compassion. The same is true of commitment based on solidarity, when it is neither social posturing nor self-satisfied management of the misery of others. In every case it is better to keep from playing on the magic of a word—the gift—and to seek above all to understand how, whether the situation is individual or social, a generous aim is directed toward the appropriate action—whether reciprocal, gracious, or based on solidarity. We cannot claim that the ceremonial gift is the foundation of human society, but only that it reveals what lies at its foundation.

CHAPTER 3

Levinas:
Beyond Reciprocity—
For-the-Other and the Costly Gift

I am responsible for the Other without waiting
for reciprocity, were I to die for it.

EMMANUEL LEVINAS, *Ethics and Infinity*

No face can be approached with empty hands.

EMMANUEL LEVINAS, *Totality and Infinity*

While the question of the gift is at the core of Levinas's thought as an in-evitable aspect of the question of the Other, it does not appear immediately in his writings. The distance with Others is such that it precludes any idea of exchange. The otherness of Others is literally absolute, and from the outset it entails a rupture. The recognition of this otherness precludes any return to the self, which would be a return to the enclosure of the *Same*. The radical character of this requirement explains Levinas's constant suspicion against the very request or even expectation of *reciprocity*. It is on this question that Levinas expresses his disagreement with Martin Buber's conception of the relationship between "I" and "Thou": "One may, how-ever, ask if the *thou-saying* [*tutoiement*] does not place the other in a recipro-cal relation, and if this reciprocity is primordial."[1] Here reciprocity means the symmetry, equality, and reversibility of the I-Thou relationship; what is lacking here is the Infinity that Others reveal to us; our responsibility to others is thus erased: "I am responsible for the Other without waiting for reciprocity, were I to die for it. Reciprocity is *his* affair. It is precisely inso-far as the relationship between the other and me is not reciprocal that I am subjection to the Other."[2] It is clear that Levinas understands reciprocity as a pure equivalence, as shown also by the following proclamation found in one of his early works: "In the reciprocity of relationships characteristics of civilization, the asymmetry of the intersubjective relationship is forgotten";[3] this view is later reasserted in the following terms: "Politics tends toward reciprocal recognition, that is, toward equality; it ensures happiness."[4]

Those various writings testify to a remarkable consistency in Levinas's conception of reciprocity, and they allow us to understand what is at the core of his conception of the gift. For him the gift is always—or rather cannot be anything else than—unconditional oblation, boundless largesse toward Others. This conception precludes any idea of exchange—be it generous and festive—and probably explains why Levinas never discusses the ritual gift Mauss discusses, defined by the triple obligation to give, accept, and reciprocate.[5] Only the first obligation could make sense to Levinas, whereas the third can only turn the gesture of giving toward what he calls the *economy, the Same,* and *happiness.* On this point his position—no matter how original and powerful its expression—is not heterodox; as we saw above, it belongs to the lineage of a well-established philosophical *doxa.* This raises a question: What alternative way of thinking can our reading of Levinas offer if the obligation to reciprocate, which is present in the ritual gift, is not the expectation of an advantage on the part of the giver, and if the reciprocity involved is not a symmetry between the parties involved, but an alternating dissymmetry, an irreversible movement, and if it takes charge of an essential conflict that cannot and must not be eliminated. If reciprocity is a challenge rather than a withdrawal, then the entire question of the gift with its diverse forms—including reciprocating—must be raised in a different way. Furthermore, in this debate it is important to reexamine the nature of the goods exchanged, so as to establish a distinction between those goods that fill a need (such as food, which sustains life) or provide worldly joy (as does the gift as a gesture), and those, ignored by Levinas, that are primarily mediators of recognition (*Anerkennung*) and guarantees of peace among the parties, according to a non-Hegelian logic. The question of the third party thus becomes unavoidable: Neither complementary nor external to the relationship between I and Thou, the third party operates through symbols as the most constant and perhaps secret mediation (or articulation) in this relationship, even when it seems absent from it. We must therefore determine if it is possible to free reciprocity from the malediction Levinas seems to cast on it, and if the theoretical difficulties he raises might not fall away once a different perspective opens up on the relationship between the Self and Others, without in any way erasing the ethical responsibility of the Self.

The Self and the Other: With and beyond Buber

The continuity that exists between Buber's and Levinas's thought seems obvious. While Levinas underlines differences just as serious between them, he recognizes a true filiation; this will make it possible to shed light on the whole of the theoretical stakes we have been discussing. Let us begin with the question of the agreement. In several writings[6] Levinas pays a tribute to the breakthrough achieved by Buber in viewing the fact of saying Thou as the primordial fact of speech as a direct relationship, a relationship of "rectitude" that affirms the existence of a distance between the Self and the Other: "The pronoun *you* is not put in place of some noun to designate a substance: A *this* or a *that* that would in addition be qualified as *you*. Here the nominative of the noun is left behind by the vocative, which is not the denomination of beings."[7] Buber discusses the I-Thou (*Ich-Du*) relationship[8] as a fundamental word—*Grundwort*—different from the other fundamental word I-It (*Ich-Es*). This involves at the same time an opposition and a dual entailment: I and Thou cannot be conceived of independent of one another. There is a Thou only for an I, and vice versa. This is also true of the I-It relationship, but in a different way: The I-Thou relationship preexists the I-It relationship and is not dependent on it; unlike the latter, the former commits a being (*Wesen*) in its entirety, and it is dialogic rather than monologic (whereas It cannot reply). To say that I-It is a fundamental word is to proclaim that the world exists as a relationship to the I, the latter being primarily a relationship with the Thou. The world of the It is made up of things that can be added up, compared, and replaced; they are the object of an experience—*Erfahrung*. The Thou is the object of an encounter; it is unique, incommensurable, and part of a relationship—*Beziehung*. Whereas the experience is accidental, the relationship is constitutive of the self. According to Buber this relationship commits the two parties in an equal and radical way: "Relation is reciprocity"[9] (*Beziehung ist Gegenseitigkeit*). Subjects are not monads; their being is defined as a relationship to Others. Every human is necessarily at every moment I for an Other and an Other for an I.

For Levinas the most important aspect of the I-Thou relationship as defined by Buber is that it is not subordinated to the I-It relationship. In other words, this relationship is not just one chapter in a general ontology; it does not stand out on the background of *there is*;[10] from the outset it stands outside this neutrality; it is affirmed independent of the It (here Levinas clearly distances himself from Heidegger). Those points constitute the core of his agreement with Buber; beyond them disagreements begin. Although in his writings about Buber Levinas takes up the term I-Thou, he probably does so more as a tribute to the title of Buber's most famous work than out of a personal conviction. It is remarkable that Levinas almost never calls on this binomial: He always talks of the Self and the Other; we sense why this is the case: I-Thou appears as a relationship of entailment; Thou is presupposed, grammatically constituted, and uttered by I. What is missing is thus the affirmation of the otherness of Others, which requires that their existence be posited as separate. Buber's Thou is summoned in the I that addresses Thou. For Levinas, Others exist before I say *I*. It is the precession of Others over me that makes it possible for me to say *I*. This radical quality of the separation stands in opposition to the model of the dialogue, where call and reply presuppose parity in the relationship and testify that I and Thou are equals in terms of freedom and simultaneity. While Levinas does not deny those dialogic values, beyond them he invites us to conceive in absolutely different terms the very fact of the existence of the Others who face us: not primarily as interlocutors, but as the source of the most imperious ethical commandment. This constitutes a break not only with the thought based on the I-Thou relationship, but also with some aspects of Buber's thought that Levinas chooses not to comment on because he feels no connection to Buber's "animism": the possibility for the plant and animal worlds to gain the dignity of being Thou.[11]

From Buber's work, Levinas keeps this decisive result: From the outset the existence of Others must be posited as facing the Self. We cannot underestimate the importance of this shift, since from Descartes to Husserl, philosophy in its quasi entirety appeared as an egology. Levinas is fully aware of this since his first adventure in the realm of thought was his encounter with the founder of phenomenology ("It is probably Husserl who is at the origin of my writings"[12]), and very early on he translated into French Husserl's *Cartesian Meditations*.[13] Buber made possible the affirmation of the anteriority of the I-Thou relationship. Levinas goes as far as to posit the anteriority of the Other over the Self (we will see how this position overcomes the paradox it entails); this nonparitary and nonsymmetrical relationship brings about a whole set of questions: the ipseity of the subject (uniqueness and unicity); the independence of the subject as a separate Other (exteriority); the direction of the relationship (in which the for-Others defines the Self)—in short, a relationship incommensurable to the dialogic relationship between I and Thou. At this point the very idea of reciprocity comes under question: "So I wondered whether the true relation to the other rests on that reciprocity that Buber finds in the I-Thou relation. [. . .] In that I-Thou relation, we are immediately in society, but in a society in which we are equal in relation to one another. I am to the other what the other is to me [. . .]. This concept of reciprocity bothered me, because the moment one is generous in hopes of reciprocity, that relation no longer involves generosity but the commercial relation, the exchange of good behavior."[14] This is a remarkable reasoning: The reciprocal character of the specifically ontological I-Thou structure comes under question on the basis of a moral argument about gift and exchange: the suspicion that every generous gesture that involves a reciprocating gesture amounts to a form of trade. We will have to discuss this point.

Reciprocity in Question: Immanence, Totality, and Justice

Levinas never wrote anything—not one chapter, not even one paragraph— that explicitly deals with the problem of reciprocity; this is a transversal but recurrent motif whenever he must define the relationship of the Self to the Other. Levinas restates his reticence with respect to this concept central to Buber's thought with unimpeachable consistency. Yet no explicit definition clarifies this reticence. As often in Levinas, the status of concepts emerges from their interweaving in the proliferating network of the argument; we must therefore reconstruct its articulations.

Levinas's conception of reciprocity is highly restrictive, as shown by an allusion found in the paragraph of *Totality and Infinity* titled "Enjoyment and Nourishment," which discusses our relationship to the world as the sum total of our activities within the limits of what is available and can be handled; in this relationship we are already facing an exteriority that escapes us and imposes itself on us: "To assume exteriority is to enter into a relation with it such that the Same determines the other while being determined by it. But the way it is determined does not simply bring us back to the reciprocity designated by the third Kantian category of relation."[15] Kant defines this category in his *Critique of Pure Reason* as follows: "All substances, so far as they coexist, stand in thoroughgoing community, that is, in mutual interaction."[16] As early as the "Analytic of Principles" Kant formulates his principle on the analogies of experience, called "Principle of Coexistence, in accordance with the Law of Reciprocity or Community."[17] Levinas specifies that even on the level of simple physical life this universal causal interdependence is called into question by an element of exteriority;

here circular reciprocity reaches its limit. He thus transgresses Kant's definition, but the fact that Levinas mentions it as a kind of reference position is illuminating, all the more so because this definition has no relevance to the realm of ends, of the action of free causalities, which comes under the jurisdiction of practical reason. Yet this is what is at stake in the relationship between the Self and the Other. Levinas does not propose to examine any further the possible status of a reciprocity released from the determinism of substances in space. We will see that this is precisely the form of reciprocity presupposed and activated by the relationship among the parties in the ceremonial gift, which opens entirely different perspectives. The reason why Levinas keeps to a restrictive conception of reciprocity, however, is presumably not the choice of an easy opponent, but the more decisive choice to reject the very hypothesis of any form of reciprocity in the relationship between the Self and the Other. We thus need to follow the argument underlain by this radical requirement.

In Levinas the idea of reciprocity is always associated with a set of notions that configure the order of immanence; this order has three levels; the first involves the domain of knowledge: our relationship to the world as defined by the cognitive aim; the second has to do with needs and the economy, domain in which our relationship to the world takes the form of the production and enjoyment of goods; the third is that of justice and politics. This world is perfectly legitimate, since first we must work toward knowledge and science, or "formalism." We must also take care of the necessities of life, and even strive toward happiness. Finally, we must organize life in common and make sure that rights are guaranteed and respected; the purpose of politics and its institutions is to promote and stabilize this life in common. The order of immanence is also the order of equivalence. It is endowed with the innocence of life in its will to subsist. It tends toward reasonable equilibrium and the reversibility of relationships. This circulation and circularity, this closure within synchronicity, is what Levinas calls reciprocity: "Need opens onto a world that is for me—it returns to itself [. . .]. Need is return itself."[18] A world so defined aims at self-sufficiency and the securing of happiness within the bounds of positive knowledge, fulfilled utilities, and human relationships ruled by justice. It constitutes a totality; this is what Levinas calls the *Same.*

Like Husserl, Buber fails to consider our needs in relationship to the world (a fact that Levinas underlines).[19] Those needs constitute the field of concerns and questions that will lead Levinas in directions entirely different from Husserl's intentionality, and even from Heidegger's being-in-the-world. For Levinas, the thinking Self, aware of his/her freedom, cannot be separated from the Self subjected to the necessities of bodily life and existence along with Others. The world and the objects that constitute it concern us as living beings, in terms of food, shelter, health, and movements. Here the otherness of the world takes on the figure of use, and it calls for *economic activity*. This fundamental dimension is analyzed in the second—and rarely discussed—part of *Totality and Infinity*: The world of use is the locus of labor, technical transformations, acquisitions, and exchanges, where we seek the enjoyment of goods, the comfort of home, and, ultimately, equitable life. Yet it is within this world of need and through relationships other than justice that Others usually call on us; this call is especially urgent in situations of deprivation, where it summons us to provide the only possible reply: support and generous giving.

Before considering this gesture, we must examine what Levinas calls *giving*, while taking care to avoid ascribing to him a kind of pietism of the oblative gesture, which some authors claim to detect in his conception of our relationship to the world.

Object, Intention, and Desire: What Is Given-to-Be-Grasped

Like the concept of reciprocity, the concept of the gift remains transversal in Levinas and is never the occasion of a specific development. Reconstructing its network of references may help clarify the way he takes up the heritage of phenomenology and moves beyond it, raising new questions while dodging others. We may, for example, ask if there is in his work a continuity between the given as discussed by the phenomenological approach and the gesture by which a giver gives a good to a recipient. Although Levinas does not raise this question directly, he considers it, and his answer is profoundly different from Derrida's and Marion's, for example.

It is remarkable that in his first writings on Husserl, Levinas appears to ignore the theme of givenness—*Gegebenheit*—which other authors view as essential to the definition of the phenomenological project. Thus in his dissertation on Husserl's theory of intuition[20] and his later study on "The Work of Edmund Husserl"[21] the very term "given" is used only two or three times, and it never occasions a specific development. As for the term "givenness," it is found nowhere in the text. The same observation applies to his writing on Heidegger in the same book.[22] It is clear that in those two authors (whom he was among the very first to bring to the attention of French readers) Levinas found nothing that would lead him to focus on the question of givenness. This question does appear in some of his later writings, but always in isolated remarks or brief paragraphs. Those passages, however, display a powerful thought articulated in an original way with Levinas's entire problematic.

The theme of the given is the object of a brief specific analysis in *Existence and Existents*, in the "Light" section of the part on "The World," which begins as follows: "The world is the given. The form wedded to an object delivers that object to us."[23] This statement calls for two remarks: (1) In the context of this section it is clear that "given" means: What presents itself as available to our perception (what Maurice Merleau-Ponty later calls the "already-there"); no oblative connotation is present here; (2) We must understand the verb *deliver* in its literal sense. We generally consider form—*eidos*—as the theme of the theoretical aim, and we separate it from the relationship of desire, Levinas explains; he adds: "In the given which we have taken as our point of departure practice and theory meet. Contemplation is turned to an object as something given. It is hence more than 'pure contemplation'; it is already a factor in an action. And not action taken metaphorically only, for contemplation is an intention, that is, a desire, a movement to take hold of something, to appropriate something for oneself—but to take hold of what is given in advance."[24] This is an original thesis: What is given in the intentional aim is not merely a distant view; it is offered to be *grasped*. Husserl, Levinas says, teaches us something essential: "The given is not ourselves. The ego possesses the given, but is not overwhelmed by that possession and keeps a distance from the object, an attitude of reserve, which is what distinguishes an intention from enjoyment. This possession at a distance, keeping one's hand free, is what constitutes the intentionality of intention."[25] Objectivity is disinterested: It is the primary expression of the non-Self. The situation is thus paradoxical: A distance remains with the world as given ("What is given is not a weight on our shoulders; it is yonder, put down, a weight put in the baggage room");[26] but, at the same time, "An object is given, but awaits us. That is the complete concept of *form*. A form is that by which a thing shows itself and is graspable."[27] The passive (*given*) becomes active (*gives itself*), which for Levinas means that it delivers itself to be grasped. The form is already in itself that which, beyond contemplation, makes apprehension possible. Through its encounter with our intentionality, which aims at it and grasps it, the intelligibility of the world constitutes the environment—the common space—that Levinas calls *light*: "Light makes objects into a world, that is, makes them belong to us."[28] Gaze and desire, theory and practice, thus articulate giving and grasping, intention and action, in the element of light: "In existing an object exists for someone, already leans toward an inwardness and, without being absorbed in it, gives itself."[29]

This calls for two remarks: First, by continually associating grasping with givenness, Levinas clearly distances himself from Husserl's *Gegeben-heit* and Heidegger's *Es gibt* ("Being in its presence offers itself to a taking in hand, is a giving.");[30] second, instead of characterizing the other pole of the relationship as *receiving* or reception (according to the classical schema of the gift), he chooses the terms *grasping* and apprehension, as if the action had to be dual, situated at the same time on the side of the object—which gives itself—and the subject—which grasps the object. We can therefore assume that the passivity whose importance will soon be made clear is not situated in this articulation. This *grasping*, which shows that the relationship involved is not a gift relationship, carries nevertheless—and this is crucial—no connotation of appropriation, even less capture; it is the act of grasping expressed by the German term *begreifen*. A slightly later writing[31] reaffirms this approach, where the argument recurs as follows: "The being that appears to the knowing subject not only instructs it, but ipso facto *gives* itself to it. Perception already grasps; and the term *Begriff* echoes that connotation of grasp."[32] This giving-itself-to-be-grasped is alien to the giving/receiving relationship.[33] The continuation of Levinas's writing reinforces this interpretation: "Through its 'transcendence' the 'giving-of-itself' promises a possession and enjoyment, a satisfaction."[34] But this appears to be how Levinas describes the realm of need: "the thought of and psyche of immanence, or self-sufficiency. This is precisely the phenom-enon of the world: the fact that an agreement is guaranteed in the grasp between thinkable and thinker, its appearing also a giving of itself, and its knowledge a satisfaction, as if it fulfilled a need."[35] This, Levinas adds, is probably the meaning of Husserl's idea of a correlation between thought and the world, and more specifically of the fulfillment of the intentional aim; it is not certain that Husserl would agree. This giving-itself-to-be-grasped demonstrates the adequacy of the known to the knowable and the object to the need. We are once again in the closed world of circular-ity, equivalence, and reciprocal relationships. This is explicitly stated in formulations such as "thought of immanence" or "self-sufficiency," which Levinas also calls the "Neutral" (a term he consistently uses to characterize Heidegger's ontology).

Let us take stock of our reading. We might have assumed that the dar-ing transmutation of the *given* into *giving itself* would lead us away from the polarity between known and knowing, but in fact it only adds to it the dimension of action. The French term *com-prendre* (to understand or comprehend) literally means to grasp completely. To grasp is to appropri-ate the world perceived; this sphere of appropriation remains the sphere of enjoyment. The given as giving-itself-to-be-grasped keeps us within this closure. This is a world conceived of outside or prior to the irruption of the Other. What happens, then, when this irruption occurs? How does it change the relationship of knowledge?

This is the question raised in *Totality and Infinity* with respect to the problem of expression. Expression is the presentation of Others to us, and as such the event from which meaning originates: "To comprehend a signification is not to go from one term of the relationship to another, apperceiving relations within the given. To receive the given is already to receive it as taught—as an expression of the Other."[36] Levinas's choice of the word "taught" is not trivial; to be taught, he recurrently explains, is to receive every meaning from the *height* of the face of the Other.[37] This changes everything in our relationship to the given: "The world is offered in the language of the other [. . .]. The other is the principle of the phenomena."[38] This highly daring statement is justified as follows: Levinas's aim is not to deduct phenomena from Others as if identifying the addressor of a sign or going back from an effect to its cause. This is not a retrospective operation, but the realization that no phenomenon appears as such outside of our relationship to Others: "This relationship is already necessary for a given to appear as a sign, a sign signaling a speaker, whatever be signified by the sign and though it be forever undecipherable [. . .]. He who signals himself by a sign qua signifying that sign is not the signified of the sign—but delivers the sign and gives it. The given refers to the giver."[39] This is a novel and powerful assertion: Nothing in Husserl or Heidegger would have made possible this shift from the given (object of the eidetic reduction in Husserl, and referring to *Es gibt* in Heidegger) to a particular giver. For those authors the givenness of phenomena remains a process, a movement without an author. What is for Levinas the meaning of this irruption of the giver? Should we view it as the gift as a gesture in the accepted oblative sense? We should not, since, he explains, his purpose is not to attempt to identify some mysterious power—whether divine or not—that would send us signals through the mediation of the world. We should instead accept that every perception or understanding presupposes our relationship to Others, not as a dialogic structure, but because Others interrupt immanence. They are constitutively that which allows us to see, feel, and above all speak. Prior to every encounter, and making it possible, this otherness alone pulls our gaze, knowledge, and desire away from the circularity of the given world, giving rise in it to the unrepresentable figure that gives it to us. Givenness thus has the ancillary function of revealing this otherness: It signals the precession of Others in our relationship to the world. What is given is no longer there to be grasped; instead it testifies to the very separation between us and Others. The irruption of the giver is the irruption of Others, which suspends the reciprocity between giving and grasping. It intervenes not as a condition, but as an event that gives rise to this now-dissymmetric relationship. It is in this sense that Others are the height that teaches us, occurring to us from the outside through the epiphany of the human face.

Otherness and Separation

Our inquiry on reciprocity and the gift has led us to the node of Levinas's approach: the question of Others. Levinas makes a radical break with every form of egology (of which Husserl is the last great embodiment), but also with every ontology (although Heidegger, in question here, would reject this categorization); in spite of his kinship with Buber, Levinas moves away from the dialogic conception, which he deems overly dependent on the schema of reciprocity. He invites us to enter the new and yet unexplored landscape of the absolute otherness of Others, which forms the nonconceptual core of his thought and to which Levinas gives a name unheard of in philosophy: the face. It might seem that by doing so he secures a specifically phenomenological resource, but this is not the case. From the outset his question is strictly ethical; it entails a reexamination of every concept from this perspective, as well as the introduction of a different requirement with respect to the gift. The question no longer is whether the world must be theoretically understood as given (available to be grasped), or even as given by Others (as "principle of the phenomenon"), but what is ethically incumbent on us to give unconditionally to Others when the world of ordinary goods—bread or shelter—fails them. The ethical gift is "the costly gift." We must resume this itinerary.

The otherness or the world—as an object of knowledge and use—tells us nothing of the otherness of *other humans*. The otherness or the world already manifests an exteriority at the same time imposed on and offered to us; it remains within the immanence of "light"; but what is the status of Others? To describe it in terms of theoretical aims reveals nothing about their existence. Our relationship to Others is resorbed neither in knowledge that neutralizes nor in need that equalizes; it is carried by a different power that runs across them: *desire*. Levinas's definition of desire breaks with an entire tradition originating in Plato, which views desire as the sign of a lack that the object of desire is called on to satisfy. For Levinas, on the contrary, desire asserts itself only beyond its object, beyond any care for the self. Desire is a positive power, and most strongly so when it is a desire for others: Desire for the Other proceeds from a being already fulfilled and independent, which does not desire for itself, in a being that does not lack for anything; more precisely, it is born beyond anything that could fulfill it.[40] Others do not come to occupy in us a space left empty; what desire reveals is the requirement to recognize their situation outside of us and affirm their *exteriority*. To desire is to desire those other than ourselves, while preserving their otherness. Even more, it is to recognize that we are Ourselves only when facing Others who we are not: *facing* them, not *with* them. There is no logical or ontological entailment here; thus emerges the essential dissymmetry that underlies the entire critique of reciprocity as presupposing an equal back-and-forth between us and Others. Symmetry is impossible, because Others come to us from an elsewhere that both escapes and grabs us. Our necessarily dissymmetrical relationship with Others proceeds directly from their radical otherness. The movement that leads Us to Others is nonreversible; it is entirely incomparable to the movement that leads Others to us. This situation is primary, as an "in-condition"; let us identify its levels—or stages—as Levinas articulates them. They arise from two questions: What does "Others" mean? What does "Us" mean?

"Others" means above all an exteriority, and testifies from the outset to a *separation*. But in a first approach Others are conceivable only from the position of the self; only the self can speak of Others. "Others" is a concept necessarily referenced to a speaking subject (in the same way that within language Thou can be uttered only by I, can be viewed and designated only from the position of a speaking subject; we can at least grant Levinas this linguistic point, even if he does not make it himself).[41] In the relationship between Us and Others there is from the outset a perspective-related constraint: "Alterity is only possible starting from *me*."[42] It is because of this constraint (which emerges as a *philosophical event* in Descartes's *Cogito*) that in the fifth of his *Cartesian Meditations*, Husserl attempts to introduce Others from the position of the constitutive Self as what must be recognized in an exteriority that is not produced by the Self, but noetically constituted by its own approach (which Husserl calls an *appresentation*).

Levinas at the same time endorses this approach and profoundly calls it into question. He endorses it in the sense that he raises the question of the Other *from the position of the Self*; there is an irreducible fact of perspective that originates in the self. Furthermore, the identity of the self must be affirmed, since there cannot be an Other without a stable self whose identity endures through time. Levinas frequently states that "The I [. . .] supports the world."[43] The Other is unquestionably another I recognized only by

a being who says *I*. But regardless of the approach through which we try
to constitute Others, our attempt fails, because Others as existence cannot be the objects of a constitution. They are given to us, occur to us, and
precede us. Our relationship to Others does not explain the fact that we
recognize them; it is instead their exteriority to us that makes the relationship possible. Others are an event, and as such they necessarily escape our
knowledge, will, and power.

On this first level (first only in the order of approach) the *exteriority* of
Others emerges. This is how others reveal the Infinite. Here "infinity"—
understood in Descartes's sense—designates the entity that remains absolutely exterior to the order of immanence.[44] Another level (a level primary
in terms of foundation) is interwoven here: This perspective-based privilege, the fact that Others only appear from the point of view of a Self, also
means that we are responsible for Others, since only a self can recognize
Others; hence a uniqueness that does not derive as in Leibniz from the
absolute uniqueness of substances, but from the nondelegatable responsibility of the self. No one can reply *in* our stead, because no one can do
so *from* our position. We are unique, and as such are ourselves, because of
the position assigned to us by the fact that we *face* Others. This makes us
nonsubstitutable, from a perspective that is not ontological but primarily
ethical (and this is the starting point of ethics as the primary philosophy).
This is why it is incumbent on us to substitute ourselves for Others. There
is a one-way relationship, not out of choice or through the acceptance of a
heroic requirement, but because since Others are Others only for us, our
responsibility to them is absolute. We will see how Levinas takes this position to its outer limits, but we can already better understand the extent to
which the idea of reciprocity—even in Buber's sense—is alien to Levinas's
radical dissymmetry.

The Face beyond Intentionality: For-Others without Reciprocation

The fact of the existence of Others, which constitutes the moment of differentiation, the movement away from the niche of the self, is for Levinas
the decisive moment when the entire thought of the Same as the order
of totality collapses; here arises the central motif of the *face*. The face of
Others, Levinas tells us, is the revelation of Infinity; the desire for Others
is a desire for Infinity. This exposition of his conception of the face, begun in *Totality and Infinity* and taken up again in many others writings,
has occasioned numerous commentaries, many of which repeat Levinas's
formulations in an incantatory mode. Let us reexamine some of those ele-

ments, more precisely if possible, and without losing sight of the question of reciprocity. Several levels of approach are articulated here, interwoven in a novel way: phenomenology, first philosophy, and ethics.

By stating that we experience Others through the irruption of their face, Levinas performs a profound break with the phenomenological approach. Through their faces we grasp Others as bodies, but not as mere objects of an intentional aim. The perception of the face transgresses the relationship between noesis and noema according to Husserl. It is even situated beyond the bodily relationship to Others as described by Merleau-Ponty, for whom this relationship is played out primarily in the reciprocal perception of bodies. Others perceive us on the level of bodies: "It perceives its intentions in its body, and my body with its own, and thereby my intentions in its own body."[45] From the outset our gaze is "at grips with a visible world, and that is why for me there can be another's gaze; that expressive instrument called a face can carry an existence, as my own existence is carried by my body, that knowledge-acquiring apparatus."[46] Understood as such, the face, just like the body as a whole, is captured in a multiplicity of perspectives that remain a form of knowledge, no matter how physically embodied. This probably explains why neither Husserl nor Heidegger, for example, grants a particular status to the face.[47] Levinas, for whom the face is from the outset a central focus, might be expected to apply the phenomenological methodology and provide a patient description of the originality of the human face; he does no such thing. When discussing the face he does away with this approach in which knowledge—no matter how "physical" or "sensory"—is granted priority. From the outset the face appears altogether in its ethical presence. It occurs, suspending every claim to a description and to every purely cognitive intentional relationship: Nothing is said of eyes and gaze, mouth, age, gender, or the diversity of facial expressions;[48] or even of the face as a whole, as a typical and aesthetic form; or of what distinguishes it from any animal face. It is as if for Levinas the human face was the object of an iconic prohibition. The face of the Other appears as a strict *analogon* of the face of the Almighty. It could be designated, paradoxically, as an empirical transcendental instance, in the sense that every face is the Face: What we encounter in the face of every Other is the very presence of the Other.

Because the face cannot be described objectively in the way the rest of the body can, it cannot be reduced to a system of relationships. From the outset it is something entirely different, situated beyond perception: "The face rends the sensible."[49] On an even more essential level, the first meaning of Levinas's statement that "the face has a meaning that starts from itself" is that the face cannot be understood based on a context; the second is that the face is not an object of representation that would presuppose a difference between a signifier and a signified. It is not a sign of the Other; *it is the Other*, it occurs to us as such, without any mediation; it addresses and compels us even if we do not see it. The face does not mean anything: It is the presence of the Other, and it carries his/her speech. The face cannot be explained by anything else; it is not predictable; it cannot be anticipated through a diversity of profiles; it occurs, and as such it is an event.

This event makes it possible to better understand the movement of desire mentioned above. Contrary to the neutrality and deontological suspension that characterize knowledge, desire is a real movement expressed by the *act* that carries us toward Others. But this act that takes us away from the circle of the Same is not a mere decision we are free to make or not make; it is *compelled* in us by the *face* of others, which calls and summons us unconditionally;[50] this summons defines the unique character of Levinas's approach. Exempt from every intentional description, cognitive approach, and psychological interpretation, the face of others forces its entry in our thought just as it occurs and surprises us in our encounters. From the outset, without mediation or relaying image, the face of Others summons us to reply and designates us in the accusative. This accusative is therefore the opposite of the intentional movement that carries us outside ourselves. But whereas in the world of immanence the outside remains caught in a back-and-forth movement, a reciprocity where the given is offered to our grasp and capture, the face does not reply to us in a symmetrical way where the movement that carries us to it would be reversed into a movement from it to us. From the outset the face summons us, designating us as responsible for Others. Yet this summons is not authoritarian; on the contrary, it derives from the fact that in worldly terms Others are powerless and always subjected to the threat of rejection and aggression.

This is what Levinas means when he speaks of the *nakedness* of the face. The face is no more unprotected and exposed than the rest of the body; its nakedness is not the nakedness of skin; it is not visible; it is the very otherness of Others, which comes to us "defenseless." This nakedness is thus above all a form of vulnerability. Paradoxically, it is what endows the face with the power to carry this injunction: Thou shalt not kill. As Ricoeur comments, "Each face is a Sinai that prohibits murder."[51] This is a powerful philosophical decision; before Levinas no Western thinker had dared claim that one part of the body—the face—is the embodiment both of Others as persons in their infinite otherness and of the prohibition that constitutes the absolute condition of the existence of every community.

This claim is the foundation of a thought based on the idea of an unconditional summons, and it states an absolute imperative of reply. We now better understand why the conventional idea of reciprocity is strictly alien to Levinas's thought. Our question is the following: What happens to this exclusion if such a thing as a nonsymmetrical and nonretributive form of reciprocity exists that carries an imperative as high as the unilateral requirement posited by Levinas? But first we must specify the dimensions of this passivity of the Self that designates it in the accusative.

Passivity, Accusation, and Ingratitude

On the question of passivity it is clear that Levinas breaks with phenomenology (in either Husserl's or Merleau-Ponty's version). In Husserl the question of the passive synthesis is inseparable from the fundamental receptivity of the subject of perception; this is a condition associated with ordinary experience and, on an even more essential level, to the subject's belonging to the world, the pre-predicative experience that forms the environment of a primordial self-evidence. Something always precedes the intentional act, and this precession marks the foundation of an *I am* prior to any form of *I think*. Here sensory experience, the powers of the senses— seeing, touching, hearing, tasting—communicate with one another in a passive experience that forms the texture of the "flesh" (*Leib*) of the world. This primordial passivity makes us experience our belonging to that which we are not, which we have not chosen, and which happens to us from the outside, merging with our most intimate sense of our own bodies; this constitutes our experience of the world. Passivity thus means primarily that the Self does not constitute the foundation of things; the world is already there, and it is other than us. Husserl's term passive synthesis, however, indicates that this receptivity is still an *act* that remains within the intentional relationship, although on a more concealed level. This entailment is precisely the point where Levinas distances himself from Husserl by introducing, prior to this passivity at the same time pathic and cognitive, a more radical passivity that is a good illustration of his affirmation of ethics as the first philosophy: Our situation as we face Others is such that we are obligated to a reply. This is the primary sense in which we are passive: We are designated by Others; as we face them we have nothing to ask. From a different perspective this confirms that we exist only in the accusative. This is the radical position presented in *Otherwise than Being*.

Levinas affirms once again the theme of nonreciprocation, carrying it to the level of a challenge: Because we are summoned in the accusative, that which we give Others, we owe it to them. Furthermore, what we give does not entitle us to their gratitude. Many commentators found shocking the following sentence from *Humanism of the Other*:[52] "The Work thought all the way through demands a radical generosity of movement which in the Same goes toward the Other. It demands, consequently, ingratitude from the Other. Because gratitude would in fact be the return of the movement to its origin."[53] This is the type of statement that makes Ricoeur call Levinas's position paroxystic.[54] In fact this statement conveys Levinas's thought perfectly and without any exaggeration. It is found in a chapter that constitutes a meditation on "meaning and work." We must reexamine its argument, which insistently resorts to a kind of kinetics of endless progression.

The concept of *meaning*, Levinas reminds us, is inseparable from the idea of *direction* (in the sense of the direction of a stream or a road). Because it is a direction, meaning signals a movement toward *elsewhere* or, better said, an impulse toward that which is other than us, a risky venture toward the unknown and away from the meanings already commonly established and exchanged (what he calls the Said). This imprudence marks a youthful character of thought distancing itself from a "philosophy" complacent in its "allergy" and its overly appeased and perhaps already senile clearsightedness, which moves outside itself only to bring back the outside toward itself.[55] *Meaning* as direction is above all the rejection of this return; it is a "motion from the identical toward an Other that is absolutely other"[56]: that is, toward the improbable and indeterminate, toward an end-point not given in advance. "An orientation that goes *freely* from Same to Other is a Work." Against every dialectic conception that views in the transformation performed on the world the ceaseless "negativity" that ensures the reintegration of substance into the subject and of the non-Self into the Self, Levinas defines the work as a thrust away from the enclosure of the Same by which the Self abandons itself to exteriority, throws and forgets itself in this exteriority. "The Work thought radically is a movement of the Same toward the Other that never returns to the Same." It is a radical generosity that "demands [an] ingratitude from the Other."[57] This is not just a desirable condition; it is an imperative. The term chosen by Levinas is not *entails* or *calls for*, but *demands*; this is thus neither a process nor an open option; it is an injunction. This ingratitude, however, introduced as it is by an indefinite article, is not said to be "radical" in the way generosity is; it is partial or specific; above all it has nothing to do with moral pettiness. Ingratitude thus means the irrelevance as a matter of principle of every expectation of a reply or retribution. The movement is one-way, "pure diachrony."⁵⁸ Although it presupposes the absence of a return to the self, this is not a random movement or a gratuitous expense;⁵⁹ even less does it generate a possible advantage. Once again (Levinas's critique is recurrent) this explicitly calls into question any form of circularity. If it expected a generous gesture from Others as a reply to our own gesture, "The one way would be inverted into reciprocity."⁶⁰ For purposes of clarity Levinas uses the language of the economy: "Looking at the work's start and finish, the Agent would resorb in calculations of deficits and compensations, in cost accounting."⁶¹ More than once, but without exaggerated emphasis, Levinas refers to the commercial relationship as the accomplished form of the reciprocity he rejects. But what if a different figure of reciprocity were to stand as the polar opposite of this accounting balance? Before considering this question we must understand the meaning of "the gift," or rather understand what giving means for the Self responsible for Others.

The Good: The Astriction to Give and the Costly Gift

What is the nature of our answer to the call—or rather the summons—that the face of the other constitutes? It can only be the movement by which we conform to that which in this face tears us away from the immanence of being. This power, Levinas tells us, is the Good. It is not a medieval heritage, one of the universals that, along with Truth and Beauty, form a trinity. It is not a category; instead, as in Plato, it is beyond being—*epekeina tēs ousias*. This situates us from the outset in the ethical sphere, short-circuiting or transgressing every cognitive condition or category. This movement runs through—pierces—knowledge; it is completed through the gesture that expresses the preeminence of the Good over being. Ethics thus takes on the status of first philosophy; its inaugural thesis is the following: "To be for the Other is to be good."⁶² This statement must be understood in its strong sense: "The relation with the face is produced as goodness. The exteriority of being is morality itself."⁶³ Here goodness does not designate a form of altruistic benevolence, but a radical attitude that realizes and completes the movement of Desire that is transcendence. It is not the ultimate completion of intentionality; it breaks with intentionality, affirming a Good that no knowledge about the world predicts or even conceives of: "Goodness in the subject is anarchy itself. As a responsibility for the freedom of the other, it is prior to any freedom in me, but it also precedes violence in me, which would be the contrary of freedom."⁶⁴

At this point Levinas introduces the gift as a gesture: a concrete and direct form of gift that has nothing to do with the—metaphorical—givenness of phenomena that is merely the offer of a grasp ensuring our relationship to the world. What kind of gift does Levinas refer to? This is certainly not the public and reciprocal ritual gift (which he does not even mention), or even the gracious gift of precious things (which remains playful, associated with celebrations and aiming at happiness), but the "costly gift"[65] (the third type in our categorization above: the gift out of *solidarity* or for support). This *costly gift* testifies to the constitutive goodness that the face of the Other reveals in and demands from us. *Otherwise than Being* takes to its outer limits this oblativity that is neither a merely generous availability nor an admirable gesture, but that which strips the Self of its possessions: "Here I am—is saying with inspiration, which is not a gift for fine words or songs. There is constraint to give with full hands, and thus constraint to corporeality [. . .]. It is the subjectivity of a man of flesh and blood, more passive in its extradition to the other than the passivity of effects in a causal chain, for it is beyond the unity of apperception of the *I think*, which is actuality itself. It is a being torn up from oneself for another in the giving to the other of the bread out of one's mouth."[66] In other words, "It is the passivity of being-for-another, which is possible only in the form of giving the very bread I eat. But for this one has to first enjoy one's bread, not in order to have the merit of giving it, but in order to give it with one's heart, to give oneself in giving it."[67] Those statements reflect with a striking contrast the following remark from *Totality and Infinity*: "*Dasein* in Heidegger is never hungry."[68] This "constraint to give" is expressed by a boundless hospitality without any expectation of reciprocation.

Let us assess the itinerary we have traveled along with Levinas. Unlike Derrida, in calling reciprocity into question Levinas does not proclaim that the gift is impossible because of a claimed aporia between the gift as phenomenality and the gift as a concept; on the contrary, he affirms the necessity of the most tangible and substantial form of generous gift—embodied by the gift of bread—in support to Others in need and regardless of the cost incurred: "Speech is not instituted in a homogeneous or abstract medium, but in a world where it is necessary to aid and give."[69]

Levinas's itinerary has taken us from the simple given of intuition offered to be grasped, through the thesis that only through Others does the world appear given in its very phenomenality, to the imperative of unconditional oblation that the face of the other requires of us. This is an original and demanding trajectory. The preclusion of reciprocity seems to be one of its essential aspects, but is it sustainable?

Questions and Objections I: Symmetrical
Reciprocity and Agonistic Reciprocity

Our reflection on reciprocity has led us to a transversal exploration of some of Levinas's essential writings. For him the inaugural reference is unquestionably Kant's definition of the third category of relationships, discussed above: reciprocity understood as the interdependence of substances within a whole.[70] It is thus clear that *for Levinas reciprocity is not a face-to-face*. This is why the concept of reciprocity, which for him is not agonistic, is assigned one and only one kind of content: a return to the self, which can be the quietude of immanence, the selfishness of happiness, or the balance of justice; but also profit, advantage, and interest.

The entire problem lies in this restrictive view that amounts to a conception of reciprocity based on the model of symmetrical exchange alone; in the end—as Levinas explicitly notes—its typical form is commercial exchange. In this view exchange comes under a more general model: the *contract*. A contract is defined as an explicit agreement between two parties that, through an exchange of goods or services, aims at generating an equal advantage for each party: This is indeed reciprocity based on equivalence; it is perfectly legitimate and healthy within the economic sphere, and it defines justice in exchanges. But an insistence on detecting in every practice of reciprocity the contractual model (with the intent to denounce it) is necessarily problematic; it is even an abuse that gives rise to misunderstandings. There is nothing new about this misunderstanding: It is part of a long tradition that could be called Jansenist (exemplified by Pascal's denunciation of selfishness and La Rochefoucauld's denouncement of interest, and also observed in Derrida and Marion). But this tradition is even older; we saw at the beginning of this essay that it had gained philosophical legitimacy in Aristotle and above all in the Stoics (Seneca in particular) and the Church fathers. More broadly, it can be viewed as one of the best-established topoi of the great moralistic traditions.

Levinas thus did not feel compelled to reflect on the ritual gift as described by Mauss (whose work he did not discuss and even appeared to ignore). If he had, it is likely that—like Derrida—he would have considered the requirement of reciprocity only in its more conventional form of symmetrical exchange, instead of the agonistic relationship it actually constitutes as a gesture of challenge that generates a reply—gift/countergift, *dosis/antidosis*—and whose stake is reciprocal *recognition*. The affirmation of honor and the granting of respect thus involve the very dignity of the parties. Furthermore, what is given in the thing given is the *self* of the giver: The risk he incurs generates and meets the risk the receiver accepts to take. In this relationship the *face* that calls cannot be separated from the *hand* that gives and the *thing* that testifies. But this form of gift is not meant to support Others—for Levinas the only appropriate purpose of giving. What is it then? Is it legitimate to reduce this gesture to the realm of closed equivalence?

In the ritual reciprocal gift the thing given is precious not as a good to be consumed or bartered, but as witness to the trust granted. It symbolizes—in a literal sense, as a *symbolon*—what is brought together, or what brings the parties together. It carries the giver to the receiver as his *guarantee* and *substitute*; it is the sacrament of the Self. Failure to reply would be an expression of contempt and would amount to choosing violence. The synchronic moment of alliance is necessary to open the diachrony of peace, just as the moment of reciprocity is necessary to break the groups' inward withdrawal. What the movement of time generates is not the internal reciprocity of tautological circulation; it is instead challenge and reply: not the symmetry of a back-and-forth, but the alternating dissymmetry of a call and reply.

The purpose is not the support of life under threat of starvation or the circulation of goods in the cycle of economy and happiness. In a way the very term "gift" is misleading. The offer involved here testifies to the founding convention: the opening of the times of peace, the choice of a difficult agreement over a self-evident conflict. What is given has no function in the realm of need; it is a guarantee of alliance, a part of the Self of the group offered to the other as a part of the group itself. To call it a symbol is to point to a fragile conjunction of the Same and the Other, We and You. This reciprocity has nothing to do with a return to the self or a circular movement. What it involves is not the enjoyment of benefits, but the venture of a gesture of reciprocal recognition and acceptance in a context of uncertainty, and the securing of guarantees for this recognition and acceptance.

In the same way that it would be a mistake to subject the ritual gift to the criterion of givenness in the phenomenological sense, it would be another mistake to subject it to the single criterion of the "costly gift" based on a spirit of solidarity and meant to support "widows and orphans." Those two forms of gift are not incompatible; the mistake lies in assessing one by the criteria applicable to the other, thus viewing every form of reciprocity as a return to the self.

Questions and Objections II: For-Others and Recognition

The requirement of recognition at stake in the ceremonial gift opens the pact that founds the very possibility for humans to live together. This recognition is not of a Hegelian type; it involves no dialectic—and neither does it for Levinas. There is an obvious reason for this: If we are responsible for Others, then there can be no confrontation between their consciousness and ours. We owe them recognition from the outset, but it is not for us to request or even expect it for ourselves; what Others grant us is up to them. For Hegel the conflict lies in the fact that every consciousness *demands* recognition as something more precious than life itself, without considering the hypothesis that this demand could be preconditioned on an offer of recognition. Every consciousness views others only as mirrors of itself and aims to bring them to or into itself. In others we see the same thing that we are; they reflect our desire. Hegel's others are not the other as such, but the Self as Other; in them we recognize only ourselves. The struggle this generates inevitably results in the domination of one consciousness over the other. Confronted with the dead end presented by this face-to-face, Levinas does not consider the hypothesis of a dialogue leading to the possibility of a *reciprocal* recognition that allows each party to recognize him/herself in the other, for the following reason: The defining element of the self is its subjection to Others. In no way can we presuppose that Others must or even wish to recognize us. Whereas for Hegel there is a demand without an offer, for Levinas our offer preexists any demand, because we are not Others, and because the mere expectation of this recognition would amount to delaying or negotiating the unconditional recognition that we owe others, and that constitutes us as unique Selves.

The objection could be raised that such a world would be unlivable. But for Levinas the only thing that makes the world livable is precisely the gesture by which each Self recognizes Others without expecting to be recognized. Could this recognition be the secret of peace? We must take care, however, to avoid thinking in terms of a global complementarity or eventual equilibrium that would be the integral of all unilateral recognitions: We could imagine a kind of reversed invisible hand—a situation in which everyone acts for Others instead of for him/herself—thanks to which everyone would end up recognized without asking for or even expecting recognition. This would amount to restoring as a global effect a form of reciprocity rejected with respect to the unique encounter between us and Others. The unilateral quality of the relationship between Us and Others does not disappear in the community of subjects. If Levinas could consider the possibility of a community, that would be instead on a paradoxical mode, as a community of Others[71] that would preserve for everyone the imperative of recognition without any expectation of reciprocation. It would be a community of pure dissymmetry and unilateral recognitions: a boundless nonclosure. This is why the hypothetical integral of those relationships of recognition does not create a social order and cannot give rise to the Law as the institution of the group and as a process of self-transcendence.[72] For Levinas the Law can derive only from the height of the exteriority of the Face. It must be taught. The ethical bond is and remains beyond the political realm, situated as it is on a level impervious to symmetry. For him reciprocity can find its locus only in the political realm—the field of equivalence and profitable exchanges where justice grants everyone his/her due.

Concluding Remarks: Right of Reply and Alternating Dissymmetry

Let us, however, ask the following question: Can there be a form of recognition where the encounter starts with an offer without precluding a possibility and even a duty for the other party to reply? Furthermore, can recognition ensure a reply without presupposing submission and dependence on the part of the other? Such is the challenge implied in the ceremonial gift, where the offer involves at the same time a game, a convention, a ritual, and also an excess. If the ceremonial gift can invite this reciprocity, this is because it is not primarily a form of equivalence, but an agonistic relationship. What it presupposes is not symmetry, but on the contrary a perpetual unbalance in the movement of gifts and countergifts. It should thus be said, in a paradoxical way, that by positing the otherness of the Other as radical and even infinite, Levinas situates himself de facto in the space of *agōn*—what he calls the *face-to-face*—with the reservation that from the outset he disqualifies conflict, advocating instead an unconditional recognition of the Other by the Self.

For Levinas every institution, legal system, social organization, or plurality of humans forming a group—that is, every mutuality accepted in the mode of the *third party*—must face the unique ordeal of the dual and asymmetric relationship since "The third party looks at me in the eyes of the Other."[73] The entire articulation of responsible subjectivity and social plurality is encompassed in this central statement.[74] It should thus be said that, because of its very asymmetry, for Levinas the face-to-face relationship remains the only relationship where the ethical stake emerges. But the face-to-face is par excellence the dual relationship of agonistic reciprocity.

Does the preclusion of every expectation of a reply on the part of Others, the exclusive consideration of our unconditional duty toward them, then amount to a denial of their right to be others? This is the risk involved, in two ways: first, from the specific perspective of the logic of the I-you relationship, which presupposes an essential *reversibility* without which the relationship itself disappears. It is in the nature of the pronouns "I" and "you" to occupy exchangeable positions; this does not imply that the persons represented are substitutable. Yet this reversibility is not regressive, but always caught in a temporal progression (this is constitutively entailed by every sentence uttered in a relationship of interlocution).[75] Second, the preclusion of the expectation of the Others' reply amounts in a way to a denial of their uniqueness, as if there were only Others in general, even though the faces of others call for our absolute respect. This would be the most serious reservation we could raise against Levinas's ethic of the face: It is as if the face was affirmed primarily in its pure radicalness—as the Face—before it can be the face of a particular human being; it has become the figure of the Law.

Yet Others are always unique beings, even if their faces tell us the Law; faces are inseparable from proper names. As living beings and as embodiments of freedom they must reply to us; they must uphold their names. The fact of their reply constitutes them as others according to the very uniqueness we recognize in them. Their reply can only be unique, meant for us and no one else; only by its uniqueness does it designate us just as uniquely as responsible toward them; this defines the Self as nonsubstitutable. Reciprocity is thus a face-to-face in the fullest sense. By replying to our generosity, Others do not turn our gesture into trivial exchange and contractual symmetry. On the contrary, their reply—like the countergift, which is a gift of the Self carried by the thing given—restores the autonomy of the Others who face us and makes us other than ourselves. The privileged perspective of the *I*, which Levinas along with Husserl situates in the wake of Descartes's *Cogito*, is thus not denied; it is instead relayed and revived by a temporal law that is not circular, but that operates instead as an endlessly progressing spiral: The reply of Others does not bring our gesture back to its starting point; it moves us forward along the diachronic line; but this is a bifurcating line. When Others reply to us, they have already been turned into others by what they have received, just as we become others through their reply: In interpersonal relationships there is an essential otherness; in the unfolding of time each of us becomes other. This is the *alternating dissymmetry* mentioned above, the nonreversible relationship internal to the reversibility of interlocution, which situates it in temporality. This relationship of challenge and reply, where the reply unbalances the initial call, affects and even diverts the line of time. The exchange does not return us prior to the nonsubstitutable position of responsibility that for Levinas must be the condition of the Self; neither can we merely object that to Others we are Others (which would precisely amount to a reduction to symmetry). Because *others can reply and in fact do reply*, our principle-based summons is continually displaced and renewed in every new circumstance; furthermore, it is disoriented and exposed to the unpredictable. The reply of the others creates a bifurcation, breaking the curve. Diachrony is not unilinear; it is an arrow that flies across bifurcations and connects them to one another. To fail to expect a reply from others is to view them only as a Face in general, as a figure of the Law, instead of unique beings we recognize here and now. Reciprocity then means only a dissymmetrical intercrossing of desire in the enigma of the face-to-face. Without their reply Others would remain indeterminate—a kind of nature or principle—instead of the unique beings who speak to *us* and summon *us*, a unique You to whom we can give a name and who, here and now, turn us into nonsubstitutable selves with our own names and unconditional obligations.

CHAPTER 4

Propositions II:
Approaches to Reciprocity

Preliminary Questions

Let us begin with the following and perhaps surprising observation: Whereas many philosophers tend to understand reciprocity as a form of equivalence and a return to the self, many theorists in the social sciences—economists included—view it as a synonym of generosity or a figure of altruism. This divergence should lead us to recommend a dialogue between the two fields to avoid such misunderstandings. But above all this invites us to recognize that the concept of reciprocity is not well defined and that we need to clarify its status, which is at the core of philosophical reflections on the relationships with Others, norms of morality, the social bond, and ultimately the gift itself. We can thus hope that reciprocity will cease to be a source of endless mistakes with respect to those various notions.

We will need to step away for a time from the specific field of philosophy and consider what sociology and anthropology can tell us about the question, since it comes under the purview of those disciplines to investigate the nature of the relationships observed among members of social groups and attempt to define them. What can they teach us about reciprocity that could rejuvenate philosophical questioning? Let us choose as our guides two authors whose analyses on this point have marked the debates of the past few decades: sociologist Alvin Gouldner, author of a seminal article on the norm of reciprocity,[1] and anthropologist Marshall Sahlins, whose book of record *Stone Age Economics* dedicates an entire chapter to defining the nature of practices of reciprocity.[2] Philosophical questionings on interpersonal relationships have much to learn from the analysis of specific social practices.

To clarify the stakes of this debate we must recall Gouldner's central thesis: "I suggest that a norm of reciprocity, in its universal form, makes two interrelated, minimal demands: (1) people should help those who have helped them, and (2) people should not injure those who have helped them."[3] We can assume that Gouldner was aware that he stated as an observation what the Golden Rule states as an imperative (with a positive and a negative side: "Do to others . . .": "Do not do to others . . ."). This rule is observed in numerous traditions; it has been formulated long before the Common Era: over six hundred years earlier by Zoroastrianism, about five hundred years earlier by Taoism, the Babylon Talmud, and Buddhism. According to Darwin it is even inscribed in the process of hominization, as an effect of evolution.[4] Gouldner is silent on this dual heritage, and he does not appear to remember that both of those formulations are found in Luke's and Matthew's Gospels, the latter of which also includes the following commentary: "On these two commandments[5] hang all the law and the prophets" (22:40). This would deserve at least a passing mention. Furthermore, just before this thesis (trivial because of its age, but remarkable as a conclusion reached by a sociologist), Gouldner proposes another thesis just as important: The norm of reciprocity is universal, for the same reason as the prohibition of incest. Here is another reason to be surprised: At the beginning of his article, Gouldner lists Lévi-Strauss among the major theorists of reciprocity, yet in situating this norm on the same level of universality as the prohibition of incest he fails to realize that for the author of *The Elementary Structures of Kinship*, those two problems are one and the same. Lévi-Strauss's novel hypothesis is his identification of this prohibition, rather than as a moral or biological interdiction, as *a universal and positive rule of reciprocity* that alone makes it possible to understand the noless universal phenomenon of exogamy in human societies. The daughter or sister that the group denies to itself is, through this very denial, guaranteed as a potential wife for other groups that follow the same rule. The enigma has thus shifted; it involves less the prohibition itself that the very requirement of reciprocity that is its foundation.

Lévi-Strauss does not hesitate to call this requirement a *principle*, including in the title of the chapter where he discusses the question.[6] But what precisely does reciprocity mean? How is it part of fundamental human behaviors? Lévi-Strauss attempts to explain this through the simple example provided by a situation he witnessed. In the south of France he observed the following scene: In certain modest restaurants with a single menu, where a great diversity of people come to have lunch, small wine flasks, whose price is included in the fare, are placed in front of every plate. The customers often find themselves sitting facing or next to strangers. A remarkable event ensues: Every customer pours the content of his/her own flask into the glass of the customer facing or next to him/her, who then reciprocates the gesture; this leads to a conversation. What has happened? Almost nothing—and almost everything: As the permutation of an identical good the exchange is a zero-sum gain; and yet through this gesture each participant expresses to the other his/her wish to recognize him/her and honor his/her presence. Each has told the other: You exist for me, I demonstrate this to you, and I respect you. We have reached the core of a problem at the same time social—the genesis of the relationship to others—and ethical—the immediate requirement of respect in the presence of Others and, ultimately, the interrelational genesis of the social bond as a fact of convention—that is, as the invention of an implicit alliance that commits persons or groups whose *otherness* is irreducible, and whose autonomy must be accepted, to a life lived together.[7]

Through its implications this apologue suggests two types of considerations relevant to the general problem we will discuss.

From an *epistemological* perspective it raises the question of reciprocity as an *exchange*. Exchanges are often interpreted as being exchanges of goods, and thus implicitly trade. This amounts to claiming that reciprocity is based on self-interest—bringing back to the self what went to others. As we have seen, this suspicion runs across our entire philosophical tradition, and it has been enhanced by the emergence of political economy. We will thus need to understand reciprocity based on a concept of exchange freed from those presuppositions or prejudices.

From a perspective that could be called *ontological* we will have to determine the implications of the universality of the norm of reciprocity. Can we presuppose that it has a metasocial status of a moral type (this is Gouldner's conclusion) without first considering the logic of human relationships, such as the requirement to reply—a blow for a blow? This consideration would be the best way to grasp how the norm emerges from the relationship to Others as an interaction.

Reexamining the Approaches of Gouldner and Sahlins

Let us briefly return to Gouldner's writing to better understand how he reaches the conclusion mentioned above. From the outset he underlines two important points: (1) the idea of reciprocity is observed in and central to all kinds of present and ancient societies; (2) this idea, however, is one of the most obscure and ambiguous sociological concepts. Gouldner dedicates the first third of his article to situating the concept within the framework of functionalist theory, then dominant in American sociology (under the leadership of Robert K. Merton and Talcott Parsons). Let us recall that the functionalist approach—which claims in part the heritage of Weber and Simmel—is a theory of action. It understands every social transformation as an interaction among agents. For functionalism the essential problem is *social stability*; it is thus important to determine the extent to which every interaction is reciprocal. But what does reciprocity mean in this case? Is it the causal interdependence that creates an effect of global equilibrium? Or exchanges of services among agents? Gouldner notes that Parsons appears to grasp the importance of the concept of reciprocity when he claims: "It is inherent in the nature of social interaction that the gratification of either party's needs is contingent on Alter's reaction and vice versa."[8] This conception perfectly satisfies the functionalist requirement of social stability; reciprocity is thus at the core of every interaction. But doesn't Parsons understand this, Gouldner asks, as a mere phenomenon of symmetry that ignores the degrees of relationships among agents? According to Gouldner this reciprocity is reduced to a *complementarity* defined by logic: Rights x of Ego match duties $-y$ of Alter; conversely, duties $-x$ of Alter match rights y of Ego; those are, Gouldner notes, mere *analytical* propositions that state that a specific right on one side *entails* a matching duty on the other. But the pragmatic approach requires more than this formal view: It refers *empirically* to the fact that every agent has at the same time rights and duties situated on different levels and involving different roles. The system is therefore more complex, as is also the interaction.

To face this complexity Gouldner supports his thesis on Bronislaw Malinowski's synthetic book *Crime and Custom in Savage Society*,[9] rather than on Malinowski's earlier *Argonauts of the Western Pacific*.[10] Malinowski asks why in primitive cultures the members of a given society obey rules. What is, for example, the source of the sense of *obligation* in the relationship of reciprocity? Malinowski's answer is from the outset explicitly anti-Durkheimian: What generates conformity to the norm is not a transcendent representation of society on the part of its members, but the fact that *every agent experiences the obligation as a reply to a specific party.* In more general terms this is an obligation determined by the relationship to Others in every situation of exchange. Malinowski's is a clearly pragmatist position (but this does not tell us on what logic the obligation is based).

According to Gouldner we have moved beyond Parsons's position, since what Malinowski discusses is not a formal complementarity of rights and duties (which is an analytical proposition), but an exchange of goods among agents who need the products offered by others. There is therefore de facto interdependence among separate agents; in certain Trobriand islands, coastal villages thus exchange fish for yams grown by inland villages. All sorts of other useful exchanges take place within groups in the same spirit of reciprocity (they are thus something else than the famous *kula* exchange among the islands discussed above). Gouldner then asks if the reason for being of this reciprocity might not have to do with two specific elements: an obligation defined by *statuses* (such as the relationships among agents bound by kinship or their functions as chiefs), or an effect of the *division of labor*. But those are two very heterogeneous aspects. Yet in both cases reciprocity appears to function primarily as a reply to the actions of Others as such. The conclusion to be drawn, Gouldner believes, is that reciprocity has a general character, and the obligation that characterizes it is not a primarily social feature. Only one option remains: Here reciprocity has an essentially moral character. Having reached this conclusion, Gouldner presupposes its universality and from then on systematically talks of the *general norm of reciprocity*. He proposes the formulation quoted at the beginning of our presentation, which so surprisingly matches what the tradition calls the Golden Rule. Let us recall this formulation: "I suggest that a norm of reciprocity, in its universal form, makes two interrelated, minimal demands: (1) people should help those who have helped them, and (2) people should not injure those who have helped them."[11]

This shift from the social to the moral realm may seem quite hasty—and it is, even though it may be legitimate in some respects. Without entering this debate let us note two highly problematic points in Gouldner's analysis. First, nowhere does he consider the possible existence of the slightest difference in reciprocity between useful exchanges and gift exchanges (which is the entire argument of Malinowski's *Argonauts*). This confusion is so widespread that Gouldner can hardly be blamed for it. Second—to preview questions we will consider later—we can ask if the moral conclusion he proclaims sheds any light on the case of the exchange of wine glasses Lévi-Strauss describes, since—to refer to both formulations of the norm—the purpose of this exchange is neither to help the other party nor to avoid harming him/her. We sense that, even though Gouldner deserves great credit for underlining that behaviors of reciprocity take on a primarily pragmatic mode as replies to the attitudes or actions of Others, he misses something crucial.

Before returning to the broader debate and specifying its stake, we must discuss Sahlins's writing, "On the Sociology of Primitive Exchange," Chapter 5 of his *Stone Age Economics*.[12] The title of this chapter could have been, "General Figures of Reciprocity." It is important to note that this writing comes after several chapters dedicated to the primitive economy—its forms of subsistence and practices of exchange—and that the topic of the previous chapter is the ritual gift. In this chapter Sahlins's intent is to discuss exchange in general in those societies. He takes up Polanyi's distinction between systems of reciprocity and systems of redistribution. Whereas the former are the more general and concern all sorts of traditional exchanges, the latter presuppose the emergence of regulating powers—such as chiefdoms—that centralize resources before distributing them; they can be viewed as the germs of the central state. Sahlins intends to analyze systems of reciprocity, which are de facto preserved in redistribution systems. He observes that the idea of reciprocity pervades all the activities of traditional societies. The economy cannot be set apart as an autonomous realm; it remains enveloped or embedded in the social interactions whose purpose is to reinforce the bonds among the members of the group. Based on those observations Sahlins proposes to develop a general model of reciprocity, in the same way that Gouldner—whom he cites—attempted to identify a universal norm of reciprocity; Sahlins could thus somehow provide empirical support for Gouldner's hypothesis.

Sahlins describes this general model as comprising three main levels or fields, which constitute different poles. He calls the first pole *generalized reciprocity or pole of solidarity*. This involves all kinds of exchanges marked by sharing, hospitality, and the free gift (described as free of any expectation of reciprocation); they can take the form of the sharing of food and the provision of services; reciprocation is possible, but not imperative, and is at most a distant perspective; the relationships among agents are personal and warm. Sahlins calls the second pole *balanced or symmetrical reciprocity*. This involves direct exchanges; the relationship is simultaneous; it can take the form of gifts, matrimonial alliances, or useful goods (such as barter); those relationships are more formal, almost impersonal, and more distant; the reciprocating gesture is most often imperative and usually expected within a short time frame. He calls the third pole *negative reciprocity or nonsociability*. Rather than giving, this involves taking, or at least harsh negotiations;

in the final analysis it defines an economy whose only purpose is in itself, and which ignores social relationships. For Sahlins negative reciprocity means an absence of reciprocity in the sense discussed in the first pole. He proposes a kind of summary of his model characterized by "swings from disinterested concern for the other party through mutuality to self-interest."[13]

This approach raises a number of problems. Even though many of the analyses presented in Sahlins's chapter are fertile—on currency, genealogical ranking, or dissymmetrical exchange, etc.—it is questionable whether his model provides adequate tools to grasp the phenomenon of reciprocity. The main objections that can be raised are the following:

—The first pole is supposed to present the most favorable forms of reciprocity. Yet it includes the most debatable examples, in the sense that here generosity is deemed positive only if it involves no expectation of reciprocation—that is . . . no reciprocity. Let us acknowledge that Sahlins chose his concept poorly. What he discusses here is in fact the generous, unilateral gift: either gestures of gracious gifts or practices of solidarity (actual forms of gifts, whose specific feature is that they do not presuppose or require compensation);

—The second pole involves situations of giving and reciprocating, gift and countergift. Here reciprocity is obvious, but Sahlins suspects the exchange of being overly restrictive, symmetrical, and hasty (which is sometimes true). The requirement to reply is often an imperative, whether in the gift or in barter. It is clear that Sahlins finds this obligatory aspect of the gift suspicious. According to him this is what distinguishes the second from the first pole. The expectation of reciprocation appears contrary to the generosity of the gift. Sahlins does not attempt to shed light on this paradox, or to establish a distinction between the reciprocity of the gift and the reciprocity of barter;

—With respect to the third pole the phrase *negative reciprocity* is surprising, since this means nonreciprocity; its canonical expression is the gesture of taking. Negative reciprocity is a form of predation. It is surprising that Sahlins situates trade within this category, since it is well-known that contracts are a major and entirely positive form of reciprocity that, though belonging to a different order than the ritual gift, nevertheless presupposes a negotiation between two partners, and is a crucial source of civil relationships. This reciprocity normatively falls under the order of justice in exchanges, even if in

practice some exchanges may turn out to be unequal. In fact the term
negative reciprocity is more relevant to the case of so-called violent
reciprocity, as in the blow-for-a-blow of vindicatory reply. This form
of violence tends to be rigorously coded and limited. It constitutes
the fundamental form of justice in traditional societies without state
organization.[14] Oddly, Sahlins does not even mention this.

How can those shortcomings and contradictions be explained?

First, it seems obvious that Sahlins uses the concept of reciprocity in a
somewhat loose or indeterminate manner, as a quasi synonym of generosity, yet unreciprocated generosity (as defined in his first pole) is not reciprocal. By hypothesis, reciprocity is dual and presupposes a reply, as Sahlins
himself states on several occasions, without showing any awareness of this
contradiction. What he describes in the first pole is not reciprocity, but
solidarity and mutuality (concepts to which we will soon return).

Another major problem already mentioned remains, found throughout
the chapter and even the entire book: a tendency to ignore the difference
between gift exchange and commercial exchange. The gift is viewed as
such only when it is unilateral; whenever it is reciprocal, it is categorized
as an exchange of utilitarian goods. This confusion can be explained by
the apparent lack in Sahlins of a clear categorization of the diversity of the
forms of gifts and of a consistent concept of reciprocity. Just like Gouldner's model, Sahlins's does not make it possible to understand the gesture
of the restaurant customers who exchange their glasses of wine, or of the
Japanese drinkers of sake who must wait for those seated next to them to
serve them, as they too must do. Those cases do not come under either
the moral rules of symmetrical reciprocation (as in the Golden Rule) or of
solidarity or social and mutual aid. Sahlins would situate those behaviors in
his second pole, since they can apparently be viewed as mere symmetrical
permutations of a good—a kind of purely formal barter; they are in fact
something else entirely. What the guests seek is not to obtain one good in
exchange for another, since the goods exchanged are exactly identical. To
them their gesture means something completely different: reciprocal recognition and acceptance, bonding, and ultimately the expression, through
the thing exchanged, of this bond and of the trust granted.

The Components of Reciprocity: An Attempt at Categorization

The ordinary use of the term "reciprocity" seems so loose that it allows
for a shift from one sense to another to fit the needs of an argument. It is

indispensable to preclude this double dealing, which can lead only to sophisms or paralogisms. Let us begin with the necessary task of establishing distinctions. The concept of reciprocity presupposes two fundamental and embedded levels: complementarity and reactivity. Each of these levels has two aspects: weak and strong, static and dynamic, or analytical and pragmatic. Let us propose the following presentation:

COMPLEMENTARITY: SYMMETRY AND INTERDEPENDENCE

(1) *Symmetry*. The relationship of reciprocity is clearly symmetrical in the sense of a complementarity of rights and duties that Parsons identifies and that Gouldner designates as an analytical proposition. This is a relationship of reversible entailment of the recto/verso type. It is also the concept of symmetry found in formal logic: When p and q are equivalent, the reciprocal proposition of "if p, then q" is "if q, then p." In linguistics also this reversible entailment is called "reciprocal": If case presupposes number, then number presupposes case. The mathematical use of this concept is also well-known, as in the following geometrical theorem: "If a triangle is isosceles, then it has two equal sides," whose reciprocal proposition is: "If a triangle has two equal sides, then it is isosceles." This is the symmetry of every converse proposition where the attribute becomes the subject and the subject the attribute without affecting the truth value of the proposition. This reciprocity understood as the reversing of logical statements is relevant to us by default: While relevant in and of itself, it says nothing about intentional relationships between the agents involved. The formalization of symmetry tells us nothing about the reasons why choices are made.

(2) *Interdependence*. Here complementarity is exemplarily situated within the social realm: It is associated with the distribution of functions or the specialization of tasks. This is already present in Aristotle's definition of *koinonia* as a community of interests capable to provide equivalence within the diversity of trades (where the function of money is to perform proportional equivalence among the goods created and among the producers of those goods, which would otherwise remain heterogeneous).[15] This reciprocity amounts to the interdependence of the parties involved in an organic whole. This is the kind of totality Kant has in mind when—on a formal level—he defines this reciprocity as the third analogy of experience, or simultaneity of actions among substances: "All substances, so far as they coexist, stand in thoroughgoing community, that is, in mutual interaction."[16] This principle is echoed in our beliefs with respect to the natural order, which lead us to assign intentionality to the elements of the

world, as in classical or medieval doxographies and in Panurge's praise of debts,[17] which assigns to celestial bodies and every element of the universe the need to depend on one another to preserve their unity. This parody teaches us by implication that on a certain level reciprocity presupposes *intentionality* and involves *human action*. From this perspective—the perspective of action—the notion of complementarity has only limited relevance. It testifies to the interdependence of functions or activities, but does not explain how they reply to one another. We remain within a circular model, the logic of entailment, a synchronic order.

REACTIVITY: ALTERNATION AND REPLY

(1) *Alternation*. On a second level reciprocity is understood as a movement of reciprocation: the movement of a mobile or agent who leaves his initial position before returning to it. This definition, however, designates nothing more than the *commutativity* of an alternating movement, a back-and-forth. Yet this makes an advance possible, in the sense that the relationship between the two terms is characterized by a clear initial separation. There are two different locations, mobiles, agents, and trajectories; this takes us beyond the realm of analytical entailment. This separation, however, remains primarily temporal, and it occurs within an already constituted space: The reciprocating movement is expected, but it presupposes a time-lag. We must recognize that the Latin term *reciprocitas* was already frequently used in this sense (forward and back; back and forth; ebb and flow); but this is not enough to account for *intentional actions*. Once again we run the risk of describing nothing more than a rotation of the respective positions: to each his turn. Two important elements emerge, however: First, an action occurs following and because of another; it is a reply to the initial action. Second, there is successiveness, which must be accepted as event-based and a temporal order that must be abided by; this is probably the meaning of the famous statement *kata tēn tou chronou taxin* in Anaximander's *Fragment IX*.[18] "To each his turn" is not a mere mechanism; it is a form of justice, an assignation associated with our finiteness, the recognition of our place in the universe and in time. While we must wait for our turn, we must also take it; finally, we must leave it to others once the time comes. Once again, however, this is an unavoidable objective process, not an action decided by an agent.

(2) *Reply*. We must therefore reach a level that incorporates in an *intentional* action both complementarity—which remains static—and temporal alternation, making the action of an agent a *response* or *reply* to the action of

another. This provides us with a more consistent and complex definition of reciprocity. From Sahlins's analyses let us keep the notion of *asymmetrical reciprocity*, which entails that the aim of a countergift is not to extinguish the relationship by establishing exact equivalence. The purpose of upping the ante is not to crush the other party, but to restart the exchange. This asymmetry is clearly a wager on time: By postponing the return it preserves the will for partnership. It makes possible the formation of more extended and sustained systems of alliance. This shows that the groups involved have strong internal cohesion (as demonstrated by "generalized exchange" according to Lévi-Strauss).[19]

This is the basic conceptual system that we can reconstruct to clarify our use of the term "reciprocity." Two concepts now require a clarification as conditions of the reciprocal relationship: obligation and otherness.

Obligation. The idea of obligation can have relevance only with respect to intentional actions; this is thus the most complex level of reciprocity. What is the meaning of the *obligation* to reply in the ceremonial gift? This can be neither a physical necessity to react (as when organisms are subjected to external stimuli), nor a legal obligation (which includes sanctions when commitments are breached), nor an ethical requirement (in which failure to react would be immoral). As we saw, the example of games with two players sheds light on this logic: Failing to reply amounts to removing oneself from the game and challenging the convention of exchange; replying amounts to confirming and activating the convention. The obligation to reply is the first rule of the game—the game being by the entire set of its rules; this is entailed by hypothesis in the gesture of the agent who enters the field where blows, balls, goods, or words are exchanged. This brings us to Charles Sanders Peirce's model of the triad,[20] where the relationship engaged between the parties through the thing exchanged forms an indivisible structure. When the "game" is a social one, what is at stake is the acceptance (or rejection) of the requirement to recognize the other and the possibility of living together. The ceremonial gift relationship is from the outset a social pact; it is the very model of the convention. This value as a model constitutes our focus; it can allow us to understand the genesis of the specifically political bond.

Otherness. It is a fundamental fact that in human action every form of reciprocity is dual, since it always involves two parties, whether persons or groups. First, this points to the very existence of Others outside us and facing us. Second, this relationship between the Self and the Other (the I/You of language) raises the question of the acceptance or rejection of Others. This is a relationship between two freedoms; in other words, the relationship is always characterized by a fundamental indeterminacy; even when the norm is prescriptive, the reply is unpredictable. Interactions are reciprocal; this does not mean that they are mechanical and computable, but that we act based on what others have done or are doing. Because the otherness of Others is an absolute limit to our own action, the relationship of reciprocity is present from the outset, inevitable and unpredictable. It freely offers a pact; it calls for a convention. At stake is the recognition of both parties, of each party by the other. This dual relationship of challenge, this agonistic face-to-face, opens the way to plural mutuality, as we will see—a plurality that begins with two parties, and then extends to several. Yet the dual relationship already includes a third party: the thing offered and received, element from the world that symbolizes and bonds together the two parties in a triadic relationship (in Peirce's sense).[21]

This clarification has hopefully helped us understand that before hastily conferring on the concept of reciprocity a moral content (whether altruistic or selfish) we need to identify its logical structure and functioning.

Agonistic Reciprocity and Contractual Reciprocity

The analyses above refer to a social form of reciprocity that is agonistic and defined as a reply, sometimes a riposte to a particular action, and that can generally be called a *reaction*. This reaction involves a fairly broad range of social behaviors, from the most peaceful to the most violent: On one side, friendly exchanges of services as replies to services received, reciprocated invitations, and of course gift exchanges; on the other, aggressive forms of action such as duels between individuals, vendettas between kinship groups, and wars between ethnicities or nations. Parallel to this dual range of reciprocity (situations of generous replies or, on the contrary, violent and sometimes lethal replies such as reprisals), let us also mention *playful forms of rivalry* such as athletic competitions, team games, and ceremonial jousts. The simulated rivalry displayed in games and rituals teaches us several lessons: It provides an effective model of formalization of social relationships of reciprocity. On a social level reciprocity functions as a cathartic *mimesis*: a procedure of substitution where the conflicts of the group are staged and symbolically resolved.

The specificity of those types of agonistic reciprocity is that they call on a form of temporality that we have called the *alternation* principle. There is a dual dynamic of reaction: First, an action follows a blow, or is a reply to an action by the other party. In games this creates the rule called *to each his turn* (in chess, for instance, playing twice in a row is cheating). Second, the logic of consecution between action and reaction entails an endless capacity to generate movement: Vendettas might never come to an end; ball games could go on until the players are exhausted; wars could be constantly restarted—hence the invention of rules whose purpose is to bring closure to this dialectic of endless reply. This is why vindicatory gestures abide by ritual procedures of resolution, called "compositions,"[22] and games have limited durations ("prescribed durations"), which impose specific functions on the participants and preclude others. In exchanges among groups this temporality has two sides: a positive one in exchanges of gifts, and a negative one in vengeance or war. In both cases, however, this temporality preserves an endless potential for restarting. In the case of positive reciprocity it matters that this openness is guaranteed and preserved by institutions (thus the exogamic alliance continually indexes the renewal of matrimonial unions on the renewal of generations and the reproduction of life); in the case of negative reciprocity, on the contrary, it is important to impose time limits on the logic of reply (endless vengeance occurs when the rules are no longer understood and accepted).

Unlike the conflictual types of reciprocity that we have just considered and that require procedures of resolution to prevent an endless reigniting of rivalry, from the outset *contractual reciprocity* assigns itself all kinds of precise limits. To understand this let us keep to contracts of purchase and sale: Since they involve exchanges of goods they will be easy to compare and especially contrast with gift exchanges. Let us recall that the stakes of the latter are not goods, but the relationships between parties that are made possible by those goods.

—From the perspective of the status of the *goods exchanged*, in contracts (unlike gift exchanges) the goods are chosen by the purchaser; their quality and amount must be defined by formal agreement (guaranteed by signing or other reliable procedures) with the seller. In no way are the goods symbols of the parties involved in the exchange; their status is thus neutral; the Selves of the parties are not involved as such in the things sold (whereas they are in the things given), even though the sale of particular personal goods can sometimes generate intense feelings.

—From the perspective of *time*, the time of finalization and the duration of the transaction between the parties are precisely defined; an appointed end is explicitly agreed upon under legal constraint (with the possibility of a tacit renewal for a specified duration). Contractual relationships are assigned a precise calendar with respect to the time sequence of the operations: beginning, unfolding, and conclusion.

—From the perspective of the relationships between the *parties*, although those relationships are by hypothesis proper and courteous, they can remain indifferent; they can also be friendly— friendliness often plays a part in successful negotiations. The final criterion, however, is not the friendly or unfriendly attitude of the parties, but the quality and amount of the goods provided for the price agreed upon.

—From the perspective of the *reciprocal obligation*, this is a strictly legal obligation. Specific sanctions are set by law in case of breach of contract by one of the parties. Here also, while the presence of trust can be crucial when entering negotiations and respecting the commitments made, wrongs will be redressed either by mutual consent or by legal procedures.

—From the perspective of the *social bond*, contractual relationships are primarily legal and therefore formal relationships; their purpose is not to create or develop bonds between persons or communities, but to guarantee the proper functioning of the exchanges.

On every level and with respect to every point, gift/countergift relationships stand in contrast to contractual exchanges. The latter are symmetrical. They are ruled by notions of equivalence and equity. They make possible an order of justice within the general framework of a legal, political, and ethical system.[23]

From Reciprocity to Mutuality

It should now be clear that reciprocity is *dual*, whether in rivalry—be it generous or violent—or in contractual exchange. Can there be a bond that includes offer and reply in a commitment not just dual, but plural, a commitment of each to everyone that makes it possible to understand the internal formation of groups? Is this not precisely what characterizes the relationship of mutuality? But how is this relationship different from the relationship of reciprocity? At first glance the two concepts appear interchangeable. What difference can there be between reciprocal love and mutual love? A more precise analysis, however, brings to the fore a clear distinction. Some authors, such as Ricoeur, have considered this distinction.[24] The core of their argument is most often a moral one: According to them, because reciprocity brings or expects a reply it tends to drift to the seeking of an advantage; it remains combative and expecting, whereas mutuality is more oblative and associated with solidarity—in short, more disinterested. This criterion, at times clearly moral, at others implicitly so, seems insufficient, or even misleading. Reciprocity itself includes a moral aspect; this is presupposed by the Golden Rule, which calls on a spontaneously experienced requirement of equity. The difference between the two concepts is found on other levels: the number of agents, the relationship to time, and ultimately the nature of action.

The Number of Agents. It can be said that reciprocity is *always* dual; it is a relationship between two parties—whether individuals or groups—that can involve either conflict or alliance. This is always a face-to-face, whether benevolent or hostile, that covers precisely the field of the Greek *agōn*. It can be expressed by the following formulation: 1 vs. 1. Mutuality, on the contrary, is more open—or more indeterminate. It can be dual, as in requited love, but in this case duality is only the first unit in a plural relationship. This can be formulated as 2 + *n*. Mutuality circulates among the many members of a group. It is understood as an association of several parties (including on a legal level, as in mutual insurance companies). It involves the ideas of *solidarity* rather than conflict (although mutual enmity can exist), and sharing rather than reciprocation. Mutuality forms networks; it calls for a logistic of coordination and an ethic of cooperation. But it is not more oblative or moral by nature: There can be solidarity in crime and mutuality in vice. An analogy with games between two teams (such as soccer) can shed light on the formal distinction between mutuality and reciprocity: There is reciprocity in the confrontation between the two groups, but there is mutuality in the internal coordination within each group.

The Criterion of Time. Because relationships of reciprocity are based on the alternation of proposition and reply or offer and response, they cannot presuppose a continuous time. There is a *successiveness* of actions, and therefore a continuous movement of engagement and reengagement, sending and return. Through this very alternation a movement forward occurs. In relationships of mutuality a more homogeneous and regular circulation is observed, and thus a continuity through time that has to do with the very consistence of the group; mutuality generates a condition, confirms a stability, an established situation, whereas reciprocity consists of the endless re-anteing of the relationship.

Finally, with respect to the *nature of the action* the difference is even more striking. In the case of reciprocity the action of one agent is continually suspended upon the action of the other. There is indetermination in terms of events, uncertainty, and risk, even if the parties interact according to rules agreed upon. Actions take place within a permanent imbalance; they belong to an *alternating dissymmetry* (as in the succession of turns in ball games or ceremonial gift exchanges). Mutuality, on the contrary, establishes balance and homogeneity among all the members of the group: *multiplied symmetry* (such is the Hobbesian peace contract *of everyone with everyone*, which excludes the third-party sovereign, arbiter and dominator, to whom violence is delegated).

Let us note that those two concepts of reciprocity and mutuality, which belong to the Latin heritage, are explicitly expressed in French and English, but less so in Greek and German, although they are present in the former: The Greek language indicates reciprocity through the prefix *anti* (as in *dosis/antidosis*: gift/countergift) and mutuality through the preposition *pros* (*pros allēous*, i.e., the ones for the others; in German there is a comparable distinction between *gegen-* and *zueinander*). Reciprocity thus appears primarily as a form of logic or mechanism—call and reply, action and reaction, attack and riposte—whereas mutuality is a form of coordination and points to a chosen disposition. Whereas reciprocity is necessarily dual, mutuality is plural and can theoretically extend indefinitely to new participants.

As we will see, Ricoeur was one of the few philosophers who paid attention to this difference when he established a distinction between the "logic of reciprocity" and the "phenomenology of mutuality": Because mutuality is not predictable it must be observed and described empirically. Mutuality appears more comforting, or even more generous: It presupposes that conflicts have been overcome; it assumes that we have moved beyond the agonistic space. It appears as a literal *state of peace* in Ricoeur's sense. It might be more accurate to describe it as a state of equilibrium that presupposes an established agreement and can exist only because something shared—*mutuum*—has already been recognized among the members of a community. In this sense mutuality presupposes that the difference between the self and the alien, between ipseity and otherness, has been assumed. It belongs to the realm of accepted convention, the space of the third party as arbiter: the space of justice. But it even is more: It is shared benevolence—or complicity. It thus operates over time, and it aims at continuity. Mutuality is trust confirmed, and even trust instituted, whereas reciprocity indicates that trust is being sought, in the process of being established, but can still be lost. Reciprocity is the moment of the encounter and the face-to-face—of persons or groups—and thus of genesis and risk. Mutuality is the time of the result: the equilibrium reached; ordered plurality.

In Conclusion. Prajâpati's Feast: The Inaugural Gesture of Reciprocal Recognition

Let us return to the ceremonial gift. Once again, can we identify what binds reciprocity and recognition? Lévi-Strauss's description of the exchange of wine glasses and the account of the encounter of New Guinean villagers with an Australian civil servant give us a clear image of this bond. There is no better way to grasp it than to examine another story, this one from the *Satapatha Brâhmana*, one of the great writings from the *Veda*. According to this narrative the first man, named Prajâpati, is also the entire universe; he is the earth and the sky, air and fire, water and wind; he is every being, and he is the first man. But he finds it difficult to distinguish among the spirits the gods from the demons. To establish this distinction he decides to give them a feast. When the food is offered, while some begin eating each one for him- or herself, with great appetite or even gluttony, the others do something odd: They give food to one another, placing it in one another's mouth. Prajâpati then understands that the latter are the gods, the ones humans should imitate. Let us call this Prajâpati's test. If we read this narrative from the perspective of rational choice theory, the demons are right in two different ways: (1) They eat as much as they want and as they wish; (2) they can choose their favorite pieces; in short, they are maximizing their interest. The gods, on the contrary, appear to lack common sense: (1) They perform an action that, in physical terms, brings a zero-sum gain; (2) they also deny themselves the enjoyment of choosing. What then does their gesture bring to the act of eating that causes Prajâpati's admiration? The following: Through this gesture, through the reciprocal offer of food and through the food itself, *they recognize* one another; they proclaim the existence of a bond among them, and their interdependence. What is at stake is not charity or solidarity (they are not needy, and food is plentiful), or the gracious unilateral gift (the gift is reciprocal), but the decision to form a community. Prior to any war, they do what Hobbes's contracting parties do to bring war to an end: They establish a pact with one another by turning what could have been a mere gesture of individual consumption into a reciprocal gesture of giving. The gesture of recognition appears to bring nothing, and yet it changes everything: It institutes a community; it inaugurates or reaffirms a *politeia*. It can do so only because it is *reciprocal*.

Others exist as other than us, for us who recognize them with their otherness; they stand in front of us with their irreducible autonomy and authentic freedom; this is what obligates us to proclaim our awareness and acceptance of this autonomy and freedom, and as a consequence to choose alliance over conflict. This constitutive reciprocity remains at the core of the modern expressions of intersubjective recognition; it is the source of every public convention; it is almost always viewed as a demand; yet it can be so only by being above all an offer.

CHAPTER 5

Marion:
Gift without Exchange—
Toward Pure Givenness

The gift, to be given, must be lost and remain lost without return.
The gift, of itself, never permits access to givenness.
The staging of the phenomenon is played
out as the handing over of a gift.
JEAN-LUC MARION, *Being Given*

Wir sagen nicht: Sein ist, Zeit ist, sondern: Es gibt Sein und es gibt Zeit.

MARTIN HEIDEGGER, *Zeit und Sein*

Jean-Luc Marion's approach to the question of the gift, presented in several of his books, finds its primary source and resources in Husserl's phenomenology and—less ostensibly but perhaps more radically—in Heidegger's thought.[1] Marion's entire phenomenological endeavor can be summed up in his statement: "As much reduction, as much givenness." The term "reduction" must of course be understood here in the precise sense Husserl gives it. As for "givenness," it becomes the key word that dominates Marion's work. Although in Marion, Heidegger's presence is always discrete, it is more insistent here. To try and understand how for Marion this relationship between reduction and givenness is established, we must—at least briefly—enter along with him the field of phenomenology. But before doing so we need to point out the kind of difficulty our questioning will have to confront in Marion's work. Our crucial task will be to determine whether the use of the term "givenness" to describe our experience of the world—as proposed by phenomenology—can, without an illegitimate shift from one field to another, apply to the oblative relationship between one person and another and, even more problematically, become a criterion of exclusion of specifically social practices of gift exchange. An unavoidable question will emerge in our discussion of the very use of the term *givenness* and its specific field of connotations, which can be stated as follows: Is it legitimate to claim a continuity between the givenness of phenomena—or even of their very being—and the gift from one human to another, or is such a continuity a mere illusion facilitated by a terminology whose relevance remains local?[2]

The question of this linguistic distinction cannot be dismissed from the outset as expressing a dubious relativism, since even among European languages a problematic discrepancy appears between, on one side, the German *es gibt* (literally, "it gives"), and on the other, the English "there is" and the Romance *il y a, c'è,* and *hay* (as we already mentioned with respect to Derrida). To summon this *es gibt* as a kind of wild card in the statement of existence of every being, action, and event, amounts to securing the use of a multipurpose interpretive tool that guarantees that its users will always find what they seek: givenness. Doing so also risks making it impossible to grasp the specificity of the gestures of gifts among persons or groups that seek a bond or are already united by existing commitments through specific symbolisms for which no reduction can account, and which can be deciphered only through empirical descriptions that reconstruct unique historical or ethnographic contexts. In other words, we must ask if what those gestures and practices—which belong to the realm of facts—call for, rather than phenomenology, is the resources of a hermeneutic based on empirical forms of knowledge. The lexicon of symbolisms is always contingent, local, and nondeductible. In no way does this lead to relativism: The logic of a symbolism participates in an intelligibility that illuminates operations associated with mental resources that can be observed everywhere.

To grasp the essence of Marion's argument, we need to situate its development primarily within the framework of Husserl's phenomenology, whose method and language Marion claims, even though he brings to this approach a new inflection and a redistribution of the field he revisits.

Husserl: Intuition, Reduction, and Intentionality

Let us recall that after working in the fields of logic and mathematical philosophy, Husserl proposes in his foundational writings[3] nothing less than a radical renewal of the philosophical enterprise[4]—a project that from the outset appears akin to Descartes's in that it proposes to set aside all acquired knowledge and received opinion and to take up every question based on the experience of the world as a phenomenon. Phenomenology is at the same time a change of attitude, a method, the rejection of certain modes of analysis, and the development of a theory of knowledge. It is a new attitude, brought about by a transformation in the gaze, that consists of freeing oneself from the supposedly common sense attitude that clings to the object and takes it for granted, thus falling victim to the illusion of an empty immediacy. Everything thus begins with a break; method alone makes it possible to receive phenomena with all the wealth of their givenness, which can be grasped by description through multiple approaches and various perspectives—by making intuition explicit. At this stage the obstacle or direction to be avoided consists of keeping to a psychological account and identifying lived experience with a state of consciousness. Both the objectivism of the common sense attitude and the psychologism of empirical description must be rejected. In positive terms the goal is to determine how, based on the conscious experience and through it, a relationship is established between the act of knowing and the object of knowledge; this relationship is said to be "intentional."

Through his inaugural decision to begin with the phenomenon—that is, the world as it appears to us—Husserl both asserts the priority of constitutive subjectivity and suspends or even rejects every ontological position.[5] Through this analysis of phenomena he proposes to establish a transcendental science of subjectivity. This means that, whatever the world may be, we can discuss it only based on our experience and consciousness of it. From the perspective of this *experienced* consciousness the world appears to us not only as an objective reality whose composition and laws can be determined by science, but as a reality that affects and concerns us—that is, that has *meaning* for us, not in a psychological sense, but in the sense that consciousness is the affirmation of a perspective, the perspective of an *I* for which and for which only the world is a world. To discuss meaning amounts to establishing the content of phenomena in terms of their essence for a consciousness. Husserl calls *reduction* the extraction of the logical element from this lived experience of consciousness.

Husserl thus raises a radical question. In no way does he deny the legitimacy or fertility of objective knowledge. His intent is to establish that this objectivity is empty if we do not bring to the fore the process through which it presupposes the existence of a prior relationship to the world; without this no knowledge could develop or even be formulated. Against the objectivist thought that discusses the world as if we were not in it, and the solipsistic thought that views it as if it did not need to be, Husserl, after Brentano, shows that consciousness is not a self-sufficient spiritual substance endowed with internal certainty confronting an external

scenery; instead, consciousness is defined by the fact that it is consciousness of something; it is thus an intentionality, which means that it *aims at
what is not itself*; it is this relationship. As a consequence, what Husserl calls
meaning cannot be reduced to a subjective interpretation of what occurs in
the world; on the contrary, meaning is the articulation of intentional consciousness with the world itself, described also as the articulation of the act
of knowledge—*noēis*—with the content of the thing known—*noēma*. This
experience of the world as the aim of consciousness—which Husserl designates as *lived experience*—constitutes transcendental subjectivity, not in the
Kantian sense of the a priori categories of understanding, but in the sense
that subjectivity asserts itself in the movement of consciousness *toward* that
which is *other* than itself and of which it is the necessary correlate. This
assertion is the movement of transcendence. Here the term transcendence
is understood literally, as a movement beyond oneself, toward an outside,
toward something other than the self. Reduction makes emerge that which
exists prior to any objectal construction; it thus gives us access to the self-
evidence of lived experience as the truth of this relationship.

This genesis grants a specific status to *intuition*—that is, the act by which
the world is perceived, or in more general terms, received, by consciousness. Husserl proclaims the importance of this act of reception, calling it
the "principle of all principles";[6] this is a surprising formulation on the
part of a thinker who, reactivating Descartes's gesture, intends to take up
the entire approach of a new philosophical beginning by dismissing the
metaphysical heritage altogether. Yet this formulation is legitimate since
this principle character applies to an essentially empirical activity shared
by every subject of perception: Intuition is the act of a subject, but in the
sense that it is primarily the reception of a world that occurs to the subject.
It testifies that the world exists prior to consciousness, for which it is an
already-there, a given world.

This is a question of principle, since regardless of the results gained
by objective knowledge this knowledge is created by a subject; no matter
how autonomous it may be or tend to become, the world this knowledge
describes and transforms always remains a world received by consciousness
or, in more general terms, by subjective experience. In other worlds, no
matter how constructed the world produced by our science may be, it still
remains the aim of consciousness as the world we experience. There is thus
an original ground of givenness prior to any science, logical construction,
artifact, and action. To conceive of the world as no more than the object
of our objective knowledge amounts to failing to see it and to recognize its
meaning. It is to forget that our consciousness is precisely this relationship

to the world, concealed by the illusion that knowledge about the world a sufficient to saturate this original bond. Our entire knowledge about the world—the hard sciences—presupposes the original layer of the world perceived, and even more broadly of the world experienced, the *Lebenswelt* that includes the social and historical world itself.

Marion's Approach

Those are a few of the main lines of Husserl's approach. Without entering the questionings and developments this approach made possible, we already have a sense of how the theme of givenness as appearance of the given will come to the fore in Heidegger's thought (who prefers the term *giving*), in a more limited manner in Merleau-Ponty, Levinas, Ricoeur, and Henri Maldiney, and in a still different way in Derrida and Michel Henry. More recently this theme has taken on an insistent role in Marion's thought. We must therefore give it closer consideration, since it takes a central place in his questioning. Marion's approach can be described as moving along three major steps; a fourth step remains, however prospective—or suspended— which involves the outcome; this is perhaps where Marion wishes to lead us, and it might be his starting point.

The first step consists of his entire effort at articulating reduction and givenness; this leads us to the verge of *pure givenness*: "What *shows itself* first *gives itself*—this is my one and only theme. I have endeavored to stick to it and orchestrate it the entire length of this work."[7] It remains for readers to follow Marion with respect to the implications of the concepts of *showing* and *giving* and the consequences of his use of the reflexive *se* [itself]. Marion clearly presents his program, or rather his method: His approach will be that of a phenomenologist, heir to Husserl. This means that he proposes to question phenomena in their self-evidence as being given. Instead of claiming to constitute phenomena, however, he intends to let them show themselves "in and by themselves"—following the way opened by Heidegger. This is no mean claim: It involves the "possibility of radicalizing the pure reduction to the given as such"[8] and thus to reach givenness itself through the reduced given, which becomes possible once—after Heidegger—reduction is no longer prisoner of the realm of being.

The greatest risks Marion takes are situated in his second step, since it consists of attempting a shift from pure givenness defined in strictly phenomenological terms to an analysis of the gift as a *gesture* among humans— that is, of an act by which a giver gives something to a recipient. This is a highly risky operation—*saltus mortalis?*—since it shifts reduction from the field of the original experience of the world to a specific experience within the world, based only on a linguistic kinship between *gift* and *givenness*, and with the aim to *reduce* the gift as a gesture itself. Marion must thus target one after the other all three terms of the relationship, to dismiss, he says, everything that has to do with *exchange, reciprocity,* and *the economy* (in which his approach meets the suspicion expressed by Derrida).

The third step, continually foreshadowed by the second, comes closer to integration; the reduction of the gift to givenness being assumed achieved, the only remaining task is to grasp the identity of given and givenness. The final result was there from the beginning: "*In principio erat donum.*"

This leaves us on the edge of the fourth and highly hypothetical step of the experience of an excess of intuition—or rather an overflowing of intuition—part of what Marion calls *saturated phenomena.* Are we coming close to the mystery? Marion does not tell us. We are still dealing with phenomena, but of a different type; Marion's approach never proposes to move beyond their realm; but can it really avoid doing so? It may be that he had crossed this border from the beginning. We will need to discuss this. For now let us follow this itinerary.

"As Much Reduction, As Much Givenness": Toward Absolute Givenness

Marion clearly states that he intends to bring to the fore the "fact" of givenness and its ultimate consequences. If phenomena must be not only constituted (this is the aim of Husserl's transcendental reduction), but also questioned in their being (according to Heidegger's existential reduction), then, in a more radical way, they must be conceived of as *pure givenness,* the ultimate limit of reduction. This is the meaning of Marion's *motto:* "As Much Reduction, As Much Givenness." It also means that there is nothing beyond givenness, which opens and closes everything.

This phenomenological approach that intends to give access to "the things themselves" must be defined based primarily on Husserl's concept of intuition. Intuition is assumed to constitute this access: It makes us see the thing because it fills an intentionality of object; it finds its order in the object. This is the movement of transcendence, literally *ex-stasis* toward the world. From this perspective Husserl stays within the limits of his method, since phenomenology claims to be a rigorous science; its demonstrations must follow a nonmetaphysical mode—that is, they must not require a foundation. It must therefore ensure that the phenomenon is grasped as it appears; this is a formidable requirement.

The question Marion asks is if intuition meets this requirement: What does this mean, to let the phenomenon manifest *itself*? Intentionality is the aim that reaches appearing in appearance; phenomenality must therefore be understood as manifestation. Intuition, however, seems to situate the entire activity on the side of the subject; but what of the thing itself? How can we understand appearing if it does not come from itself, if it does not have the initiative? By its own requirement the method must make possible this initiative of the appearing of phenomena and give way to it: "The methodological beginning here establishes only the conditions of its own disappearance in the original manifestation of what shows itself."[9] There is no such thing as preestablished meaning or rather there is no meaning prior to the appearing: "Constituting does not equal constructing or synthetizing, but rather giving-a-meaning, or more exactly, recognizing the meaning that the phenomenon gives from itself and to itself."[10] (Let us note in passing Marion's use of the reflexive pronoun throughout his book; we will return to this.) The first task of the method is thus to let the manifestation occur, to remove the obstacles that would limit its possibility (and even its right—here, like Husserl, Marion resorts to a legal language whose preexisting legitimacy he does not question).

To say that phenomena manifest themselves beginning with themselves is to say that their appearing is not suspended on a sufficient reason that guarantees their belonging to a foundation (of a Leibnizian type) or a system of categories (of a Kantian type). This autonomy of intuition leads Husserl to designate it "the principle of all principles." Here Marion asks Husserl a radical question: "Does the constitution of an intentional object by an intuition fulfilling an objectifying extasis exhaust every form of appearing? And even more, we must ask if intuition should be restricted to the limits of intentionality and the object's transcendence, or if it can be understood within the immense possibilities of what shows *itself*."[11] Husserl thus appears to enclose intuition within intentional fulfilling, and, ultimately, within objectivating representation. Furthermore, according to Marion, since intuition is posited *before* reduction, we can ask how intuition can lead to a specifically phenomenological form of knowledge possible only through reduction. This amounts to presupposing that the result of the operation is given before the operation itself. The hypothesis of inaugural givenness (that is, giving as contemporaneous with reduction itself) must make it possible to overcome this contradiction; hence the term "so much" in the formulation, "So Much Reduction, So Much Givenness." Husserl was aware of this possibility, but he immediately restricted it, positing that

"*Every originally giving intuition is a source of right for cognition*, that *every-thing* that offers itself *originally to us in intuition* [. . .] *must simply be received for what it gives itself*, but without *passing beyond the limits in which it gives itself.*"¹² What Husserl generally calls a "pure phenomenon" is not its mere appearing, but the phenomenon as grasped through reduction. To say that the phenomenon is given, is to say that it is given as reduced. Marion thus identifies in Husserl the essential association between reduction and given-ness. Reduction brought to its term manifests givenness; givenness is that which calls for the operation of reduction: "The reduction never reduces except to givenness [. . .]. There is no givenness that does not pass through the filter of reduction; there is no reduction that does not work toward a givenness."¹³ This is the first point of Marion's argument.

The next step consists of establishing the autonomy of the movement of givenness. To do so Marion questions Husserl's claim to the primacy of *intuition*. Intuition as the movement of consciousness toward its other is defined by intentional filling. When reduction has been brought to its term, however, only the given remains, not as an object, but as an appear-ing, or as the given in the sense that it is given: givenness; intuition thus has an ancillary function. Furthermore, the emergence of phenomena involves an excess beyond the intentionality of the object. What is given does not depend on this intentionality; it is thus given by itself: "What gives itself, insofar as given in and through reduced givenness, by definition gives itself absolutely. To give itself admits no compromise, even if in this given one distinguishes degrees and modes: Every reduced given is given or not. In contrast to intuition, givenness is not reducible except to itself and is there-fore carried out absolutely. Reducing givenness means freeing it from the limits of every other authority, including those of intuition."¹⁴

It is clear that, in contrast to Husserl, Marion operates a shift from the constitutive subject to the phenomenon of givenness. But he does so by using the resources provided by his master: His aim is to conceptualize the correlation between givenness and the paradox that reduction is the act of consciousness while givenness occurs *by itself*, based on itself. This is Hus-serl's concept of "intentional immanence"—that is, "immanence within transcendence"—which makes it possible to hold both sides together. The following claim must thus presuppose a "correlational a priori": "Given-ness arises precisely when appearance gives, besides itself (genuine imma-nence), the object, which without it could never appear even though this object does not amount to it (intentional immanence)."¹⁵

Marion talks of a "right of the phenomenon to manifest *itself*," and claims that it manifests *itself* "in person"—the usual translation of the German *selbst*, which raises some difficulties. Things are different with respect to the term "principle," which he explicitly discusses. To talk of givenness as the "final principle" runs the risk (as it does in Husserl) of being trapped in a metaphysics of which phenomenology aims to free itself. The principle escapes this trap, Marion explains, because it is canceled as a principle in givenness itself, since givenness is not situated within the order of representation to which the use of self-evidence in its classical form remains subjected. Givenness belongs to the order of *performative effectiveness* (this is the meaning of the term "by itself," and this legitimizes the term "in person"); givenness exists only as an operation. We now better understand the equation that relates reduction to givenness. What is said to one also applies to the other: "The reduction is not defined; it is performed as an act."[16] This brings us to the following axiom, whose echo we recognize: "Givenness is established as its own criterion as well as that of the nongiven."[17] We have reached a limit where discourse fades away, accomplished or exhausted in the act it describes. In this sense this situates us as much in the ultimate (the "final principle") as in the inaugural. There is nothing beyond givenness: "The reduction reduces everything, except the given; inversely, what it cannot reduce it admits as given. The reduction does not reduce givenness, it leads back to it."[18] This is a transposition of the essence (if we can say so) of the Heideggerian moment: Thought does not represent (itself); *Dasein* is as such the question itself; it is being, opening to the understanding of being; it is this understanding in the process of occurring, the locus of unveiling, and as such it is atemporal. This brings us back to *Es gibt*.

Everything Is Givenness: An Incomparable Privilege

Whereas Marion has so far followed Husserl's approach very closely, he now diverges from him on an important point. According to Marion, Husserl did not ask in a consistent way the question of being, and he remains—primarily, it seems, based on methodological requirements—within the paradigm of the object. In Husserl phenomena belong to the realm of beings, and they appear within the field of objectness. Although Husserl did raise the question of phenomena based on the requirement of givenness, his project remains incomplete. Here Heidegger makes it possible for Marion to go further—that is, to conceptualize being based on givenness.

What makes Heidegger unique is the importance he gives from the outset to *Es gibt*, a formulation without counterparts in other languages. A passage from *Being and Time* gives the following formulation: "Being lies in the fact that something is and in its Being as it is; in Reality; in presence-at-hand; in subsistence; in validity; in Dasein; in the 'it gives.'"[19] Marion chooses to translate *es gibt* as *cela donne* [it gives], rather than to use the standard French translation, *il y a* [there is].[20] As we will soon see, he explains his choice in detail (while also examining the suspicions his translation generates). Here everything turns on the articulation between being and beings. Even before presenting his demonstration Marion already states its result: "Being, insofar as it differs from beings, appears immediately in terms of givenness."[21] This claim is supported primarily by a reference to Heidegger's *Zeit und Sein* (1962)—a writing that reverses the terms of the title of his 1927 book and includes this decisive claim: "We do not say: Being is, but rather: It gives Being and it gives time. For the moment we have only changed the idiom with this expression. Instead of saying 'it is,' we say 'it gives.'"[22] *Es gibt* instead of *es ist*. This is a careful choice (at least if we accept Marion's translation of *es gibt* as "it gives" instead of "there is").[23] If we cannot say that being *is* (in the mode of subsistence), then we must claim that being *is not*; only beings *are*. *It gives being* is then the right formulation. It remains for us to understand "it" in this formulation. To give *what is not*, is this not to give the very retraction of being? To give thus necessarily amounts to relinquishing, which Marion states as follows: "Being withdraws from beings because it gives them [. . .]. Being advances in its own withdrawal—this paradox is illuminated only in terms of givenness."[24] An enigma remains: What is this *it* that gives? Is this an identifiable figure? Here Marion exercises his critical vigilance, escaping the temptation to designate an "ontic agent" or a personal transcendence. *It* must preserve the anonymity, or rather the unstatedness of givenness. But Heidegger, Marion notes, does not show the same caution when he conceals "it" under a name: *Ereignis*, the Advent, "indeterminate power that one must avoid substituting for the 'it'"[25] (the discrepancy between this noun and this pronoun would still need to be defined). It thus remains for us to consider a givenness that is its own horizon. This is the ambition that propels Marion's entire book: "From here on out, it is a question of defining givenness in itself and on its own terms."[26] This is the "privilege" of givenness.

In *Being Given* this privilege reigns sovereign: "It belongs to givenness to give [itself] without limit or presupposition because it gives [itself] without conditions. [. . .] in whatever way and by whatever means something can relate to us, absolutely nothing is, happens, appears to us, or affects us that is not first, always, and obligatorily accomplished in the mode of a *givenness*."[27] Here the phenomenological position is indicated by the "us" of the beneficiary. Thus stated Marion's thesis is irrefutable, and as a consequence it can be extended to its outer limits: "Nothing arises that is not given. And even nothing."[28] If everything that occurs, in any mode (whether being, experience, thought, possibility, or hypothesis), is said to be "given," then there is nothing outside of givenness, not even its denial (since to deny it is still to confirm it), death (as the possibility of the impossibility of receiving), nonsense, or misunderstanding. This is why for Marion it is important to free phenomenology from the hold of intuition and to be open to the power of "saturated phenomena." ("Phenomenology does not come to an end when it is set free from the primacy of intuition—it begins.")[29] There is nothing outside givenness. Marion's syllogism is clearly visible: From the phenomenological perspective nothing can be received as anything else than a phenomenon; nothing can be received that is not given; and nothing can be given without a process of givenness. It thus seems legitimate to claim that "Givenness opens the unsurpassable space of the given in general."[30]

This argument is clearly vulnerable to the accusation of tautological circularity, as in the old phrase "everything that is." What is not *is*, as nonbeing. This brings to mind Hegel's critique at the beginning of his *Phenomenology of Spirit* of the category of being as the most general and therefore the most empty. Let us also mention the risk of a purely nominalist operation that calls "given" everything that is not as well as everything that is. There is then no chance that anything can escape the selected category.

We must credit Marion for anticipating this—very obvious—objection and not giving in to this simplification. The reason why he does not explicitly mention this difficulty, however, is that he probably takes it for granted that the term "given" has nothing to do with the *datum* of empirical experience, and even less with *data* understood as statements of observable situations or balance sheets of information, or even the "data" of a problem (as in mathematics). The given he discusses is the *reduced given*. For Marion this is more specifically the given as conceived of through the articulation—*the fold*—between given and givenness; it is the given of givenness—and no other. In other words this given is received only to the extent that it is sought. For it to be given one must seek it; this is the polar opposite of the natural attitude. Point taken.

What is at stake is the *act*. At this ultimate stage of the reduction, at the end of the movement, confronting the unsurpassable horizon of givenness, the concept gives way to its absolute limit: the very operation it states. This brings us back to an argument already encountered: Discourse gives way to *performance*: "If [givenness] makes the given appear and sets the stage for the phenomenon—it must therefore be understood as an act. Givenness comes forward and accomplishes, arrives and passes, advances and withdraws, arises and sinks away. It does not subsist, persist, show itself, or makes itself seen. It is on the make; it makes the event without itself making up an event."[31] The narrative and dramatic status givenness takes on here is surprising. Givenness, which is not even supposed to be designated as a figure of thought (such as Heidegger's *Ereignis*), is presented as a conceptual agent endowed with exceptional energy: It "sets the stage for the phenomenon" that carries it, arises, passes, shows and removes itself. The term "stage," already found on several occasions, introduces an artificiality that detracts from the rigor of reduction. We seem to observe a kind of movement of impatience on the part of givenness, but against whom or what is this impatience directed? Givenness, which functions as a nonfigure, seems continually tempted to become a character. The verbs that qualify it come close to allegorical hypostasis. We observe a kind of dramatic acceleration in which the given provided by givenness follows a genuine kinetics—or even a ballistics—of the strong gesture: "The arising of the given makes it visible, because the movement of appearing ends by bursting on the depthless surface of consciousness like the impact of the gift, which precipitates and bursts there. The projection of the gift onto the conscious screen is enough to provoke appearing. The given is exposed because it explodes."[32] So be it. It is apparently time for givenness to *give*—that is, to make a gesture. This gesture had already been foreshadowed for a while: "The staging of the phenomenon is played out as the handing over of a gift."[33] Let us now see the show. The stage manager has been expecting us.

What the Gift Can Offer to Givenness

Between on one side givenness as it can be conceptualized based on Husserl's approach and surpassed through a more radical attitude, on the other the gift as the gesture by which a giver gratifies a recipient, Marion asks, is there more than a mere lexical resemblance [*paronymie*]?[34] This is a very scrupulous suspicion, since the lexical kinship between the two is undoubtable, but does this deserve philosophical questioning? Our question is all the more legitimate because the gift as observed in its empirical forms carries with it everything from which the effort at reduction has attempted to free itself, beginning with the metaphysical presuppositions of efficiency, causality, and subsistence. Moving from one field to the other appears risky. But this difficulty is also an opportunity to move further ahead. The aim so far has been to free givenness from any outside intervention. Marion now clearly states: "This new model of givenness will come from the gift."[35] He adds that it is surprising that so few phenomenologists have been intrigued and interested by the obvious kinship between givenness and the gift. The most prominent among them is Derrida, who in *Given Time* attempts to situate the question of the gift at the core of his reflection on givenness. Marion therefore proposes to follow him—but not all the way: He intends to turn off fairly soon, taking up in a different way the analysis of the terms of the gift relationship, lest their questioning lead to an aporia that would erase the phenomenon of the gift given, and at the same time givenness itself. The reason for Marion's reservation is clear: If the new model is to be provided by the gift, then we must be able to move beyond Derrida's argument, whose intention is precisely to demonstrate that the gift as gift—as a phenomenon—can be conceived of only as "*the* impossible," and that the very claim that one is giving is enough to cancel the gift.

Marion begins with a tribute to Derrida's endeavor, in particular for bringing to the fore the "metaphysical" presuppositions of the most famous essay on the gift, Mauss's *The Gift*. Marion unquestionably shares Derrida's reservations with respect to Mauss, and he agrees with Derrida's claim that Mauss remains within the order of causality (following very precisely its four classic modalities: efficient, physical, formal, and final), and therefore within the order of sufficient reason. What must be questioned, Marion tells us, is the very idea of exchange, the idea of reciprocity that entails the obligations to give, receive, and reciprocate. The obligation to give eliminates from the outset gratuitous generosity, while the obligation to reciprocate generates a debt. Marion thus grants Derrida the claim that this exchange involves an economic logic: calculus, interest, and utility. This is manifest in the reevaluation of every element involved in the exchange: Givers know that they are giving and that their gift will be reciprocated; recipients know that they are obligated to reciprocate and that they are in debt; the things given in their visibility and subsistent physicality are different from the goods exchanged in commercial relationships. From this perspective, according to Marion, Derrida is right to end up claiming that for a gift to exist the givers would have to be unaware that they are giving, the recipients unaware that they are receiving, and no debt should force them to reciprocate.

Marion and Derrida are clearly in agreement regarding the gift exchange described by Mauss—an exchange entirely subjected, in their opinion, to the mode of subsistence and the most metaphysical causality. Based on this agreement it is not entirely clear why Marion does not accept Derrida's conclusion with respect to this type of gift: "If [the donee] recognizes it *as* gift, if the gift *appears to him as such*, if the present is present to him *as present*, this simple recognition suffices to annul the gift."[36] Marion objects: "Such a non-appearing of the gift in no way implies renouncing its phenomenality."[37] It is true that Derrida's conclusion precludes the possibility of any phenomenological approach; it presupposes that the very visibility of the gift is what objectifies the gift, equates it to economic exchange, and ultimately takes it away from givenness. This precludes the progress toward givenness through the reduction of the phenomenality of the gift. For Derrida it is as if—in and only in the case of the gift—the phenomenon is in excess, hence the aporia whose terms are now familiar to us.

For Marion this aporia of the gift is tenable only if the appearance of the gift is subjected to the mode of presence (causes, subsistence), in which case the gift disappears with the deconstruction of this very mode. But according to him this subjection is inappropriate, since to occur, the gift does not need presence: "But in thus disappearing as a permanent present, the gift is not lost as given; it loses only the way of being—subsistence, exchange, economy—that contradicts its possibility of giving itself as such. In losing presence, the gift does not lose *itself*; it loses what is not suited to it: returning *to itself* [. . .]. The initial paradox—the present (the gift) cannot be present in presence—is now transformed into another: The present (the gift) is given without presence. The impasse becomes a breakthrough."[38] This is a remarkable reversal: Marion's aim is to reject nothing in the phenomenon of the gift; he even proposes to seek in the phenomenon what opens to givenness. Derrida himself seems to consider this breakthrough: "There would be, *on the one hand*, the gift that gives something determinate (a given, a present in whatever form [. . .]) and, *on the other hand*, the gift that gives not a given but the *condition* of a present given in general, that gives before the element of the given in general."[39] But for Marion to discuss this condition in these terms is to enter the problematic of foundations—in other words, to resort once again to a "typically metaphysical function."[40] This critique amounts to accusing Derrida of falling into the trap of that which he never ceased to deconstruct. It is because Derrida was trapped by his debate with Mauss on exchange and reciprocity (which according to Marion have nothing to do with the gift) that he can conceive of the possibility of the gift as givenness only in terms of its impossibility as an exchange. But "this contradiction states the essence of nothing at all, therefore not that of any gift whatsoever."[41] Why not? Because the thesis that the gift-as-exchange constitutes a gift should have been rejected from the outset. We must thus renounce the economic horizon of exchange and think the gift from the starting point of givenness (let us note that this entire line of reasoning becomes fragile or even irrelevant if it turns out that the reciprocal ritual gift discussed here has nothing to do with an economic exchange).

The way is now open for a phenomenological approach of the gift as the act of giving.

The Triple Epokhē, or the Suspended Relationship

Marion clearly states his approach: His purpose is to think the gift based on givenness—and thus outside the mode of causality—that is, the "metaphysics of presence" presupposed by exchange; it remains to be determined how to overcome the obstacle exchange constitutes. He must demonstrate how the gift given according to givenness is not by its very nature suspended on the intervention of the parties in the exchange or even on the thing that circulates from one of them to the other. This task is highly problematic from the perspectives of both the theory of action and phenomenological reduction. With respect to the former, to eliminate the agents of a relationship is to presuppose the inexistence of the gesture that bonds them, as well as that of the relationship itself. This is a daring wager (and attempting it may also be contradictory). The latter brings us to a classical difficulty of phenomenology: Its effort at reduction always involves lived experiences of consciousness rather than practices. It can approach practices only from the perspective of the lived experiences associated with them. This is why, although Marion does not specify this verbatim, an approach to the gesture of the gift as a relationship between parties cannot begin with a direct attempt at reduction; it requires a prior bracketing operation, an *epokhē* that suspends the data or sediments of history or experience. This is the task Marion takes on, which he expresses as follows: "To speak of a gift, what lived experiences are required? It is of course necessary to make a distinction between the lived experiences of the gift affecting a consciousness playing the role of giver and those affecting a consciousness playing the role of givee."[42] Each of those "roles" raises a specific problem of perspective relatively easy to account for in turn, but what of the thing given? Should it be reduced to the consciousness of the giver or the recipient? It cannot be reduced to both at the same time without rejecting the very principle of the phenomenological approach: Reduction occurs through and for a conscious I. We must thus assume that each consciousness takes on in turn the function of the transcendental I. Marion senses the tortuous character of this operation, and he makes this clear in a footnote. We will return to this point, since the stake of this discussion is the status of the relationship between the parties involved in the gift *that* is given and the indivisible structure of this triad. It is actually important to conceptualize this triadic unity as such—a concept entirely alien to phenomenology.

To proceed with this *epokhē* Marion proposes a sequence of analyses of typical situations, each of which involves one of the poles of the relationship—situations that show a withdrawal or, rather, a nonactualization of the standard figure. With respect to givers something remains impossible to identify as long as they are anonymous or indeterminate (as when a gift is sent to a population through an association). In the same way recipients who proclaim themselves enemies of the givers can reject the gift offered, and ingrates can be indifferent to the givers. Givers can be absent for the recipients, as in the case of inheritance. Most of the time, the givers (of a show, a work of art, or an emotion) have no idea of what the recipients will receive. No exchange takes place; no symmetry can be conceived of, not even in the case of endebtment, since even if what is owed is repaid in the end, it is never entirely so. The very postponement is the measure of a want that can never be filled. "All debt, like all credit, amounts finally to time given and lost—but never repaid. In short, all debt is temporalized, whatever its object may be; therefore one is never free of it."[43]

Marion's argument is constructed as follows: If what we identify as the phenomenon of the gift can be preserved in spite of the scarce reality of the giver and recipient, does this not point to an intention to give that preexists—or exists beyond—the relationship between the consciousness of the giver and that of the recipient? In this case the various suspensions are indeed capable to open to reduction and give access to givenness; but what of the thing given? When the giver and the recipient fade away, does the thing not resist this *epokhē*, thus testifying to the physical existence of the gift and the reality of the exchange?

This physicality is precisely the target of Marion's suspicion. Nothing, he explains, forces us to grant priority to tangible and visible goods; those are after all merely "simplistic gifts, and the poorest ones."[44] Many other types of gifts are far enough from this empirical schema to allow us a different view of the presupposed physicality of the thing given—for example, the gestures by which power is granted or one's word is given, as well as the gift of oneself. In those three cases no identifiable and measurable good is transferred: Power is a function and prestige; the word given is a promise; the self expresses the essence of a person. For Marion "it must be suggested as a fundamental rule that the more considerable a gift appears, the less it is realized as an object and by means of a transfer of property [. . .]. In the realm of the reduction, the gift is accomplished all the better when it is not reified in an object."[45]

This is a very appealing statement, since a gift, no matter how physical and regardless of its type (whether reciprocal, gracious, or out of solidarity), never consists only of the transfer of a property. As Mauss says, the thing given always testifies to the self of the giver, which is what confers on it inestimable value, a priceless character that cannot be accounted for by any commercial model. This value and this aura transfigure the "thingness" of the thing offered. But if the nonphysical essence of the gift derives precisely from the fact that it carries the self of the giver, then it is problematic or even absurd to dismiss the thing given. Is it necessary to resort as evidence to the argument to the examples of the gift of power or of one's word? Furthermore, are those really gifts? Both cases are designated by single-set phrases that can be replaced by synonyms in which a different verb can be substituted for "giving" (we will examine below the very specific status of this multifunctional verb). Power can also be said to be granted, entrusted, or passed down; this involves not oblativity (no more than do such phrases as: to give way, permission, or food for thought). Giving power is a duly established legal procedure that merely designates the entire set of gestures and words required by the accepted protocol (whether in the political field or any other institution). Here the term "giving" has the neutral status of a verb that indicates the procedure by which authority is established or transferred; in no way does it express a gift. The same can be said of the single-set phrase, "to give one's word." That this phrase is not used as a noun phrase ("the gift of one's word"), but only as a verb phrase that includes a possessive that reflects the self ("to give *one's* word"), clearly shows that this operation can be conceived of and performed only in the first person by the speech act, "I give you my word," where the very utterance constitutes the act. To give-one's-word is a single-set phrase that can be substituted for by terms such as to *promise* or *swear*. Here "to give" is the equivalent of a verb whose grammatical object is not a noun ("one's word"), but a clause (to swear that . . .; promise that . . .; guarantee that . . .; etc.; "giving one's word" is therefore not equivalent to "the gift of one's word"). The choice of those verb phrases can be convincing only if supported by a precise analysis of the grammatical functioning that determines their semantic status. To play on the similarities generated by verbs (such as: to give, to do, to make, to get, to take) that function as multiple-purpose instruments and tend to lose their semantic value or become stereotypic, generates contrasts that force us to think, but also runs the risk of creating mere paralogisms.

Let us go further back in our examination of Marion's remarks on the gift of goods he views as "primary and poorest." First, as we saw, as guarantees to the self of the giver, those gifts always involve something beyond their mere physicality; they are thus never primary or impoverished. Above all, when the purpose is to give bread to the hungry or assist "widows and orphans" (to use Levinas's Biblical language), it is much better to keep to the natural attitude than to examine the gesture "in the mode of reduction" (our purpose is not to simulate a phenomenological *Witz*). Levinas calls "costly gift" a gift whose priceless value cannot be separated from its physicality. Let us recall this statement from *Totality and Infinity*: "*Dasein* in Heidegger is never hungry."[46] Marion would probably endorse this claim, while noting that the phenomenological reduction of the gift in no way precludes the empirical gesture: It merely extracts its ultimate instantiation. So be it. But this does not justify rhetorical shifts that underestimate the powers of language. Polysemy, so crucial to poetic expression, can become a fatal trap to philosophical argument.

An important point remains, which Marion designates by the concept of *givability*; how should we understand this term? What is it that is givable? This is neither a feature of the thing given (since the gift would thus result from a quasi-mechanical necessity) nor a mere perspective on the thing (which would remain purely subjective). Beyond the polarity between subject and object, givability must be understood as a "positive potentiality" that runs across and affects at the same time the agents of the gift and the thing given. Givability leads the givers to let the gift move without them, to "lose" it for it to be given. This is an appealing idea with respect to the gracious gift; it points to the essence of beautiful gestures. The counterpart on the recipient's side is *acceptability*: the disposition to recognize and welcome the incoming gift. Marion shows this in a beautiful analysis of the figure of Percival, where this acceptability appears in the inverted form of the surprise and fear that grasp the knight at the moment when he witnesses the Grail carried by a procession; those reactions cause him to fail to ask the nature of the marvel that is moving away from his grasp. Percival is not able to recognize that this grace is intended for him. The word "Grace" is precisely the one Marion does not write. Yet this is the only appropriate word here, since the idea of grace is continually and profoundly associated with another "positive potentiality" that runs across his entire book and remains unnamed: oblativity. It is not named because it is perhaps that which operates at the articulation between given and givenness, which Marion designates as a *fold*, and which we will soon discuss.

Returning to the Ceremonial Gift and Its Misunderstanding by Phenomenology

With this attempt at a triple *epokhē* Marion aims to "reduce" the two poles of exchange and the thing exchanged to make the gift more clearly emerge as givenness, which should make it possible for givenness to appear as a gift; his approach is thus clearly different from Derrida's. For Marion Derrida's error lies not in his failure to see that Mauss distorts the nature of the gift (on this Marion confirms Derrida's critique), but in his subjecting his approach to the gift as givenness to a confrontation that has nothing to do with the gift—that is, reciprocal exchange. We must agree with Marion, but for opposite reasons, which require that we vigorously call into question the claim by the phenomenology of givenness to account in epistemologically acceptable terms for the gift-exchange practices discussed by Mauss as well as all the authors who have studied similar data. Two types of problems must be considered: the first involves the concepts of exchange and economy Marion calls on; the second concerns the specifically social nature of the ceremonial gift, as opposed to the individual gift to which Marion, like Derrida, continually refers, even when discussing forms of the gift that are collective and ruled by different types of logic.

The type of gift described by Mauss is the ritual gift: offerings provided by characters endowed with a specific status—such as the head of a lineage, clan, or any other form of organization—to characters with comparable status. They occur in certain precise circumstances, according to procedures known to both groups, and involve the exchange of precious goods whose symbolic value is defined by traditions. The ritual gift is therefore not a gift given by one individual to another out of generosity or of a wish to receive a gift in return, yet this type of private gesture, free of all circumstances and context, is the one Marion, like so many other philosophers, continually presupposes in his analyses. Although on other points he breaks with Derrida, from this perspective he reiterates and appropriates Derrida's analyses in *Giving Time*, and he shows caution in avoiding an extensive discussion of Mauss's positions.

It is clear that—as, once again, so many other authors do—Marion reduces the concept of reciprocity to the idea of a self-serving return: "The gift, to be given, must be lost and remain lost without return."[47] "The gift demands, in order to give *itself*—therefore to make its own decision about itself—giving without return or response."[48] "It [the gift] excludes the reciprocity that the other demands."[49] "If the truth of the gift resides in the payback, the truth lowers it to the status of a loan."[50] Those claims would be entirely convincing if they applied exclusively to the gracious gift, unilateral by hypothesis. If the gracious gift came with an expectation of reciprocation, it would indeed betray its own requirement and go against its essence. But this is not the case of the ceremonial gift, reciprocal by definition since it is primarily a procedure of alliance and public recognition between groups. An alliance presupposes an agreement between two parties: an offer and a reply; an unreciprocated alliance would be an alliance without allies. Derrida's failure to understand this—simple and clear—situation leads him to go astray in his comment on Mauss; on this point at least Marion follows in Derrida's footsteps when he views this type of reciprocal gift as an exchange in the economic sense. This form of gift is in fact the glorious and generous expression of the respect granted to the other party. The goods offered are thus not "things" in the legal or even physical sense, but goods with a particular status, precious goods whose role is to symbolize the alliance and manifest the agreement. In addition, the parties involved are not just any parties, random individuals who take the initiative to give; they are agents with a specific status, entrusted with a function that involves the entire group and participants in ceremonies defined by precise procedures that follow an accepted calendar. To discuss those as simple economic exchanges shows a regrettable misunderstanding. Marion and Derrida appear willing to consider only one sense of the term "exchange": profitable exchange; they echo a linguistic use that has prevailed only over the last two centuries, but that obscures a large variety of very different senses: exchanges of gazes, blows, messages, favors, points of view . . . and of course gifts. To consider only the commercial sense is to confirm the very standard view that one intends to call into question.

Based on this prior simplification, Marion sets up the argumentative configuration at the core of his critique of the Maussian gift—that is, in more general terms, the ceremonial gift. This configuration is a deconstruction of the concepts originating from "metaphysics," which according to Heidegger must be understood as the whole of the ontic concepts passed down by the Western tradition since their emergence in Greek philosophy with Plato and Aristotle. In proposing to deconstruct (*umbauen*) or undo those concepts, Heidegger does not merely take on a project of simple critique; he intends to perform a task of dis-obscuring of being as buried—*forgotten*—in the arrangement of beings, a task Derrida ceaselessly takes up again and radicalizes. This deconstruction begins with the

concepts of principle and foundation that presuppose the closure of a sufficient reason dominated by the schema of causality. Marion emphasizes
this point: "Givenness is never defined as a principle or ground precisely
because it delivers the given from any demand for a cause by letting it deliver itself, free itself."[51] If the topic of the discussion was gracious giving,
one would have to agree with Marion's claim. But is this claim relevant to
the ceremonial gift? After a reference to Mauss's *The Gift* Marion develops
his critique as follows: "This system in fact remains thoroughly metaphysical: the giver gives the gift in the role of efficient cause, mobilizing a formal
cause and a material cause (in order to define, reify the gift), and pursuing
a final cause (the good of the givee and/or the glory of the giver). These
four causes enable givenness to satisfy the principle of sufficient reason.
Reciprocity repeats this sufficient reason to the point of perfectly apply-
ing the principle of identity by bringing the gift back to itself."[52] So be
it; but if it turns out that in the ceremonial gift the good offered is in no
way a physical good merely "reified," that it functions on the contrary as
a guarantee of alliance, that reciprocity constitutes an act of recognition
continually renewable and renewed, that nothing returns to beginning because things proceed through alternating dissymmetry, that the exchange
involves an open temporality and, even though its procedures are predictable, it remains undecidable as an event, then we must recognize that to
view this as a "thoroughly metaphysical system" that activates the four
modalities of causality is to provide an argument on the wrong object.
The only thing the critique has destroyed is the ghost it had constructed.
Although Marion's critique is irrelevant in the case of the ceremonial gift,
however, it is entirely legitimate in the case (and only in the case) of the
individual gift claimed to be gracious (and thus unilateral) while being in
fact self-interested. In other words, we must always return to the heterogeneity of the orders of the gift (a. reciprocal; b. gracious; c. out of solidarity), which almost all the authors who discuss the gift continually confuse.
The paradox is that the form of the gift that constitutes the primary target
of Marion's critique—the reciprocal gift, whose most typical form is the
ceremonial gift (and which is necessarily an exchange, but in an agonistic mode, and is an exchange of symbols)—is precisely the form furthest
away by its presuppositions and its logic from the "metaphysical system,"
whereas the gracious gift is much more liable to fall into the trap of this
system, to the extent that this form of the gift surreptitiously aims at reciprocity while removing it by hypothesis from its horizon.

The more general problem we face with this critique of a specifically
social type of gift (such as the ceremonial gift) is that it views things in

terms of purely individual relationships. Thus, when Derrida and Marion comment on Mauss, they always discuss an indeterminate giver and recipient: you or me or anyone, facing an Other considered in general, outside any specific situation or belonging to any group, ignoring the local status of the parties as well as any specific symbolism or tradition. Those are extraterrestrial parties for whom giving is an initiative available to anyone anywhere; but to whom do they give, with what aim, and according to what modalities? Is givenness the only purpose of the gift? And why make the decision to give in the general and neutral environment of this subject situated in limbo? In fact we know the identity of this—modern—subject, which is potentially us: He is a subject without qualities.

The following peremptory claim helps us understand this *ontic* indetermination: "The gift [. . .] owes nothing to any anthropological or sociological model."[53] This claim is unquestionable with respect to the givenness of phenomena in Husserl's sense or the gift of being in Heidegger's sense, and it could be argued for with respect to gifts given by individuals motivated by their own generous intentions. But with respect to the ceremonial gift, Marion's claim is untenable. It should even be reversed as follows: No phenomenological model of givenness can be applied to the ceremonial gift. In other words, shifting from an analysis of the givenness of phenomena (a valid interpretive choice if the aim is to grasp their mode of being) to an analysis of the gift as a social practice and even as a private gesture, is a fraught and arbitrary theoretical decision that tends to misunderstand the specific nature of social facts, implicitly reducing them to unmotivated and decontextualized individual practices.

The Resources of Thought Embodied in Language: The Lexicon of the Gift

Marion's following statement with respect to Heidegger's *Ereignis* is entirely convincing: "As is often the case with words, it concerns what is essential."[54] We should also mention that a theory of words is not enough; we can recognize, however, that the term "words" is only an accepted way to designate the order of language. For a long time grammarians—and more recently linguists—have made it possible for us to grasp the extraordinary complexity of the formation of sentences and the functioning of discourse within the framework of the continually updated virtual system we call language. The semantic content of terms and phrases cannot be reduced to the designations provided by lexicons or traced by philologies; it is at play in the grammatical resources called on by sentences. From this perspective we can draw lessons from the use of specific phrases involving terms such as gift, givenness, and giving *oneself*.

LEXICAL QUESTIONS I: "GIVENNESS" AND *ES GIBT*

Let us begin with the very term "givenness" [*donation*]. The difficulty lies in the dual sense this word has in French, since it designates what is given as well as the act of giving. This ambiguity is also present in German with the term *Gegebenheit*. This observation has led some translators to alternate the terms *donné* [given] and *donation* [givenness]. Marion states that it is far better to consistently use the term "givenness." He could have called on the resources of linguistics, but he prefers to keep to specifically philosophical arguments. Rather than to waver between two levels of translation, what matters according to him is to understand this ambiguity as a *fold*, the very articulation between given and givenness, counterpart of the articulation between appearing and appearance, or phenomena and their manifestation. This brings us back to the results of the previous analyses: A phenomenon is such only as it is given, and it thus carries the trace of the process of its arising: "It comes forward insofar as it gives itself."[55] This means, only because it gives itself. Marion's questioning of the choice of the term "givenness" does not lead him to a discussion of its linguistic implications, but to an additional philosophical distinction—a *fold*—between given and givenness.

Marion sticks to his guns. So does language: The choice to translate Husserl's *Gegebenheit* as "givenness" is not immaterial since we know that in German this term designates the given, or data (without the ambivalence of the French *don* or the English "gift," which designate the thing given as well as the gesture of giving). Furthermore, the French term *donation* is loaded with a legal heritage that interferes with the debate whether we want it or not. The ninth edition of the *Dictionnaire de l'Académie* gives the following definition of *donation*: "Formal contract by which an individual, the donor, divests himself irrevocably of a good, without any compensation and with a generous intent, to the benefit of another individual, the donee, who accepts the good. Donation among living parties. Donation pure and simple." It is difficult for French readers to erase from their minds this legal connotation, but nothing forbids us from freeing the term from the connotation and accepting the effort at diversion and philosophical invention Marion proposes (Levinas continually requires the same effort, and rightly so). But, as a commentator notes, to retrospectively project the notion of *donation* onto Husserl's *Gegebenheit* and Heidegger's *Geben* is

more problematic. The same commentator observes that the French translators of Husserl (Ricoeur, Alexandre Lowit, and Arion Kelkel) choose *le
donné* [the given] or *la donnée* [the datum], or even *la présence* [the presence]:
"These translations have received their legitimacy from the particular context. Yet, is the unification of this semantic sphere under the term "givenness" essential? 'Donation' in German is *eine Schenkung*. It is not at all the
same."[56] The same problem arises in a different mode with respect to Heidegger: "When we translate the verb *geben* by the substantive 'givenness,'
this verbal force of *geben* becomes overshadowed, as well as the difference
between this 'giving' and the gift (*Gabe*)."[57] To sum up, the creative distortion of language is an unimpeachable and precious philosophical freedom; but this freedom ends on the threshold of the territory of translation, which requires faithfulness to the original writing and respect for the
specificity and idioms of the language in which it is written. The lexicon of
that language does not legitimize theoretical choices based on terms taken
exclusively from the language of the commentator.

There is no doubt that "as is often the case with words, it concerns what
is essential." Language is neither transparent nor innocent—but this does
not make it guilty. Language carries a history and follows its own logic;
philosophy cannot disregard this without paying a price. In the words of
Jocelyn Benoist, another of his commentators, Marion chooses to consider
the problem as resolved: "It seems to us that Jean-Luc Marion's thought
suffers from a deficiency in the philosophy of language [. . .]. An ignorance
of language or a tendency to take it for granted (Marion's case appears
to be the second) is probably one of the most constitutive features—and
limits—of phenomenology."[58] Benoist's reservations are focused on an
exacting discussion of the relationship between intuition and meaning in
Husserl, which we do not need to consider here. The central point of his
critique is the following: In Marion this lack of reflection on language is
inseparable from a deficiency in the philosophy of meaning: "From this
perspective it can be said that his phenomenology, in what is in the end a
traditional way, is pervaded throughout with linguistic naivety."[59] Benoist's
remarks concern primarily the very specific status of language, which cannot be viewed as a "given" among others: "Between experience and language, there is an intractable problem, and perhaps a gap."[60] This is probably a figurative way to assert—in a quasi-Hegelian style—that language
brings a constitutive negativity to experience and increases a distance that
affects in a radical way our relationship to the world. Those suspicions,
however, can be steered in a different direction: the use of words, their
intrinsic power, and their reserves of thought.

This invites us to return to the question of *Es gibt*, which we already briefly approached with respect to Derrida's *Giving Time*. Marion notes that Heidegger's use of this formulation is still in its inception in *Sein und Zeit* [*Being and Time*] and that it becomes central in a 1962 writing, *Zeit und Sein*. With respect to this writing, the translation of *Es gibt* raises nearly insoluble problems. The French translation in *Questions IV*[61] follows the current use, translating the German formulation as *il y a* [there is], often complementing it with the verb "to give." Marion resolutely chooses *cela donne* [it gives], an apparently sound choice since Heidegger's formulations, in which *Es gibt* is followed by the verb to give [*geben*], remain opaque if *Il y a* is used in isolation.[62] In the following sentence from *On Time and Being*, "This 'There is being' [*Es gibt Sein*] might emerge somewhat more clearly once we think out more decisively the giving [*geben*] we have in mind here,"[63] unprepared readers will not be aware of the explicit resonance in German between *Es gibt* and *geben*; on the contrary, this resonance bursts out in the translation, "It gives being." In the latter case, however, the sense of the simple arising (or appearing) of the phenomenon is lost, whereas this sense remains present in *Es gibt* and is perfectly conveyed by "*il y a* [there is]." Every German speaker recognizes that in ordinary usage the phrase *es gibt* does not suggest in any way the idea of giving. For this connotation to be recognized requires either explicit wordplay or a theoretical reexamination emphasizing the kinship between the two terms (Heidegger provides the latter). The French translator of *Zeit und Sein* reminds us in a note that the German *geben* is a development of the Indo-European radical **ghabh*, from which the Latin *habere* originates. This linguistic filiation is interesting in the sense that among Indo-European languages, only German shows this derivation as the origin of the verb "to give," whereas other languages use two verbs that generally function as helping verbs: "to be" (there is; *c'è*; *det er*) or "to have" (*il y a*; *hay*;).[64] We now better understand why *es gibt* is an appropriate translation of *il y a* [there is], and vice versa,[65] and also why in French (as in the other languages mentioned above) the verb *donner* [to give] often designates a mere observation or an attribution completely devoid of the connotation of givenness that Marion grants it, in phrases such as "to give" a feeling, an illusion, an appointment, or a pretext.[66] The verb "to give" works in an open and indeterminate way, like the other multifunctional verbs such as "to make," "to put," and "to take" that we mentioned above. To grant this verb a primarily oblative meaning and extend this meaning to its other uses is to risk generating arbitrary semantic associations.

We also better understand the use of the terms "the given" and "the data" [Latin for "the given"] to respectively designate a verifiable situation and the information necessary to establish a research or a problem (as in mathematics). This is the primary meaning of the German *es gibt*; translating this phrase as *il y a* [there is] is thus entirely appropriate. For Heidegger to shift *es gibt* toward the idea of *geben* is an interesting philosophical choice that informs us on his own thought and suggests its originality, but this does not authorize us to generalize his choice. Heidegger himself sometimes chooses to preserve the neutral character of the phrase *es gibt*, but then he assigns this character almost entirely to the pronoun *Es* (which he proposes to capitalize).[67] At best, "there is" points to the contingent quality of the world and extends Husserl's formulation, "The world is." This explains why in the end the French translator of *Zeit und Sein* chooses the phrase *il y a* [there is], rather than *cela donne* [it gives] as does Marion, who sees in it the prefiguration of givenness. There is another reason why in French Marion's view is far from self-evident: The ordinary meaning of *cela donne* is not oblative at all; it suggests instead the creation of an effect, as does the English phrase "you get": Mix up blue and yellow, and you get green; make an offer, and see what you get—no obvious givenness here.

What conclusion can we draw from this brief lexical study? At least two points: (1) If German alone was capable thanks to its *es gibt* to designate the givenness of being, this would mean that other languages are deficient when compared to German, unless we accept to turn phrases such as *il y a* and "there is" into a somewhat forced "it gives"; (2) Thinkers have every right to call on language and push it beyond its customary uses; but whereas poets transform the very material of language, philosophers cannot lose sight of the requirements of argument, and therefore of scholarly inquiry. If their search for a new literalness leads them to an idiom without speakers, then this search is nothing more than a rhetorical feat without an audience.

Lexical Questions II: The "Itself" of Givenness

To say that givenness gives *itself* and does so *by itself* or *from itself* is to call on a particular type of grammatical construction that represents either the action of a subject, or a quasi passive. The meaning of a French sentence such as *un concert se donne* [a concert is given] is entirely different from the several possible meanings of a sentence such as *une personne se donne* [someone gives him/herself]. In the latter, *se donner* is an example of what grammarians call a reflexive pronominal construction, which is different from other types of pronominal constructions, whether reciprocal, passive, or subjective. When applied to a thing, the pronominal construction is the equivalent of a passive, as in *la tour se remarque de loin* [the tower can be seen from afar]; *ce tableau se vend cher* [this painting is sold for a high price]; or *la pièce de théâtre se joue* [the play is performed]. In a more essential way we are dealing here with the modalities of the passive and reflexive forms of diathesis.[68] It is therefore relevant to ask whether the formulation *le phénomène se donne* [literally, the phenomena gives itself] (1) is equivalent to a passive construction ("is given"), which minimizes the importance of *se* [itself], thus erasing the initiative that phenomenologists wish to grant it; or (2) retains the status of a reflexive pronominal construction, which amounts to presuppose in it a reflexivity without ipseity, or to grant it the ipseity of a quasi agent (made patent by the translation of *selbst* as "in person"). This ipseity, however, is highly problematic, and it involves a metaphoric functioning that can not be called on without critical precautions. It would be advisable for Marion to consider those questions, which are crucial to the argumentative rigor of his demonstration.[69]

Those effects are directly related to the major question that runs across the entire movement of *Being Given*: the shift from an analysis of the givenness of the phenomenon to a phenomenology of the gift.[70] Such a phenomenology can certainly account for gestures that are assigned to a subject in general and that can be described through the gradual reduction of experiences of consciousness, but it remains incapable of reducing social practices endowed with a specific institutional character. With respect to the latter the only possible approach is a hermeneutic (or some other type of well-established interpretative discipline) based on objective knowledge about this practice. A simple analogy can help us understand this: No matter however perceptive and detailed it may be, a phenomenology of speech will never be able to account for the objective phonetic, morphological, and syntactic processes that constitute the functioning of a language, and without which no sentence could be uttered by a speaker or recognized by an addressee. Furthermore, only the knowledge of those processes can make it possible to grasp the creation of effects of meaning where lies the power of the most unique and inventive forms of speech, beginning with poetic speech. The same can be said of the symbolic facts that underlie and inform social practices. Only scholarly inquiry can establish their elements—lexicon—and describe their functioning—syntax—making it possible for an interpreter to bring to the fore their logic and, more generally, their meaning (that is, their value and intelligibility for the agents involved). This is the appropriate approach with respect to ritually organized practices of gift exchange. Without prior scholarly inquiry philosophers cannot say anything of those practices beyond fruitless general statements.

Cultural symbolisms—such as languages—are always specific, local, and nondeductible. Their formation and functioning, on the contrary, are neither arbitrary no incommunicable; they reveal formal models recognizable everywhere. In this field factual analysis must come before and inform the analysis of experiences of consciousness.

In Conclusion

Being Given is built like a cathedral. The breadth of its construction cannot be grasped if we stay on its front porch or next to one particular pillar. Yet the pillar that supports its critique of reciprocity appears fragile. The need to give it close attention to examine its fissures has left us little time to visit the rest of the monument. We did not discuss the book's developments on the event, the gifted, and above all on excess of intuition and *saturated phenomena*. Some of those questions have occasioned polemics. Those are legitimate debates, but they are not ours. The discussion we have presented here is usually not entered by phenomenologists, nor more generally by philosophers, for at least two reasons: few of them doubt that there are good reasons to suspect reciprocity; thus few are aware of the complexity of the questions it involves; in addition, those questions entail a consideration of the social sciences, consideration that many philosophers view as overly risky. Their attitude is understandable given how highly specialized and narrow those disciplines may appear. Yet while philosophy must not be subjected to their modes of approach, it cannot ignore their results, especially with respect to practices that have been extensively studied and precisely problematized. Philosophy owes it to itself to seek in a new way to discover how thought moves forward in fields of knowledge where a regional intelligibility of phenomena is rigorously presented.

Let us return to our question. While a phenomenology of the gift—understood as the oblative gesture of a subject in general—is possible as a procedure of reduction of an experience of consciousness, it is not relevant to specific symbolic practices. Our consciousness of those practices can never account for the laws that rule them and the contexts that make them unique. If phenomenologists propose to evaluate them by referring them to categories loaded from the outset with inadequate content (for example, by reducing every exchange to a commercial schema or every form of reciprocity to self-interest), not only will they teach us nothing about the specificity of those practices, but on this point at least their own conceptual approaches will fail to catch. If phenomenology (or at least one of its versions) intends to subject the ritual gift to the process of reduction, thus bracketing—operating the *epokhē* of—the giver, the recipient, and the thing given, then it ignores the fact that the gift relationship constitutes an indivisible triadic structure, which amounts to conceiving or rather imagining an institutional form of gift free of relationships—where the parties involved are suspended—and a gesture without mediation—where the thing given is erased. This presupposes a gesture of recognition without recognized parties, a pact of alliance without allies or guarantees of the agreement made (a logical equivalent of Lichtenberg's bladeless knife whose handle is missing). It is not enough to object that this *epokhē* does not cancel the terms of the relationship, but only suspends them to make givenness appear; even if this is true, *epokhē* cannot suspend what it would need to suspend: the purpose sought in forming the relationship. What is at stake is not the exchange of a good or its return to the self, but the ability to generate the gesture of respect and the bond that are at the core of every alliance. The great lesson Husserl taught us is that we can reduce *our* relationship to phenomena; but to extend this operation to systems of relationships that constitute *institutions* and appear as unique symbolisms endowed with their own forms of logic does not seem methodologically tenable. The *pure givenness* supposed to emerge from such a reduction would have the unreal beauty of the "idea," unfolding like Mallarmé's flower "absent from all bouquets."

CHAPTER 6

Ricoeur:
Reciprocity and Mutuality—
From the Golden Rule to *Agapē*

In his phenomenological studies, like Merleau-Ponty, Ricoeur does not grant special consideration to the question of givenness. At most he discusses its relevance as an important aspect of Husserl's method (in fact Husserl's term *Gegebenheit* designates what is given) or of Heidegger's *Es gibt*. He does not attempt to connect those themes with the theme of the gift. Yet a questioning on the problem of reciprocity is at the core of his thought, with a demanding but also disquieting or even hindered presence—hindered not in and of itself, but because of a kind of reservation or suspicion also found in many of the authors we have discussed. Unquestionably, it is in *Oneself as Another*[1] that Ricoeur presents his most profound problematization of reciprocity, through a questioning of the concepts of solicitude, promise, otherness, and attestation, among others. His effort, however, must make its way through the lines of the resistance drawn by thinkers as diverse as Kant, Husserl, John Rawls, or Levinas, who force Ricoeur to state the question explicitly; whereas objective allies such as Aristotle, Hegel, or Heidegger, while they provide him with incomparable analytical instruments, do not allow him to reach its final formulation. This involves something beyond the mere difficulty of conceptualizing the paradoxical relationship between identity and difference, autonomy and heteronomy: the difficulty experienced since the emergence of Modernity—that is to say, the age of the *Cogito*—in conceiving of *the Other as such*, as a Self distinct from oneself, and in understanding the bond between oneself and Others as inseparable from the bond between Others and oneself, without reducing this relationship to simple symmetry.

This difficulty is not primarily conceptual; it belongs to a different order. Ricoeur suggests that it may have to do with *forgetting*. He does not refer to accidental negligence, but to a dynamic of erasure that pervades an entire age. For him this dynamic is exemplified by the emergence of the theories of the contract: fictions designed to imagine a "choice-to-live-together" understood primarily as an association of autonomous individuals constituted from the outset without considering their reciprocal bonds. This is why, "once this has been forgotten, only this fiction can make the contract the equivalent of the principle of autonomy and of the person as an end in himself."[2] The problem of the contract is only an example of this, but it gives us an idea of the stakes involved. Ricoeur's questioning on this topic demonstrates consistently what he views as his duty to counter this forgetting and shape his own writing as a medium of anamnesis of the erased question. I believe that this is why he insistently returns to the Golden Rule. Whenever his argument involves the question of otherness—and more specifically the otherness of other humans—he mentions this rule. One could almost map its occurrences in his work: They would trace fairly precisely the archipelago of his arguments on reciprocity, which is at the core of any ethical requirement.

Clearly, the question of reciprocal giving is bound to emerge in the end. It first does so in *Memory, History, Forgetting* (2000) in the context of a debate on forgiving; but it is most present in his last work, *The Course of Recognition* (2007 [2004]), where the relationship with the Other in traditional exchange practices is precisely questioned in its actualization through the symbolic operation by which goods are alternatively offered and reciprocated. Ricoeur appears to distance himself from the concept of reciprocity, and instead he promotes the concept of mutuality. He views the former as leading to conflict, and the latter to benevolence. Ritual exchanges of "mutual" gifts should then be understood as exceptional moments that lead to "states of peace," furthermore leading to the relationship of *agapē*. It is questionable whether one can accept Ricoeur's interpretation, which underestimates the element of struggle and differentiation that is a foundational factor in the ceremonial gift and underlies every bond of reciprocity, including the bond stated by the Golden Rule.

Golden Rule and Ethical Self

Let us begin by asking, what is the *Golden Rule*? This formulation attributed to Hillel (the rabbinical master whose school played an important part in Paul's education) in fact goes further back. It is already found in Zoroastrian writings (more than five centuries BCE). The Babylonian Talmud (around 500 BCE) states it as follows: "Do not do unto your neighbor what you would hate him to do to you. This is the entire law; the rest is commentary."[3] The Gospels take up this maxim in a positive mode: "In everything do to others as you would have them do to you; for this is the law and the prophets."[4] In both cases the requirement of reciprocity is understood as summarizing every other commandment. It thus forms the core of the ethical and religious relationship. Hence its exceptional status, made tangible by the metaphorical term that designates it (the reference to gold always points to perfection, as in "golden number" or "golden age"). This rule could have been expected to constitute for philosophy one of the strongest foundations of a universally shared ethic. This has not been the case; at most it has been one chapter of moral theology in medieval thinkers. Among the moderns, from Machiavelli to Hobbes and Locke to Rousseau, the question is raised only indirectly, in connection to the notions of illusion or interest. Kant is the first philosopher to take up the debate. But his apparent intention is to implicitly question the rule of reciprocity as subjecting the moral norm to a conditionality that must be strictly excluded from categorical imperatives.[5]

Either tradition was mistaken as to the greatness and correctness of the Golden Rule, or modernity is no longer capable of thinking its necessity. Among contemporary thinkers, Ricoeur is certainly the most worried about this rift or forgetting, although he does not reduce the debate to this dilemma. This concern pervades his moral as well as his political thought, insistently placing the requirement of reciprocity at the core of his questioning of the Self understood in a dialectical tension between sameness and ipseity, and, more fundamentally, between ipseity and otherness. This is not an easy journey. It requires that several corpuses of thought be taken into account and discussed. It may be that the project itself was made possible only by the results of an effort conducted over several decades, not only within the philosophical field, primarily of phenomenology, but also elsewhere, on the border of philosophy, an effort that modified an entire conceptual environment: the new instruction that ethnological research provided to modernity on the question of tradition.[6] It was necessary to reconsider in their complexity—and sometimes their strangeness—the most common and ancient practices of reciprocity, especially the ceremonial gift, to understand that the obligation to give, receive, and return has nothing to do with self-interested calculus or simple charity; rather, it implies the full affirmation of the self in the moment of the unconditional recognition of the Other, on either side—based not on a commutative equivalence, but on the contrary on an alternating dissymmetry that preserves the risk of rejection in the offer as well as in the reply.

Because modernity was defined around the question of the Subject, because the refoundation of truth was performed as a self-foundation based on the affirmation of the *Cogito* and every philosophical questioning has to be situated in relation to this focal point of perspective and reference, only by fully assuming this legacy can it become possible to move beyond its horizon, as Ricoeur well knows. Here this movement encounters a significant resistance: The existence of the Other can be posited and defined only from the position of Ego (rather than of the Self, which belongs to a different ontology). Since the relationship is situated from the perspective of a privileged term—Ego—the other becomes complementary. Reciprocity can then be viewed only as a movement toward the other and back to the self, which amounts to missing the otherness of the Other. Conversely, if the initiative is entirely granted to the Other, viewing the Self as unconditionally obligated to the other is tantamount to the epitome of abnegation, from which reciprocity is excluded.

Ricoeur's approach is profoundly different. It takes up the debate in an ample and integrating manner, placing it outside every egological problematic to question the Self in its differentiation between *idem* and *ipse* and its constitutive relationship to what it is not. He thus confronts the otherness of the world and of the Other. Most significantly, he understands the Self as the reflexive agency involved in every modality of the "who" question: Who speaks? Who acts? Who tells? Who is accountable for a choice? Ricoeur's answers involve a precise reexamination of ancient and recent debates and a recomposition of the problematic of the Self, which through a kind of necessity leads to the ethical question. It is within this framework (topic of the last two studies of *Oneself as Another*, amounting to over half the book) that, on the level of intersubjective relationships as well as the institutional level, the question of reciprocity is the question that tests philosophy's ability to move away from the egological circle within which Descartes's shift lastingly placed it.

From the outset Ricoeur declares that he situates the ethical question in the wake of Aristotle. This means that, from a methodological standpoint, he does not need to take on the task of generating the plurality of the Others from the position of Ego. By raising the question of the subject from the position of the *Self* rather than Ego, Ricoeur approaches the Self in its relationship to Others and considers the relationship itself in the context of a life in common ruled by institutions. This forms the core of his theoretical position. The statement of the Golden Rule is therefore highly significant: It condenses a very ancient wisdom that was and remains at the core of the requirement of respect that animates the moral practices and forms of justice of every society, ours included. How could this require-ment be at the same time so present and so hidden in our philosophical heritage? What is the meaning of this insistence and of this denial? To answer these questions we will follow part of Ricoeur's itinerary, focusing on three authors selected for the exemplarity of their approach: Aristotle, Kant, and Levinas. In each case, we will also present a complementary inquiry into other writings by those authors that will lead us to the follow-ing hypothesis: The core of the Golden Rule could be the relationship of reciprocal gift, a relationship at the same time called upon and ignored by our entire intellectual tradition.

Ethical Aim and Reciprocity: Questions for Aristotle

When Ricoeur proposes a clear distinction between the concepts of eth-ics and morality, he recognizes that his choice of those terms, although entirely justifiable, is not commonly accepted. There are two different traditions of thought: One, called teleological (and initiated by Aristotle), intends to *identify what is deemed good, and to determine how to achieve it*; the other, called deontological (and whose main representative is Kant), posits as essential to define *what is unconditionally* just, and whose form is there-fore an obligation stated in the imperative mode.

Ricoeur's purpose is not to draw an opposition between those two di-rections. But he favors the ethical position as broader and more complete: Rather than excluding the deontological position, it encompasses it in that, under certain conditions, the ethical position accepts to subject its own requirements to the test of the moral norm. For the moral position, on the contrary, it is inconceivable to subject the norm to any teleological aim—that is, to understand it as an adequacy of means to ends, no matter how just those ends may be.

How can the project of the ethical perspective be defined? Ricoeur sums it up as follows: "Aiming at the good life with and for others, in just institu-tions."[7] This aim presupposes a dialogical structure between the self and the Other, and an institutional framework where this relationship can be realized. The entire difficulty involves the predicate "good," which is to say the content of the ends. Ricoeur dedicates to this question precise analyses that cannot be presented in detail here. From the perspective of our question what matters is the *mode according to which the Other is presupposed from the outset in the ethical aim.* On a first level the other is presupposed through *solicitude*, which for Ricoeur is very precisely the *unfolding* toward the other of what characterizes the ethical Self—that is, *self-esteem*. What this involves is the Self rather than the Ego. What makes the Self worthy of esteem is his/her abilities rather than his/her achievements—a potential that presupposes the mediation of the other, and therefore the movement toward and from the Other. What should this relation be called? According to Ricoeur it cannot be better expressed than by the relationship of friendship—*philia*—analyzed by Aristotle in the *Nicomachean Ethics*.

For Aristotle a friend is not an *alter ego* in the sense of a double of the self, but a different self: *heteros autos*;[8] for him this founds "an ethic of mutuality, of sharing, of living-together."[9] Friendship does not pertain to an analysis of emotional states, but to an ethic, which is to say a normative relationship with Others. Self-love—*philautia*—thus finds its accomplishment in the love of others. This friendship remains therefore necessary, even to happy men, which means that the foundation of friendship is neither utility nor comfort—even if certain forms of friendship appear to exemplify those categories. Friendship is determined by what is deemed "good" and therefore by an end desirable in and of itself. True friendship can therefore only be mutual, and this is what makes it ethical. Ricoeur concludes as follows: "From Aristotle, I should like to retain only the ethics of reciprocity, of sharing, of living together." But he does so only after stating this reservation: "One will readily grant that there is no place for a straightforward concept of otherness in Aristotle."[10] One would like to encourage Ricoeur to extend that reservation and note that the Aristotelian notions that express mutual bonds are relatively weak when compared to the Greek concept of *reciprocity* as found in Homer or Hesiod and at play in the tragedies of Aeschylus, especially the *Oresteia*. The Golden Rule refers to a similar context: the context of a relationship between equal partners that takes the form of a *reply*. We must therefore extend our inquiry beyond Ricoeur's analyses and briefly reexamine the question.

Aristotle himself shows us the way. Let us begin by noting that his term *philia* is difficult to translate exactly. It means "friendship," but it suggests the broader connotations of benevolence, affection, attachment, sociability, and civility. Aristotle, however, carefully avoids confusing friendship with benevolence (*eunoia*), and above all with affection in general (*philēis*), because affection can apply to things: "Affection for soulless objects is not called friendship, since *the affection is not mutual*, nor is there any wishing good for the object."[11] The Greek term for "requited attachment" is *antiphilēis*, in which the prefix *anti* always indicates a *reply* to an action. It is precisely through such a *return* that benevolence itself, at first unilateral, changes its status: "Goodwill is said to count as friendship only when it is reciprocated."[12] Here the prefix *anti* once again marks *reciprocity* (*eunoian gar en antipeponthosi philian einai*). Friendship exists only because the Other *replies* and *requites* the affection given. This is reciprocity in the stronger sense. On the contrary, what is *mutual* is not expressed in the mode of the reply (indicated by *anti*), but in the mode of the reception by more than one other, as conveyed by such phrases as *pros allēlous*: ones for the others. This applies to all altruistic emotions and attitudes—mere benevolence—and even to the fragile friendships determined only by utility or pleasantness.[13] But true friendship is different: It is a relationship between two agents. It exists only if each of them acts with the other in mind, and replies to him. Because friendship presupposes this true reciprocity by which affection and generous gestures are *reciprocated*, friendship also implies *equality*, which connects it to justice, while making friendship between persons with a very different social status difficult.[14]

Based on those remarks, should we propose an interpretation of Aristotle's concept of friendship entirely different from the accepted interpretation, including that of Ricoeur? We could do so if Aristotle established a rigorous and constant contrast between the languages of reciprocity and mutuality, but that is not the case. On the contrary, his ethical writings can be viewed as testimonies to a shift through which those two notions have begun to blend, or even merge. In fact reciprocity itself—in the stronger sense of a reciprocating gesture—is sometimes problematic for Aristotle. That is clearly apparent in his critique of the notion of justice according to the Pythagoreans[15]: He blames them for keeping to traditional reciprocity alone—which calls for returning a blow for a blow—whereas according to Aristotle true reciprocity is proportional and allows architects to conduct exchanges with cobblers through the diagonal coupling that equalizes at the same time the products and their producers (this is the operation money expresses). In the first case Aristotle calls what is "reciprocal" *antipeponthos*, participle form of the verb *antipaskhein*, which designates any reception or subjection in return (*anti*), whether service, honor, harm, or punishment.[16] The term *antipeponthos* can also designate the compensatory action or vindicatory justice improperly called vengeance.[17] In mathematics, *antipeponthos* means "reciprocal," hence the consistency of the Pythagorean view that Aristotle criticizes. This is why in the same passage he calls *antidosis* the proportional reciprocity he contrasts with their view; *antidosis* is a fair exchange among producers.[18] This is a remarkable choice (unnoticed by commentators),[19] since in the entire tradition from Homer to the tragedians, *antidosis* designates a countergift, a reply to a gift received—*dosis*.[20] Here Aristotle takes up the language of the gift, appropriating it and translating it into the language of the exchange of goods. Yet in Homer's world,[21] as in every traditional society,[22] gift relationships are not exchanges of goods (as are barter or trade), but, as we showed above (Chapter 2), forms of reciprocal public recognition (in the sense of the granting of respect) mediated by the goods offered as *tokens* and *substitutes* of the giver. Let us recall once again that, as Mauss emphasized (but without stating all the consequences of his statement), *what one gives in the thing given is always oneself.* The reason why reciprocating is *obligatory* is not that goods must be balanced, but that there can be no recognition without reciprocity; failing to reply already amounts to offending the other. Vindicatory justice is the punitive or compensatory form of this reciprocal relationship, when a serious breach has occurred in the recognition owed between the partners in the gift. The same partners are also held responsible for restoring the reciprocity that was breached.

Why does this additional inquiry matter to us? The reciprocity Aristotle criticizes in the Pythagoreans, which he nevertheless recognizes at the root of friendship, is the reciprocity the entire tradition formulates in the Golden Rule: the *requirement of an* anticipated *reply* that can be stated in terms either positive ("Do unto others . . .") or negative ("Do not do . . ."),[23] but that expresses the necessity of the *reciprocating movement.* This is the reciprocity Ricoeur apparently has in mind whenever he refers to the Golden Rule: the obligation of a reply from oneself to Others, as well as from Others to oneself. There is no doubt that Aristotelian morality has already toned down the already-ancient logic of the reciprocating gesture. With him the *agōn* of reciprocity is neutralized in the *analogia* of proportionality, and even more so in the *homoion* of commutativity. Friendship remains a unique case, where the power of reciprocity (*antipeponthos*) is alive, but not always, or not enough. *For this power to remain fully alive would require a full recognition of the otherness of Others.* As Ricoeur rightly emphasizes, this requirement is lacking in Aristotle—and even more so in the Moderns. From Descartes on, this *absence,* like the negative shape of a forgetting, appears to deeply trouble every philosophy and lead it almost backward toward the Other that gift relationships posited from the outset in a position of otherness such that nothing less than demanding rituals could tame its distance and point to its enigma.

Reciprocity and the Test of the Moral Norm: Kant

The main obstacle the ethical aim encounters is the need to define the predicate "good" in the phrase "the good life." Facing this kind of difficulty requires, Ricoeur writes, "subject[ing] the ethical aim to the test of the norm."[24] This is no more than a test because the ethical aim keeps its privileged position, and the purely moral perspective risks becoming prisoner of the contradictions of formalism. The entire question will be to determine how to shift from respect for the law to respect for actual persons. We will need to understand how and in what terms Kant raises the question of the Other. Can he keep a space for the requirement of reciprocity without endangering the very logic of the categorical imperative?

The first test of the ethical aim is the question of *universality*. This does not mean that the ethical aim lacks universality, but that it cannot posit a criterion as powerful as "good will," as does Kant when he states: "It is impossible to think of anything in the world, or indeed even beyond it, that could be considered good without limitation, except a good will."[25] Kant calls "will" the ability of a reasonable being to act according to the *representation* of the law (rather than to be subjected to laws, as do beings devoid of reason). His question is therefore a moral one; it can be summarized as follows: "What must I do?" This will is said to be good, without any restrictions, if it is determined by reason alone—that is, by the *form* of the law— rather than by inclinations. An inclination can result from an advantage or an empirical goal; it can be good, but not *without restrictions*. To satisfy this requirement, Ricoeur explains, the maxim of the action must pass the test of universality, summed up in the statement of the first imperative: "Act only in accordance with that maxim through which you can at the same time will that it become a universal law."[26] Such an imperative is said to be categorical because will is determined based on the *representation* of a law, rather than on a goal (such as happiness) or a condition (such as caution), which define only a hypothetical imperative. By implicitly stating, "Do not . . . *if* you do not want . . .," the Golden Rule appears determined by a hypothetical imperative. It clearly fails the universality test—unless the reciprocity to which it points is understood as expressing a nonconditional necessity. Is this the case?

Before this question can be answered, Ricoeur believes, a second test must be confronted: the test of the *autonomy* of the Self in the exercise of his/her moral judgment and decisions. Unrestricted will for good must equate self-legislating will. Autonomy designates will as freedom, both negatively—as removed from natural causality—and positively—as agency capable of giving itself its own law. This definition circumscribes the conditions of formalism: Will is determined only by the form of the law. Autonomy implies that free will is not subjected to any causality external to itself, coming either from an inclination or from another subject. Hence the following question: How could Others intervene as part of the imperative without displacing free will to the side of heteronomy? Here Ricoeur makes an important remark: By positing the Self as at the same time legislator of and subjected to the law, Kant incorporates in himself the positions of speaker and addressee, giver and receiver of orders. This enables him to conceive of evil as an internal fact of disobedience to oneself; regrettably, this also allows him *to do away with the relationship to the Other.* This exclusion of otherness makes it difficult to conceive of the reciprocity presupposed by the Golden Rule. Confronted to the test of autonomy, reciprocity appears defeated once again.

Yet, through a patient and exacting reading of Kant's writings Ricoeur is able to find in them resources capable to reveal an otherness that was not immediately apparent. This otherness is manifested above all in the very antagonism that the will for good must overcome. Autonomy is affirmed in a confrontation with heteronomy—that which is other than the self. On a first level this confrontation denotes an element of *passivity* that refers to the essential receptivity of finite will. On a second level it becomes necessary to determine the situation of those concerned by the exercise of my will. This is precisely what the second imperative defines: "So act that you use humanity, whether in your own person or in the person of any other, always at the same time as an end, never merely as a means."[27] The question is thus the following: To *whom* does this statement primarily apply? It clearly applies to the humanity of every person, rather than to that person as a unique being. How can we then conceive of the confrontation of the self to the other? Isn't the element of otherness erased in this very relationship? And in this case, what does the second imperative add to the first?

This is not an easy question to answer, since, as Ricoeur notes, the idea of humankind considered here by Kant as the "object" or "matter" of moral law concerns the plurality of persons.[28] According to Ricoeur, this gives this idea the same "dialogic structure as solicitude"[29] and tempers the fact that the Self concerned by the imperative is in principle indifferent—although not contrary—to the distinction among persons. "It is here that the notion of *person* as an end in itself comes to balance that of *humanity*, to the extent that it introduces in the very formulation of the imperative the distinction between 'your person' and 'the person of anyone else.' With the person alone comes plurality."[30] This adds a powerful element to the second imperative: "Something new is said when the notions of 'matter,' of 'object,' and of 'duty' are identified with those of end-in-itself. What is said here that is new is precisely what the Golden Rule states on the level of popular wisdom, before it is sifted through the critique. For it is indeed the deepest intention that now emerges clarified and purified [. . .]. The Golden Rule and the imperative of respect owed to persons do not simply have the same field of exercise, they also have the same aim: to establish reciprocity where there is a lack of reciprocity."[31] Unquestionably, this ensures the shift from respect for the law to respect for persons, since if Kant's point of departure is the existence of morality as a "fact of reason," then this fact itself presupposes another fact: the existence of persons as ends-in-themselves. What constitutes a person is that he/she is the being capable of giving him/herself a law.

Reciprocity is thus finally capable of passing the tests of universality as well as autonomy. To discover this requires following Ricoeur in his exacting reading of Kant's writings. It appears, however, that other writings, of which he did not make use, are much clearer and more explicit—so much so that it is surprising that Ricoeur did not consider them: writings on benevolence, charity, gratitude, and respect found in the "Doctrine of Virtue," the section of the *Metaphysics of Morals* that is the counterpart to the "Doctrine of Right." Its tone may appear Aristotelian. In it Kant analyzes the diversity of duties depending on the situations. Yet it is not a textbook of ethical caution, but a theory of *virtue*— of the courage (*virtus*) the practice of duty requires as the obligation to obey the law according to which will is determined. If the second imperative defines the unconditional quality of the respect owed to every person—me as well as Others—then what happens on this side of this limit? Is there room in Kant for a more nuanced attitude than the position identified by Ricoeur? Is there a duty of benevolence? Is this duty reciprocal?

Kant's answer is very clear: "Every morally practical relation to human beings is a relation among them represented by pure reason, that is, a relation of free actions in accordance with maxims that qualify for a giving of universal law and so cannot be selfish. I want everyone else to be benevolent toward me; hence I ought also to be benevolent toward everyone else."[32] Kant specifies that to satisfy the requirement of universality this commandment must include me in the "duty of mutual benevolence." He adds that legislating reason thus "*permits* you to be benevolent toward yourself on the condition of your being benevolent toward every other as well."[33] The tone and content of the Golden Rule, already intensely present in this maxim (as suggested by the shift to the second person familiar), are even more so in the following proclamation: "Every human being has a legitimate claim to the respect of his fellow human beings and is *in turn* bound to respect every other."[34] The requirement—better yet, the *duty*— of reciprocity could not be stated more strongly and explicitly. It is not introduced surreptitiously as a hypothetical imperative, but is instead proclaimed as the legitimate corollary of the categorical imperative.

The Other in Hyperbolic Mode: Levinas

Ricoeur set aside his debate with Levinas until the last pages of the last "Study" of *Oneself as Another*. The reason for this is clear enough: Levinas takes us to an outer boundary. As we saw in Chapter 3 above, and as Ricoeur reminds us, through a very daring gesture Levinas effects a radical break with every form of egology, his master Husserl's included (even though in his "Fifth Cartesian Meditation" Husserl proposes a very innovative shift away from the Ego, through his analysis of *appresentation*—that is, an analogical transfer from the self to the Other through the experience of my body and the body of the Other as flesh).[35] For Ricoeur this break can be read in Levinas through two relatively distinct steps, the first embodied by *Totality and Infinity* (1961), and the other by *Otherwise than Being* (1974).

The essential proposition of *Totality and Infinity* is that there is no path from Myself to the Other. Every attempt to conceive of the Other from the position of Ego is in fact a representation and amounts to assimilating the other and reducing him/her to oneself. The field of Ego is the field of Sameness—that is, a self-enclosed totality that nothing that derives from itself can open or even crack. This is why this totality is also a complete separation. Only from the boundlessness of the Other can the relationship, or rather the *irrelationship*, be conceived of, and be conceived outside of any representation, through the emergence of the *face* of the other. This face comes to me from an exteriority forever distinct from my own aim. "The human face tears the tangible" to make the voice heard that comes from the face and proclaims this commandment: "You shall not kill." Ricoeur sums this up in this beautiful formulation: "Each face is a Sinai that prohibits murder."[36] Not only is the Other the source of this injunction, but he/she is above all *what makes me be* through my confrontation with him/ her in this very injunction. Through the call he/she directs to me, or rather through the commandment he/she orders me to answer, it is the other and he/she alone that constitutes me as a subject.

Ricoeur calls this thesis from *Totality and Infinity* hyperbolic in the same sense that the Cartesian suspicion is hyperbolic: It is excessive out of methodological choice. From this perspective Levinas performed an unprecedented breach in the wall of forgetting (the forgetting mentioned by Ricoeur at the beginning of *Oneself as Another*). But unlike the suspicion that in Descartes leads to certainty, in Levinas the unconditional affirmation of the Other does not lead to a reaffirmation of the self. With him the hyperbole remains the mode of a consideration of radical otherness. Furthermore, Ricoeur claims, the theses of *Otherwise than Being* become *paroxysms*. The Other somehow has "every right" over me. The other obligates me to a form of abnegation so radical that I must substitute myself to him/her when he/she suffers persecution. "A subject is a hostage," Levinas claims; for Ricoeur this is "the most excessive [expression] of all,"[37] since it presupposes an assignation and an irrefutable injunction, including when an offense was committed or when facing the worst possible threat or suffering. This involves a complete rejection of reciprocity. Ricoeur can only follow Levinas on this point. But this raises many serious questions: What happens to this injunction when, rather than a Master who teaches or judges, the Other is a humiliating oppressor, or even a torturer and annihilator? How can it be justified for the disciple to accept enslavement? Levinas grants the Other such an unconditional immunity that those questions are sidestepped. But this is probably also due to the fact that from the outset Levinas posits an equation between the Self and Ego that Ricoeur finds unacceptable. Ego can be conceived of as separate, and it may be that an egology logically leads to solipsism; all mediations—whether bodily, linguistic, or narrative—then become useless. But this applies to Ego, not to the Self. Breaking the circle of sameness of *idem*, the ipseity of the Self is reflexivity—as structure and power of reciprocation—through which the otherness of the world and of the Other is affirmed and constitutively etched in the Self. Furthermore, the world and the Other can exist only for a Self. How can the injunction of the Other reach me, Ricoeur asks, without this receptivity specific to the Self, if this ability to reply were not constitutive of the Self? But Levinas could not take this point into account without having to completely redefine what he calls "Ego" and reexamine the entire question of the relationship to the Other—in short, without having to consider a nonsymmetrical reciprocity that escapes a return to Sameness (this point was discussed in Chapter 3 above).

The Golden Rule, to which Kant's morality could have led in the end (as confirmed by an analysis of the duty of charity), remains unthinkable for Levinas, because it presupposes a reciprocity that would obligate the Other to a reply. For him, I alone have an obligation to reply to the requests of the Other. There is a complete and irreversible asymmetry: I cannot even presume that the Other is also an Ego, and that as such he/she can and should be subjected to the same commandment, since for him/her I too am an Other. Levinas rejects this reversibility: I can never switch sides in this "irrelation," even as a hypothesis, since I exist only to the extent that I am called up by the Other. What constitutes me as Ego is the absolute requirement by which "I alone have to answer." Any suggestion of reciprocity erases this possibility. Ricoeur's entire conceptual effort aims at demonstrating that the opposite is true: To release the Other from the obligation to reply is to fail to recognize him/her in what constitutes him/her as Other.

Provisional Conclusion

This is the form of reciprocity—a relationship of reply, free gesture replying to another free gesture by which the partners are obligated to each other through this very recognition[38]—that constitutes the greatness of the Golden Rule. It is the reciprocity constitutive of the Self, which Ricoeur proposes to release from an enduring philosophical *forgetting*. As we know, this forgetting is not due to a faulty argument or a conceptual failure among philosophers. It has to do with the kind of deep and slow shifts that become apparent only when major breaks occur. To talk of the age of the *Cogito* does not amount to assigning to Descartes the responsibility for an illumination or a delusion; it is only the name we give to the theoretical horizon of an age and to the operation of the multiple forces that moved across it and shaped it, as we attempt to understand its emergence and persistence. In the same way, we can wonder what has been occurring for more than a century and is still happening today that makes it possible for the question of being to be understood once again in Heidegger's terms; for the question of the Other to be raised through Levinas's radical formulation; for the question of the Self, along with Ricoeur, to be no longer reduced to an egology but shown in all its complexity as the question of a being that conceives of him/herself *toward* and *starting from* what he/she is not, as a *reflexive* relationship to the world and to Others, and for this very reason as a question inseparable from ontology and ethics. Why do we understand those issues better? Have we overcome forgetting? Those questions are difficult to answer, even if we can analyze the parameters of this event.

Yet it is undeniable that a new approach to what is given has emerged. It is as if the possibility had (re)emerged for us to conceive of the world not primarily as the object of our technical knowledge, but as what happens to us. The entire effort of phenomenology since Husserl has aimed at this openness and welcoming that Ricoeur expresses through the motifs of passivity and receptivity, always articulated with the theme of otherness. This conception involves in a crucial way the concept of *attestation*, which is introduced in the first pages of *Oneself as Another*, and reappears with every important inflection of the discussion. Thus, in Kant, morality as a *factum rationis* attested by consciousness is inseparable from the autonomy of will,[39] but this self-attestation only appears to be a self-position. What is attested is instead a receptivity through which freedom itself is affected by the law. What this attestation involves cannot be deduced; it can only be a given. The attestation is related to that which can be revealed, the alethic, but it also involves the credibility of the witness: "Attestation is fundamentally attestation *of* self."[40] It presupposes trust. To extend Ricoeur's analysis, it can be claimed that this attestation is the foundation of every pact, the unwritten preamble of every institution. It is the *fact* of the relationship between the Self and the Other; it cannot be derived from either of them. It is attested in each of them in that it is the-one-along-with-the-other, but it is not a symmetrical relationship between two positions. It constitutes a relationship of reply to a call, akin to the relationship of the countergift to the gift. This is the *fact* of reciprocity, at the same time ontological and ethical. It is embodied in the relationship of *alternating asymmetry* between every Self as another and every Other as a Self. This fact is expressed in the requirement of reciprocal *recognition*, which is unquestionably the content of the Golden Rule.

Approaches to the Gift: Forgiveness, Mutuality, and Agapē

Although Ricoeur did not appear especially interested in the question of the gift, either as a phenomenological concept or as a social practice, among the philosophers who belong to the theoretical trend discussed above he is the only one who resisted the reductionist critique of reciprocity. His last two major works (*Memory, History, Forgetting* and *The Course of*

Recognition[41]), however, show a more explicit approach to the problematic of the gift. Surprisingly, his discussion of Mauss's *The Gift* leads Ricoeur to express certain reservations about the notion of reciprocity. His attempt does not consist in reneging on his earlier recognition of its importance, but in tracing its limitations and opening it onto a relationship that appears to him richer and more personal: *mutuality*, which to him is uniquely capable to lead to what he calls "states of peace," and which, even more significantly, makes possible the form of unconditional generosity that an entire tradition calls *agapē*. This is a stimulating approach but, as do the other approaches we have discussed, it involves certain misunderstandings.

GIVING AND FORGIVING

In the final pages of *Memory, History, Forgetting* Ricoeur raises the question of forgiveness.[42] It is clear to him that, unlike justice—no matter how necessary—forgiveness is not ruled by equivalence or, in other words, by a horizontal relationship of reciprocity. Forgiveness is a gesture that escapes entirely the logic of interaction and the networks of causality; it occurs without antecedent or explanation; it is offered unconditionally; it is a relationship from Above. But isn't this a purely heroic view that requires a sublime degree of abnegation inaccessible to humans? Should the victim forgive when the persecutor has not asked for forgiveness, or even expressed remorse? This forgiveness would amount to a renouncement of all reciprocity. Such a gesture is not just a difficult one; it may be misplaced, in that it releases the aggressor from having to examine his conduct and from redeeming himself, and it exposes us to an implicit condoning of his crime. "We believe, on the level of practice, that there does exist something like a correlation between forgiveness requested and forgiveness granted."[43] This amounts, Ricoeur specifies, to situating forgiveness within the circle of exchange, supply and demand. Is this really his model? Does forgiveness belong to the realm of reciprocity?

To answer those questions Ricoeur proposes to consider the well-known example of ritual gift exchanges. This connection may seem surprising: The gracious gift would appear more relevant. Ricoeur reminds us that there is an explicit relationship between the notions of giving and forgiving (also verified in other languages: *Geben* and *Vergeben* in German; *don* and *pardon* in French; *dono* and *perdono* in Italian). But what relationship does this have with the exchange rituals discussed by Mauss and many others? Ricoeur does not intend to consider those practices in detail. What matters to him is above all a model of reciprocity, from which he draws the conclusion that those rituals presuppose an essential parity between the partners. This is crucial for the beneficiary if full equality is to be expressed and preserved between him and the giver, if he is not to owe a debt to the giver. This is required for the countergift to be genuine. This movement from one agent to the other transcends equivalence, but it remains conditional, and it embodies the Golden Rule. But can forgiveness be modeled? In the Gospel forgiveness is a requirement with a radical formulation: Love even your enemy.[44] This requires giving up the expectation of a reciprocating gesture. It does not preclude such a gesture, but it does not make it a condition of the gift.

Is Ricoeur adopting in the final analysis the radical positions of Levinas and Derrida (even though he viewed them with serious reservations), and thus underplaying reciprocity, which he was among the few thinkers to speak for—running the risk of appearing overly reasonable? He cannot be accused of adopting views whose paroxysmal character alone make them seem worthy of admiration. On the contrary, Ricoeur takes the trouble to examine in detail an exemplary field where the principles of reciprocity are called on in a powerful and disturbing fashion: the procedures of public debates initiated by the Truth and Reconciliation Commission led by Desmond Tutu and set up by Nelson Mandela after he was elected president of South Africa. The commission's public hearings and debates made possible an exceptional effort of memory, from confessions to denials, which made the participants reexperience the traumas and angers associated with apartheid. Reconciliation occurred on an emotional level through the expression of remorse and complaints, and on an institutional level through an agreement accepted by all that stipulated that those guilty of political crimes (as opposed to ordinary crimes) could receive amnesty in exchange for their confessions. This could of course generate hypocritical repentance, but the risk was negligible in regard to the extraordinary movement of realization and catharsis this "exchange" made possible. In this case, reciprocity could exercise its power to its outer limit: effecting reconciliation, but, as the commission stated, reconciliation does not amount to forgiveness. Forgiveness cannot be institutionalized; it remains beyond the reach of relationships ruled by legal procedures. It remains an astonishing decision: "In truth, forgiveness spans an interval between the great height of the spirit of forgiveness and the abyss of guilt."[45] It is thus situated beyond any model of exchange—even the exchange of gifts. It does not rely on the offender's confession; neither does it cancel his otherness. It cannot be stated in general. It remains a personal relationship to the Other who is granted forgiveness. This is why its statement is performative: a sentence that performs what it states and can be uttered only in the first person of the present indicative: *I forgive you.* Its only counterpart is another performative statement: *I ask for your forgiveness.*

Those are powerful and convincing analyses. This forgiveness that comes before it can be asked for by the offender is already, to the fullest extent, what as far back as his first writings Ricoeur called *agapē*, the generous relationship devoid of any expectation of a retribution. Yet we must ask the following question: Is the model of the ritual gift and its forms of exchanges relevant to this demonstration? The use Ricoeur makes of Mauss's *The Gift* is explicitly formal: He draws from the book only its well-established model of reciprocity. But to place the ritual exchange of gifts on the side of reciprocity understood as equivalence amounts to inappropriately situating it only on the side of justice—and this is what Ricoeur appears tempted to do. By so doing he runs the risk of ignoring the agonistic aspect of gift exchanges and, above all, of failing to identify their specific reason for being. To him they appear to have no function beyond exemplifying a value of reciprocity in human relationships and exposing the limits of those relationships.

From Reciprocity to Mutuality

Ricoeur returns to this form of exchange in *The Course of Recognition.* Here his approach is fundamentally different: The question of the gift is discussed in the final pages as the apex of the itinerary. The inquiry on recognition has begun with a consideration of the cognitive perspective (Descartes and Kant: Recognition is above all an identification), before an approach to the effort at self-recognition (confession, anamnesis), followed by a reevaluation of the legacies of Hobbes (original rivalry) and Hegel (struggle of consciousness). Only in the third and last section of the work does Ricoeur discuss recognition per se among persons; this is also the context of his return to ritual gift exchange. This passage develops four concepts: reciprocity, which leads to mutuality, which introduces "states of peace" and the relationship of *agapē*.

The title given to the entire section is "Mutual Recognition." The choice of the qualifier is not trivial, since here Ricoeur proposes an essential distinction between reciprocity and mutuality. He shows that while reciprocity belongs primarily to the logical realm, mutuality calls for a phenomenological description. Reciprocity is situated on a systemic level of global circularity, as observed in the triple ritual obligation to give, receive, and reciprocate. According to Ricoeur this process remains within the realm of equivalence and the order of the law. Reciprocity is thus more powerful than are the agents involved; it holds them within its impersonal regulation, and in a way controls their actions from the outside. To this logic Ricoeur contrasts the movement of mutuality, which emphasizes *the point of view of the agents*. Mutuality belongs to the pragmatic realm, where the gift relationship is always a personal gesture of trust, a specific reply to the gesture of the Other. Ricoeur thus declares himself "in favor of the mutuality of relations *between* those who exchange gifts, in contrast with the concept of reciprocity that the theory places *above* social agents and their transactions."[46] Mutuality therefore involves an ethic of the relationship, a freedom to choose asserted at the very core of social constraints.

There is no doubt that Ricoeur now adds a significant nuance to the concept of reciprocity as he has so far understood and articulated it in his references to the Golden Rule. His distinction between reciprocity and mutuality unquestionably makes it possible to refine the analysis of the relationships with Others. Developing this idea, Ricoeur returns to the question of the ceremonial gift. His demonstration takes some distance with Mauss by calling on the analyses found in Chapter 4 of *The Price of Truth*,[47] where ceremonial exchanges are interpreted primarily as a procedure of public recognition among groups, in which the goods offered are above all symbols of an agreement, as tokens and substitutes of the givers. This new approach, Ricoeur notes, performs a decisive break with economistic hypotheses (which view the ritual gift as an archaic form of trade) and moralizing hypotheses (which view it as a charitable gesture). This does not mean that the ceremonial gift stands contrary to trade, the generosity of mutual aid, or gracious giving. If the ceremonial gift truly is a procedure of recognition of which the goods offered are the symbolic guarantees, then it is unquestionably, Ricoeur believes, an exceptional form of *mutuality* that presupposes an interactive bond between the partners in the exchange and a free and personal choice on the part of the agents. This type of relationships is associated with specific moments in the lives of human groups: festive moments, and more precisely what he calls—in Luc Boltanski's words—"states of peace."

States of Peace and *Agapē*

To speak of *states of peace* obviously entails a consideration of their reverse: states of struggle. The latter are not necessarily violent (as are war, vengeance, or armed action of all kinds); they can be observed wherever *disputes* prevail, as is presumably the case in any legal procedure. The conflict is under control when it is subjected to rules of discussion, exchanges of arguments and points of view, and when it involves entities such as businesses, political organizations, universities, research teams, athletic groups, etc. Those states of struggle are the default situation; states of peace are rare. The former trace the world of reciprocity, whereas the latter are released from that world. For Ricoeur this exit from the circle of rivalries has a name: *agapē*, and its emblematic figure could be Prince Myshkin in Dostoevsky's *The Idiot*. The man of *agapē* neither calculates nor judges, replies, disputes, or demands anything: "Justification is entirely foreign to it, as is attention to self. More enigmatically still, *agapè* lives in permanence, in that which endures, its present knowing neither regret nor expectation."[48] His language has the form of praise or chant: "*Agapè* declares itself, proclaims itself; justice makes arguments."[49] This raises the following question: Is *agapē* capable of action? It is a crucial question, since *agapē* must deal with the same world that justice is meant to manage. Ricoeur's answer is that *agapē* does act, and that it does so through *the gift*. Unlike the reciprocal gift, this is not a gift ruled by equivalence, but a gift without expectation of reciprocation: unconditionally generous giving.

Doubts and Reservations

At this stage of the demonstration the reader of *The Course of Recognition* is inevitably puzzled: What of the requirement of reciprocity so crucial to Aristotle's *philia*, which Ricoeur identified in the end in Kant himself and strongly asserted against Levinas? What of the Golden Rule? What becomes of mutuality itself when confronted with the "sublime" of *agapē*? What is the point of recognizing that the reciprocity of the gifts in exchange rituals is primarily a mutual recognition between the partners, if this mutuality is to be devalued by the privilege granted to unilateral gracious gestures? There seems to be only one way out: to acknowledge a paradoxical situation. The countergift is thus viewed not as reciprocation but as a "second first gift."[50] This is a remarkable suggestion, since reciprocation is indeed a "return": not the erasure of a debt or the restoration of symmetry, but the taking up of the initiative to give. Nevertheless, there is a *reply*. Reciprocity and *agapē* appear therefore mutually exclusive. Rather than a paradox, it would be more accurate to call this situation a double bind, or a deadlock. The stakes now need to be clarified.

The question of the double bind is not insignificant. Ricoeur, who illuminated the foundations of reciprocity so powerfully as to show its presence in the very structure of the Self, believes he must underemphasize it

when situating it with regard to *agapē*. The question of forgiving legitimizes this relativizing. We might be tempted to follow Ricoeur's distinction. But why should we accept this contrast, and therefore this choice between reciprocity and *agapē*? It is as if Ricoeur still shares the old suspicion
we found in so many authors: In *The Course of Recognition* the notion of
reciprocity seems to imply not only circularity, but furthermore a profitable return to the self—in other words, a kind of "selfishness." At best
reciprocity remains close to the equivalence that characterizes justice. Yet,
as we saw above ("Propositions II"), the figure of the circle and the notion
of symmetry concern only a limited and preliminary aspect of reciprocity:
the static element of complementarity and the relationship of implication.
Reciprocity also has another aspect, more fundamental and dynamic, associated with the idea of reactivity and alternation through time: It then designates a relationship of reply, or even challenge. It is a constant openness
of the relationship, an invention in the unpredictability of the encounter.
Furthermore, in no way is the reply in gift relationships a compensation or
the erasure of a debt: The gift-in-return is part of the relationship itself as
a whole, which should be understood—as in Peirce's model—as a triad.
The reply is inseparable from the first move. In other words, this order
of relationships has its own legitimacy, and it should not be contrasted
with unilateral generosity—such as *agapē*—which itself should not be assessed by the standard of the gift/countergift relationship. Gracious gift
and reciprocity should not be judged based on each other. Once again it
is important to recognize the originality and autonomy of the different
orders of the gift.

It is therefore highly debatable to situate reciprocity squarely on the
side of the logic of relationships, as an abstract mechanism of a systemic
type. This view derives from the fact that reciprocity is defined as a structure and movement of reply and belongs to a dual and agonistic space. In
no way does this fact lessen the commitment and freedom of the agents:
They interact or confront each other within the framework of rules agreed
upon (as in games with two partners, whether individuals or teams), but the
obligation to reply—if one is to keep playing—that is part of the convention of exchange implies no determinism in the reply and its content. Reciprocity, dual in its very essence, is no more mechanical than is individual
action. It involves just as much initiative, event, and novelty. It is true that
reciprocity is based primarily on a fundamental disposition of living beings
to react when confronting another living being. This is even what defines
the polarity of life and leads to a tension between dialogue and conflict,
reply and riposte, agreement and reprisal. But this polarity constitutive of

reciprocity (and through which reciprocity is logical and systemic) in no way erases the freedom of the agents. It only imposes on this freedom a framework and a set of rules. From the outset it leads to the ethical order, the very foundation of the universality of the Golden Rule.

From this point of view, mutuality is neither more generous nor moral than is reciprocity. It belongs to a different relationship structure: It shifts from dual to plural relationships, from face-to-face to networks, from confrontation or adjustment to a partner—whether individual or collective—to coordination among several partners (let us recall the example already given of the confrontation between two teams, which defines a dual—and therefore reciprocal—relationship of rivalry, whereas coordination within each team defines a mutual relationship of coordination). Mutuality is not a surplus of benevolence. It has its own logic and ethic: the logic of multipolar organization, and the ethic of internal solidarity within the group. But this applies to legitimate as well as illegitimate purposes. Thus is there a form of mutuality within criminal organizations, in terms of networks and codes to be abided by (no matter how morally despicable they may be).

We can therefore question Ricoeur's categorization of ceremonial gifts as "states of peace," *mutual* rather than *reciprocal*. True—as Mauss was the first to show—the choice to give presents constitutes an alternative to war; the choice to give is a choice for peace. But it is primarily a gesture of reciprocal recognition within an agonistic space always open to the possibility of conflict. A state of peace is a moment of suspension of rivalry. We must remain aware of this indetermination or oscillation of the relationships. In traditional societies this threat is overcome through the complexification of ceremonial exchanges, the most fundamental of which is the exchange of wives: In the generalized matrimonial exchange extended over several generations, the exogamic rule presupposes enduring trust in all the other groups. This does constitute a shift from a dual reciprocal to a plural mutual relationship. Reciprocity and mutuality should not be placed on a gradient of axiological dignity or moral quality; they should be understood instead as different modes of relationship that operate on two embedded levels of complexity and call for specific attitudes and values.

Conclusion

With respect to Ricoeur's references to ceremonial gift practices a final difficulty remains. By defining those practices as exceptional festive moments—"states of peace"—when the life of the group comes renewed, he views them as privileged opportunities for the expression of *agapē*. This views seems problematic, for several reasons: First (and Ricoeur does not appear to have grasped this central point), in traditional societies those ceremonial exchanges are not mere parentheses, festive intermissions when conflicts are suspended; on the contrary, they are *foundational* procedures of *public* recognition among groups, meant to be established for the long term, primarily through marriages, but also through a large number of shared activities such as celebrations and collective work. Crucially, in societies with a central authority—such as classical cities and nation-states—this public recognition is ensured by political, legal, and economic institutions. Reciprocity among groups and individuals, however, continues to exist in the social and personal realms. Only on those two levels can states of peace be viewed as privileged moments. We must therefore identify three different levels: institutional, social, and personal. Each of those levels implies a distinct form of recognition; they cannot be merged without incurring a risk of confusion. For example, the forms of traditional gift exchanges (described by Mauss and many other anthropologists) cannot serve as a reference to understand contemporary personal relationships, or be interpreted as embodying the same form of generosity. To say that those traditional practices are public is another way of saying that they belong to what constitutes for us today the domain of institutional law. In their traditional forms those practices are always configured by local symbolisms and rituals, specificities (with respect to the representation of the group) associated with forms of kinship and authority, modes of living, and types of circulating goods (some of which are categorized as precious). The agents involved in those exchanges cannot be discussed (as philosophers often do) as if they were agents in modern societies and if those practices could be understood primarily as intersubjective experiences—to which neither the political association nor the social relationship can be reduced, regardless of the type of society considered.

It is always risky to make use of ethnographic data without taking into account the requirements of their transposition into our Modernity. But if we take care to situate ourselves in our own world and suspend our quest for geneses, it remains that the question of recognition, which is at the core of the ceremonial gift, is fundamentally implicated in the normative statement that Ricoeur formulates for any human collective as follows: "aiming at the 'good life,' with and for others, in just institutions."[51] Ricoeur is quite aware that to define a norm is not to propose an irenic project or trace a utopia, but to assign ourselves a program of action where, on every level, the requirement of recognition is at play. This implies confronting the possibility of failure. Ricoeur concludes *Course of Recognition* by lucidly noting that with every moment of recognition comes, like its shadow, a risk of misreading that is both cognitive (mistake) and interpersonal (mis-understanding). Thus a *capable man*—capable of saying, acting, expressing himself, taking responsibility for himself, remembering, and promising[52]— is always at the same time a *fallible man*.

CHAPTER 7

Philosophy and Anthropology: With Lefort and Descombes

The questioning we have developed so far on the relationships between the gift and reciprocity has focused primarily on authors from the phenomenological tradition. The reason why now appears more clearly: There has been a kind of diffuse attraction between the motif of the givenness of phenomena—the understanding of the world as given—and the gift as a gesture, whatever its modalities. Among the many misunderstandings caused by those associations or assimilations, the most embarrassing involves the reference to Mauss's *The Gift*, which has been subjected to criteria of assessment without any relevance to its own field of knowledge: practices of symbolic exchanges among traditional groups. It is therefore urgent to problematize more precisely the possible relationships between philosophy and social anthropology from the perspective of gift exchanges. In France few philosophers have attempted this effort. Two of them seem especially interesting for our discussion because of their original relationship to Mauss's *The Gift*: Claude Lefort and Vincent Descombes. Their perspectives are very different. Lefort supports his reflection on the political realm and history based on the social sciences, whereas Descombes questions the validity of the concepts of those sciences, beginning with the concepts of society and social relationship. It remains to be determined how their respective readings of Mauss's writing contribute to the development of their projects and shed light on our own questioning.

Let us recognize that reading their works after those of Derrida, Levinas, and Marion gives us the feeling we have moved to a different planet (less so in Ricoeur's case), whether in terms of style, method, or field. This involves first of all a change in perspective on what is called *the social realm*, a very broad concept that only the context defined by a specific debate can circumscribe. In the phenomenological approach *society* as a collective reality and object of thought can be approached only as the experience of a subject. The existence of the group is thus considered based on the presupposition of the autonomy of the Self, which opens a transcendental intersubjectivity. On a more fundamental level this presupposition also determines the type of relationship that any subject can have with Others in general, and with "the others" as members of the group.[1]

The question of the *social bond* is at the core of Lefort's and Descombes's inquiries. It is not enough to ask what unites a group, preserves its unity, and makes it view itself as forming a unique whole (this is the question of the community and its identity). Lefort examines whether seeking this bond entirely absorbs the energy of the members of the group and determines their choices and actions, while Descombes attempts to answer a more general question: How can an individual subject relate to another and view this relationship as being as evident and fundamental as his/her own existence? What makes it possible for a Self to bond with Others? Can this bond provide a sufficient basis to define the social fact? If it cannot, what else does this require? Can we presuppose that the intersubjective relationship is identifiable to the social relationship? It is based on these kinds of questions that the exchange practices of traditional societies are chosen as providing the very model of the strong bond and the specific level that those authors seek to define.

Lefort: Exchanges, Gifts, and Historic Forms of Sociality

In issue 64 of the journal *Les Temps Modernes*, from February 1951, Claude Lefort, then a very young philosopher, published a twenty-page-long article that established his intellectual reputation: "L'échange et la lutte des hommes."[2] To this day this writing remains frequently cited, and the analysis it presents is still admired and viewed as unimpeachable. At the time structuralism had just begun its rise. The previous year Claude Lévi-Strauss had published his *Introduction to the Work of Marcel Mauss*,[3] immediately viewed as a kind of manifesto that broadened the perspectives open by his *The Elementary Structures of Kinship*. Other writings of his were being disseminated that would become more broadly available in 1958 with the publication of his *Structural Anthropology*. But things were already being shaken. Would the field of the social sciences allow itself to be taken over by an endeavor viewed as formalist? Lévi-Strauss did claim Mauss's legacy, but he intended to move beyond it; he proposed to understand so-called "primitive" societies based mostly on their kinship systems,[4] and these kinship systems as ruled by the exogamic reciprocity entailed by the prohibition of incest—that is, the exchange of wives, which he presented as the highest form of the gift exchanges described by Mauss. Lévi-Strauss thus called on Mauss in the service of a project many authors felt had to be resisted. They wished to provide a different reading of Mauss's *The Gift*, a political reading capable of restoring the "dialectical" wealth of traditional gift exchanges, in spite of what they viewed as the insurmountable inability of those exchanges to liberate a specifically historical force. Lefort's article proposed to contribute to this clarification. This tightly written and intelligent text was granted the reception it deserved. We will soon return to its precise argument, but also to a few of its debatable presuppositions—its prejudices—and of its argumentative and above all documentary short-comings. We can assume that Lefort soon became aware of those, since as early as the following year he published another writing that corrected some aspects of the earlier publication.[5] Let us return to his 1951 article.

The Priority of the Bond among Humans over Their Bond to Things

From the outset Lefort presents some crucial propositions with respect to the work of Marcel Mauss, which he credits for moving beyond the "narrow" rationalism of his mentor, Durkheim.[6] For Lefort, Mauss's originality lies in his intention to reach "the total man," in the words Marx uses in his early writings (although in a fairly different sense).[7] Lefort does situate Mauss in the lineage of Marx as well as Hegel. He also refers to Husserl, indirectly recognizing a privileged connection with the work of Merleau-Ponty and shedding light on his own insistence on viewing the social sciences from the perspective of "concrete men." Lefort specifies: "We cannot help calling on phenomenology when Mauss attempts to remove the wall artificially raised between sociology and history, or between sociology and psychology, and affirm the reciprocity of perspectives on a reality that cannot be defined in and of itself."[8] In fact (in France at least)[9] phenomenology had not yet attempted to build bridges with the social sciences. What Lefort expressed was more of a wish than a task to be achieved; hence the theoretical interest in *The Gift*, which according to Lefort makes it possible to consider at the same time the regulations of the group and the motivations of the agents. This is what Mauss sums up in the following statement: "It is by considering the whole entity that we could perceive what is essential, the way everything moves, the living aspect, *the fleeting moment when society, or men, become sentimentally aware of themselves and of their situation in relation to others.*"[10]

The reason why Lefort views Mauss's writing as "an essay on the foundation of society,"[11] however, is not only its method, but the very object of its analysis: the system of gift exchanges as a "total social" fact—that is, a fact that integrates and directs every aspect of life lived in common. This makes progress possible with respect to this question: "What conditions make it possible for a society to exist?"[12] The answer Lefort finds in Mauss can be summed up as follows: In those societies the continual exchanges of gifts show that in every way the relationships humans establish with one another matter more than those they establish with things, so much so that the production of goods must be continually ruled by the priority given to the social bond. This is how "phenomena of exchange teach us how to read social phenomena in general."[13] Lefort adds a few highly relevant remarks: (1) this activity of exchange is sustained by a logic of challenge, rivalry, and prestige: It is fundamentally antagonistic; (2) "one does not give in order to receive, but in order for the other party to give."[14] The purpose is not self-interest, but the continual renewal of the relationship.

Those are the crucial points on which we can fully agree with Lefort. They would be more than enough to justify the title of his article. This writing, however, also includes problematic or even suspicious elements— in particular, with respect to the accuracy of the anthropological data and their philosophical interpretation. With respect to the first point, let us begin with his recurrent formulation, "exchanges through gifts." Lefort establishes a distinction between those and another form of exchange he believes to have developed later: barter. This amounts to presupposing that in "primitive" societies exchanges of goods began in the form of gifts (and therefore as exchanges *through* rather than *of* gifts) before becoming more contractual and calculus-based. Mauss himself, sometimes hesitant as to this genealogy, continually calls it into question, so contrary are the respective stakes of those two types of exchange. This is what his entire essay aims to show. Malinowski,[15] to whom Mauss owes so much, is very clear on this. As we saw above (Chapter 2), in the Trobriand Islands gift exchanges (*kula*) have an exclusively generous and glorious purpose: They weave intense personal bonds and guarantee prestige, whereas barter relationships (*gimwali*) are equalitarian and bitterly conducted, without an extended commitment of the parties. Barter (which is a form of trade with mental norms of equivalence, thus involving a virtual currency) is as old as gift relationships. The two coexist because their purposes are different: The latter are the foundation of public recognition among groups, whereas the former ensure the circulation of goods based on the requirement of fair equilibrium with the aim to meet needs. From this perspective, Lefort's analyses on the economic presuppositions of gift exchanges appear as a mere expression of old prejudices (let us note that at the time many French, English, and American anthropologists shared those same prejudices).

In addition to those misunderstandings on the economic status of sumptuary exchanges, there is a serious problem of documentation: Lefort studies almost nothing else than the *potlatch* of the northwest coast of North America; he mentions in passing the exchanges of the Trobriand Islands (mistakenly discussing copper objects that did not exist in those islands). Yet Mauss gives many other examples where gift exchanges are more appeased, while the element of challenge and agonistic reply is still present: the Trobriand *kula*, the Maori *hau*, exchanges in the Fiji islands, Melanesia, the Andamans, and Samoa. To restrict his consideration to the *potlatch* alone allows Lefort to privilege the extremely antagonistic aspect of the exchange and, as did Bataille based on the same example, to underline the potentially destructive aspect of the *potlatch*. Lefort's main philosophical argument is constructed through a reference to this *destruction*.[16]

Before dealing with this central point, let us consider Lefort's paragraph on Lévi-Strauss since, as we saw, his writing proposes a nonstructuralist reading of gift relationships in general and Mauss in particular. Lefort does not appear to have closely read *The Elementary Structures of Kinship*, which he hastily criticizes. It is obvious that Lévi-Strauss's purpose is not to describe the concrete social life of any given society, but something else entirely: to attempt to bring to the fore regularities—models of relationships—in what appeared as an inextricable proliferation of local rules. Lévi-Strauss achieves this by observing that, no matter the degree of distance involved, wives must imperatively come from another group, or at least a group viewed as other (whether clan, moiety, or lineage); this defines exogamy. The prohibition against marrying within one's own group is called the prohibition of incest; it also entails that, for every wife the members of a group deny themselves within their consanguineous group, another wife is in principle guaranteed to them in another consanguineous group with which their group has a relationship of alliance. The prohibition is thus nothing else than a positive obligation of reciprocity. Lévi-Strauss acknowledges that he found the inspiration for his hypothesis in Mauss's *The Gift*. He thus declares that exogamy is "the supreme rule of the gift."[17] We now understand how regularities form a system—cycles of reciprocity; contrary to Lefort's odd claim, to grasp the logic of this system does not amount to reducing concrete experience to a "mathematical reality" or a "mechanical-type law,"[18] but to develop a scientific endeavor and secure the means to identify the meaning and dynamic of the most "concrete" practices. This is precisely what Marx does when—through an abstract analysis—he brings to the fore the law of value, and Lévi-Strauss remains faithful to his method by avoiding confusing "the logic of things with the things of logic."

Let us come to Lefort's philosophical conclusions. There are two kinds. The first specifically involve the meaning of gift exchanges; the second, the historical fate of "primitive" societies. What is the aim of the parties in the *potlatch*? According to Lefort it is to free themselves from the many *belongings* in which they feel *lost* (an argument that rests entirely on a reference to Lévy-Bruhl, author of this condescending and perfectly arbitrary thesis).[19] But the core of Lefort's argument is the following: "By giving he breaks the bond that connects him to the thing, but this rejection can be true only if the other party recognizes it by performing it in his turn. The world of humans takes shape only through a concomitant distancing from reality; *through an identical operation, giving, men confirm to one another that they are not things.*"[20] This reading is perfectly Hegelian, but not Maussian in any way. What Mauss teaches us, on the contrary—and the entire ethnographic literature confirms this—is that to give is always *to give oneself in and through the thing given.* Lefort rightly notes this elsewhere ("To keep something from the other party without reciprocating would amount to keeping the other party himself"[21]), yet, oddly, he appears to have completely forgotten it. He confesses to being embarrassed[22] when Mauss talks of "blendings"; yet those do not involve the exchanges, but the bonds between humans and things. Far from breaking their bond with the *thing*, the giver ventures the thing into the space of the other *as a part of himself* (hence the magic meant to protect it). The thing given is a *guarantee* and *substitute* of the giver. It seals an alliance; it testifies to a pact; it symbolizes and guarantees it. To give is therefore not to "break the bond that unites the giver to the thing," but on the contrary to give oneself in the thing given, making it the precious witness to the pact and the recognition granted.

Hegelian negativity is thus not relevant here. Is it even involved in the case of the exacerbated and destructive *potlatch*? Not even then, since the purpose of the *potlatch* is not to tell one's rival and confirm for oneself, "This is not what I am: I am something else than those physical goods"; it is to secure greatness and glory by giving those goods, and sometimes to prove boundless wealth by destroying them. In this case the gesture of giving becomes a simulated conflict: The destruction of the goods is a temporary rejection of the alliance, in the form of a challenge, but this occurs instead of a war. Whatever the case, this is not the crucial point. To call those ritual exchanges a "total social fact" means that for Mauss those gift practices constitute the core and main reason for being of life lived in common. Not only does this fact integrate all its other dimensions, but above all it is what gives meaning to everything else. Those practices mean that for the group nothing is more important than to guarantee its cohesion and proclaim it through procedures that imply a necessary reciprocity.

The Expectation of History and "the Denaturing Cogito of the Exchange through Gifts"

The second theme of Lefort's philosophical conclusions involves "*primitive*" societies' relationship to history—more precisely, the fact that they "are incapable of developing a history." They do experience conflict and antagonism, but in the form of "an oscillation instead of a dialectic in which something new can emerge."[23] This oscillation is a mere back-and-forth, the repetition of a balanced interplay of exchanges, a noncumulative reversibility. For Lefort something in the ritual gift resists the transformation that opens to truly historical time. He acknowledges, however, that those societies have labor, creating in some cases a wealth of goods. His answer is a condensation of dialectical arguments: "[Primitive] production stands for something other than itself; it does not reveal any truth to men. In those societies it is as if men were concerned only with situating themselves relative to one another and feverishly repeating the *denaturing* cogito of exchange through gifts. This does not mean that there is no competition among humans, but this is an immediate competition where men are just as locked as they are in immediate cooperation."[24] Those formulations display a textbook Hegelian and Marxist inspiration. We can assume that if Lefort were writing today he would forego this discourse. He soon recognized its ethnocentric presuppositions; in a 1952 writing (which constitutes the next chapter of his book) he problematizes in a much more nuanced way the gap between "societies with exchanges through gifts" and societies that participate in history. He even begins this writing with a highly critical calling into question of Hegel's sections on India and China in *Leçons sur la philosophie de l'histoire* (Hegel's sections on Africa are even more debatable). Lefort expresses suspicion with respect to Husserl's European point of view, and he precisely defines the possibility for different societies to have diverse temporalities, each with its own legitimacy. Thus, to establish, based on documents, the undeniable distance that develops between *stagnating* and *historical societies*, he comments in detail on an inquiry on Bali by Gregory Bateson that shows that rituals and hierarchies reach there a level of complexity so astounding as to block all change, where the coded avoidance of conflict leads to a peace that stifles *dynamic oppositions*. On the contrary, by forsaking the immediate social recognition guaranteed by "exchanges through gifts," modern societies accepted and allowed the introduction among humans of the mediation of depersonalized things, thus promoting the neutral relationship of contractual exchange and the endless transformation of the natural world through the detour and reserve imposed by labor; this made possible the unlimited opening to history, the fluidity of social relationships, and above all the emergence of the new. Those views are remarkable and could inspire stimulating research, provided that we recognize that they apply not only to so-called archaic societies, but also—and even more so—to our own.

At the time, in the optimistic age of dialectics, it was still possible to talk as does Lefort of the "denaturing cogito of exchange through gifts." That age is now behind us; while it viewed itself as critical, it was unaware of its own naivety (ours will soon become apparent to others . . .). Ancient statutory blockages have given way. Boundaries among classes seem increasingly fuzzy. The speed of circulations makes positions unstable. But, rather than as the advent of *the new human being*, the triumph of *history*— understood in terms of economic production and mastery over nature— appears today mostly as the triumph of capitalism. The purely speculative money of globalized finance appears increasingly capable of reconstructing myriads of inflexible hierarchies and fierce blockages in which profit constitutes the only criterion, and compared to which the modest hierarchies and blockages of traditional societies remained quite harmless.

Descombes: The Criterion of Otherness and the Gift Relationship

On the question of the gift, Vincent Descombes presents, especially in his *The Institutions of Meaning*, an original approach entirely different from Lefort's.[25] One of the major aspects of Descombes's research involves the nature of the relationship between the Self and Others. What criterion makes it possible to designate another person not just as another self, but a self different from us? Is this operation, assuming it is successful, sufficient to define the social relationship? In this process of reconstruction, gift relationships have a privileged situation. Let us try to follow succinctly the argument Descombes develops.

PHYSICAL RELATIONSHIP AND INTENTIONAL RELATIONSHIP: MONADS, DYADS, AND TRIADS ACCORDING TO PEIRCE

One of Descombes's purposes is to clarify the notion of *Social Relationship*. The considerable diversity and fuzziness of the possible senses of this term requires a real critical effort, in particular an inquiry on the very concept of relationship. Descombes reminds us that this question has generated complex age-old debates. A consideration of one aspect will be sufficient for our discussion to move forward: the canonical difference often claimed to exist between *real relationship* and *reason-based relationship*. The latter is essentially established based on the criterion of resemblance. The old example Bertrand Russell uses is a familiar one: A white wall in Rome is in a *reason-based* relationship with a white wall in London. They share the feature of whiteness. This relationship is based on two distinct and independent facts; this is why the "whiteness" feature cannot be the basis of a real relationship. For the latter to exist requires that the shared element be inherent to both subjects. Thus (to use an example presented by Locke) when we discuss Titius as a *husband* this feature entails the existence of a *wife*. This wife is Sempronia, and she alone can be assigned this feature. This is a real relationship.

According to Descombes, the logician who revitalized in depth the debate on this problem at the turn of the twentieth century was Charles Sanders Peirce. For Peirce a relationship is real when its terms constitute a system. Thus the "husband" and "wife" features are *intrinsically* associated. This example is self-evident enough to convince us. A more interesting one—since it seems more indirect—is provided by the following proposition: *Cain killed Abel*. How do the terms of this statement constitute a system? Descombes's answer is that they are connected by a fact: homicide; Cain is a murderer and Abel a victim. Unlike the two walls above, one of which can cease to be white without affecting the other, those are not two separate and independent facts, but two connected facts—to kill and be killed—expressed by two contrary and complementary predicates.

From this Peirce draws several theoretical considerations, which Descombes takes up again. First, this kind of proposition whose terms constitute a system involves relationships based on activity and passivity rather than on amount and quality. This must be understood primarily in a grammatical sense: The phrase, "Cain killed Abel," can be stated in the passive form as, "Abel was killed by Cain." This reversibility is intrinsic to transitive verbs, of which they constitute a crucial criterion. Peirce's second important thesis is that this type of relationship manifests above all an *intentional* activity. What it designates is not merely physical facts with a neutral status (to kill and die), but the act by which polarity is brought to the fore from the outset: between murderer and victim. Based on this argument Peirce proposes a distinction between three fundamental types of propositions, which are also three levels of relationships. He calls the first type *monad*. It is associated with a statement (such as, the wall is white) that assigns a feature or defines a status; there is only one logical subject. The second type of relationship is called *dyad* because it involves two logical subjects and entails the use of transitive verbs; it thus sustains the transformation of the active form into the passive form and points to an action at least potentially intentional (it is possible to kill someone by accident). The third type of relationship, the *triad*, involves a shift of level that is also a *shift of order*: Intentionality becomes explicit. The relationship between the terms is *mental* (as opposed to a purely physical relationship); the intention applies to an *action*; the intention can be universalized (as we will see below). Above all, the proposition includes three logical subjects. The best examples are provided by verbs with dual objects, one direct and the other indirect, which grammarian Lucien Tesnière,[26] whom Descombes often quotes, calls trivalent verbs, and which express either *telling* (to assert, announce, teach) or *giving* (to bring, grant, provide, confer, award, give, offer); those verbs are called verbs of "giving"—in a broad sense, since the category also includes *to buy* and *to sell*; while Descombes ignores this not insignificant detail, we will have to pay attention to it.

This reflection on the triad, Descombes explains, is what makes Peirce's work highly original. This type of proposition operates a change of *order* (in Pascal's sense), because the triad cannot be constituted by merely adding an extra term to the dyad. The triad opens to the different space of plural relations: It is in fact nothing else than the beginning of a polyad. The existence of a dyad is a mere observation, but the triad points from the outset to a *purposeful relationship* between its terms. It is impossible to isolate monads and dyads within a triad: "No description of brute (dyadic) facts can exhaust the meaning of (triadic) intentional facts,"[27] Descombes comments, setting up a telling parallel between Russell's positions and Peirce's. In his *An Inquiry into Meaning and Truth*[28] Russell proposes to reduce complex propositions (such as those expressed by trivalent verbs) to atomic propositions. Thus the statement, "A gives book B to C," can be broken down into two basic units: "A gives B" and "C receives B." Russell acknowledges that his formulation is "phenomenistic" in the sense that it amounts to presenting the action performed as the addition of two physical facts free of intention. This amounts to "determin[ing] *the relation of the people to the objects* without mentioning *the relation of the people to each other*. The relation between donor and donee would then become a simple logical consequence of two relations to the object."[29] Russell's positions are at the polar opposite of Pierce's. For the latter no physical description or addition of raw facts can account for the intentionality that inhabits the sentence, "A gives book B to C." "Russell has failed to analyze an example of gift giving; instead he has provided an analysis of a kind of pantomime. His description would fit any operation that included, as one of its moments, the physical transfer of an object."[30] (Let us note that this statement presupposes that it is known what a *scene of gift giving* is or must be; we will have to return to this.) Here Descombes recalls a remarkable passage from a letter Peirce wrote to Lady Welby, a pioneer of semiotics:

> If you take any ordinary triadic relationship, you will always find a *mental* element in it. Brute action is secondness, any mentality involves thirdness. Analyze for instance the relation involved in "A gives B to C." Now what is giving? It does not consist [in] A's putting B away from him and C's subsequent taking B up. It is not necessary that any material transfer should take place. It consists in A's making C the possessor according to *Law*. There must be some kind of law before there can be any kind of giving—be it but the law of the strongest.[31]

We find this writing admirable, not only because it expresses a fundamental requirement of every gift relationship, but also because it reveals a type of logic inherent to every human relationship understood as a social relationship. We still need a correct understanding of what Peirce designates as coming under a *Law*. For Pierce this idea of a law is from the outset inseparable from the elements already brought to the fore: The gift relationship is a mental thing, an intentional thing—thus nonreducible to raw facts—that involves an encompassing element: the purposeful relationship between the terms of the triad. But triadic relationships such as gift relationships also involve other aspects, including the following four:

First, *universality*. Descombes sums this up as follows: "To say that there is a law is to introduce (potential) infinity. The future is determined *regardless of what happens*, which shows that the determination in question is logical and not causal or physical."[32] Second, *context* in Frege's sense, related to what Ludwig Wittgenstein designates as a *multiplicity* necessary to the manifestation of an intentional order: sufficiently frequent occurrences, but also a network of connotations—in other words, everything that makes it possible to grasp a connection between events, rather than a sequence of unconnected or merely concurrent facts. Third, the function of *mediation*. In Peirce this must be understood in a nondialectic sense. Dialectic mediation would propose to generate the triad based on a dyad, but "we are at once within the triadic. Mediation here means that the triadic relation must be conceived as including both real relations (e.g., this specific thing is given to *that* specific person) and intentional relations (governed by rules)."[33] This means that in this case it is impossible to isolate dual relationships: each term (whether it is called subject or agent) mediates the two others depending on its position. Relationships among persons are inseparable from persons' relationships with things. Let us add a fourth aspect, which also constitutes a necessary condition: *otherness*. Here Descombes calls not on Peirce, but once again on Wittgenstein, author of a text highly relevant to this discussion:

> Why can't my right hand give my left hand money?—My right hand can put it in my left hand. My right hand can write a deed of gift, and my left hand a receipt.—But the further practical consequences would not be those of a gift.[34]

We must ask, Wittgenstein says: "Well, and now what?"[35] The only possible answer is: nothing. The gift relationship can occur only among real and autonomous persons. This, Descombes rightly notes, entails at the same time freedom and the order of justice, therefore a legal system (the *law* Peirce discusses must be understood also in this sense). Descombes specifies this notion of otherness in other texts[36] where he shows that the *social relation* cannot be reduced to an *intersubjective relationship*. The latter does not require the real difference between two persons. It can occur—according to Husserl himself—as a diachronic distance between two moments of the self. The same is true of the dialogic relationship, which according to Peirce is already constituted at the intersection of two levels of the self. In short, "dialogism requires different subjects, but not necessarily a *personal* difference among those subjects."[37] Descombes thus establishes a fundamental distinction between the concepts of subject and person. The concept of subject can involve a distance between two states or dimensions of consciousness internal to the self. The concept of person designates the individual as a socially identifiable existential entity. Hence the following question: If the intersubjective and dialogic duality is not enough, then what is the criterion of a truly social relationship? "What is required for there to be another person is an otherness that moves us out of the sphere of the self."[38] Here Wittgenstein's remarks on the relationship between one's hands (where the right hand gives something to the left hand) become crucial. The possibility of giving presupposes a *personal* difference between a giver and a recipient. One cannot be the beneficiary of a gift given to oneself. In general terms this means that, contrary to phenomenology's assumption, the other person cannot be derived from *our own experience of Others*. More precisely, the relationship cannot be said to be "social" by the mere fact of our awareness of Others, no matter the intensity of our empathy. This only involves experiences of the self that Thomas Reid, a late-eighteenth-century English author whom Descombes discusses, calls "*solitary* operations" (to think, walk, feel, admire, etc.) and contrasts to *social* operations that can occur only in relation to real persons (to promise, contract, establish an alliance, exchange, or give). The latter fulfill Wittgenstein's criterion of otherness. They can never result from a combination of solitary operations, in the same way that Peirce's triad cannot result from an addition of dyads, but testifies from the outset to the advent of an entirely new order. What makes a relationship social is the fact that each person behaves relative to another according to a law, and that the other is a real person who preexists us and stands outside us.

This is the ultimate element that sums up Descombes's entire effort at clarification. This is also why the gift relationship analyzed by Peirce or Wittgenstein must enable us to grasp the nature of a system of real relationships. Those relationships amount to an *institution*: They constitute a normative order (whether implicit or explicit, spoken or written) and form mental totalities (in Peirce's sense)—that is, intentional systems that are triadic from the outset. Those systems allow for and even require a holistic conception that holds that the whole is different than the sum of its parts (in the same way that an intelligible sentence is more than the mere arrangement of its elements). The term *institution* must be understood here as a generative authority rather than in the restrictive sense of the public or private organizations that are its legal and functional expressions. This helps us understand the title of Descombes's book: *The Institutions of Meaning*. It is significant that in this book the question of the gift has such a strategic position. But this also raises several questions that we must now *clarify* by using Descombes's very method.

DOUBTS AND OBJECTIONS: REEXAMINING MAUSS AND LÉVI-STRAUSS

Peirce, Russell, and Descombes after them use the term *gift* in an accepted sense, without specifying its content or questioning its polysemy. This involves a fairly widespread paradox: the construction of a tight axiomatic consistency around a concept that remains relatively indeterminate. How is this the case here? The concept of gift is assumed to apply indifferently to all kinds of situations where a good is generously transferred to a third party. This general character may appear adequate when the purpose is to identify a formal type of relationship. But it is risky when there are *differences of order* among those situations. This is of course the case of gift relationships. As we saw above ("Propositions I") it is clear that: (1) the reciprocal ceremonial gift; (2) the gracious unilateral gift; and (3) the gift out of solidarity share only two or three of the eight variables identified in the first case. This entails significant consequences (which we already presented with respect to Derrida, Marion, and Levinas). Those distinctions justify the objection that in those three kinds of gifts the triadic relationship remains relevant. To reinforce this objection let us examine the examples Descombes analyzes. The example discussed above, "A gives book B to C," does not consider whether the action is performed by a librarian (in which case an object is merely lent to C) or A gives a gift to C. In both case the action is intentional and the relationship triadic. In terms of intentionality, however, the difference between those two cases is analogous to the difference between "A kills B" (perhaps accidentally) and "A murders B."

With respect to the term *gift* Descombes develops a rigorous argument that along the way shifts from one level to another. First he refers to the list of trivalent verbs grammarians call by convention "verbs of giving," a list that includes verbs that mean the opposite of giving, such as "selling" and "paying." We must therefore acknowledge that in both its grammatical and everyday uses, the verb "to give" has taken on an extremely broad meaning, most often implying no idea of gift, and free of any oblative connotation. Giving then becomes synonymous with providing, guaranteeing, making available, forwarding, administering, approving, or designating (a long list of those synonyms can be found in any good dictionary). To play on those nonoblative meanings when discussing the gift in the sense of an offering—or to do the reverse—is an abuse of language that it is crucial to avoid because it leads to the philosophical confusions—or even contortions—that we have already observed in respectable phenomenologists. Descombes avoids those confusions. But he does not warn us—because he does not ask this question—against the shift from the model of the book transferred by a librarian to the model of the book offered as a gift. From this perspective all *trivalent* verbs, beginning with the *verbs of giving*[39] share a perfectly neutral status: they involve gestures intentional by nature that presuppose an addresser, an addressee, and a thing transferred. We can say that selling, taking, or reimbursing show as much intentionality as do giving, providing, or assigning something to someone. But to introduce a discussion on Mauss situates the issue from the outset within the mode of the gift (and not mere transfer), and even within the realm of gift practices strongly encoded by various cultures. It is as if the shift from an indeterminate use of the term "gift" (as mere intentional transfer) to a specific use (as a gesture of generous unilateral or reciprocal gift) appears unproblematic to Descombes. Yet this is not a mere nuance but the very stake of the gift as a gesture that Mauss discusses.

Our second objection is that in Chapter 9 of his *The Institutions of Meaning* ("Essays on the Gift") Descombes moves directly from a discussion of Russell's dyad and Peirce's triad to the ethnographic materials Mauss presents in his *The Gift*.[40] Descombes convincingly confirms everything that has been said about the gift as an institutional fact, and he illuminates some crucial aspects. But the following question remains, asked by Mauss at the very beginning of *The Gift*: Why in so-called archaic societies is it imperative to *reciprocate* a gift received? What is the origin of this obligation to reciprocate? We could expect Descombes to seek in Peirce an answer to this crucial question, but he does no such thing. He trivializes and evades the problem as follows: "The diversity of usages and customs is thus not in itself an obstacle to their comprehension. If we can understand that a gift requires two operations (one on the part of the donor and the other on the part of the donee), we can, by extension, imagine a more complex rule that brings together a gift and a countergift."[41] Let us remember that the two operations Peirce posits are nothing more than giving and receiving. This does not explain why *reciprocating* is entailed by giving—in other words, why the recipient *must* become a giver. Descombes adds: "The relation will then link two operations within a rule: one prescribing giving to someone else, who will receive, and the other prescribing to the recipient to give back to the donor after having received."[42] This sentence describes a sequence of—indeed intentional—gestures through a mere narrative observation (this, then that) that does not account for the *obligation* to reciprocate. This obligation is reduced to an extension of the movement of giving. In the reciprocating gift the roles are reversed: The recipient becomes the giver. It remains to be understood what leads and even *forces* the recipient to reciprocate: This is the fundamental question Mauss asks at the very beginning of *The Gift*. What is the exact nature of the "more complex rule" Descombes invokes? He does not say. Neither does he put forward the concept required here: reciprocity.[43] Yet what is at stake in this reciprocation is the intentionality of the gift as a *reciprocal gift*.

Our belief is that Peirce's model as well as Descombes's approach can contribute to a formulation of the answer, provided that an additional condition is brought up. Let us note for now that, because he lacks a satisfactory hypothesis, Descombes finds himself in the same situation as Mauss: He observes the presence of the reciprocating gift, takes note of what happens, and pays attention to what the agents say about it—a preliminary approach indispensable on the part of any investigator or researcher working on a material to be investigated. Mauss himself follows this approach with respect to the Kwakiutl *potlatch* and the Trobriand *kula*. He describes those exchanges based on the inquiries available, and he interprets them as follows: Their purpose is to create alliances, gain prestige, celebrate the merits of the participants, and intensify the bonds among the parties involved. But in the case of the Maori *hau* something gives him pause; the stakes remain obscure. He cautiously keeps to reporting the facts as Elsdon Best transcribes them in his inquiry[44] and to presenting as according to the Maori's statements about this strange force (*hau*) by which the thing given is filled and haunted. Lévi-Strauss criticizes Mauss for his restraint: "Are we not dealing with a mystification, an effect quite often produced in the minds of ethnographers by indigenous people?"[45] Conversely, Descombes strongly calls into question Lévi-Strauss's criticism. He dedicates to this questioning the major part of his Chapter 18; at the end of this chapter, however, the question that was our starting point remains unanswered; we know only what the Maori tell us: The obligation to reciprocate has to do with the *hau*, the *spirit* of the thing given. It is as if Descombes's polemic with Lévi-Strauss allowed him a kind of diversion on an eminently thorny question. His defense of Mauss gives him cover for his lack of an answer.

We must acknowledge that this failure to move forward is probably due to a faulty formulation of the problem. This fault is both Mauss's and Lévi-Strauss's, neither of whom is able to grasp the stakes of the Maori *hau*. As does Descombes, they miss the crucial element.

In *The Gift*[46] Mauss reports the words with which an old Maori sage called Ranaipiri tries to explain to anthropologist Elsdon Best why a gift must be reciprocated: The thing given comes with a kind of mysterious power, the *hau*, which is akin to its spirit and contains a yearning to return—or rather the yearning for a gesture in return. Ranaipiri's speech includes an essential element ignored by every commentator,[47] even though it is the very purpose of his demonstration. The essence of Ranaipiri's statement is the following: If I give a gift to someone, he is now able to give a gift to someone else, who can now give one to someone else, and so on. At some point the final recipient must present a reciprocating gift to the original giver. Mauss does not notice this point; he even deems useless this intervention of a third party in the interplay of reciprocity.[48] What is then the meaning of this system of postponed exchange? It is surprising that Lévi-Strauss also fails to grasp it, since he is the one who theorized it; this is the very logic of the *generalized exchange*, which constitutes the most seminal section of his *The Elementary Structures of Kinship*: Group A gives a wife to group B, which gives a wife to group C, which gives one to group D. At a—sometimes much—later point group A receives a wife from group D or some other group in the network of exchanges. This system, Lévi-Strauss explains, is the expression of a circulation that commits exogamic groups to one another over the long term, and thus presupposes trust among the parties and strong bonds with the entire society (whereas a direct exchange of wives, called "restricted exchange," involves only two groups over a short term, preserving them from future risks).

Ranaipiri's message is now clearer: His aim is to explain to the foreign visitor that the obligation to reciprocate is not diluted when it moves to a third or fourth recipient; reciprocation to the originator of the cycle must be guaranteed. Let us note that, contrary to the belief of many commentators—which contributes significantly to the misunderstandings on this question—what is reciprocated is not the object originally given, but the *hau*, the spirit of the thing given. This is in fact what a few years later Mauss himself calls "indirect alternating reciprocity."[49]

How can this help us understand the obligation to reciprocate? We have already seen in Chapter 2 above that the ceremonial reciprocal gift is a public procedure of recognition among groups, which can be clearly observed in first encounters, and is extended and renewed in the longer term through the exogamic alliance and exchanges of presents in conventional circumstances. We also identified in Chapter 4 the precise meaning of the "reciprocity" involved: The ceremonial gift is above all an implicit but highly consistent pact, in which the goods exchanged are the guarantees and substitutes of the parties. By definition a pact (just like a contract in the realm of commercial exchanges) presupposes two parties, sides, or groups. The obligation to reciprocate has to do above all with the necessity to abide by the pact (just like a contract can exist only if the signature of one party replies to the signature of the other and the payment of one matches the goods provided by the other). *To reciprocate a gift is to accept and preserve an alliance.* This is the logic that must be displayed in every ritual public exchange of gifts. Lévi-Strauss is right to expect Mauss to identify this logic. But he fails to recognize it in the Maori *hau,* even though he continually discusses it throughout the six hundred pages of his *The Elementary Structures of Kinship.* The *hau* is an example of *indirect reciprocity,* analogous to the postponed exogamic exchange Lévi-Strauss calls generalized exchange. Peirce's model is entirely relevant here if it is extended to reciprocity. As we saw in "Propositions I" above, this model makes it possible to understand the unity of the act of giving (according to a law); receiving (according to a law); and above all reciprocating (according to a law)—to *abide by the pact.* This is the sense in which an *obligation* exists. In the same way that a tennis player returns the ball to remain in the game, the requirement to reciprocate a gift is entailed by the original gift. Reciprocity thus presupposes the reversibility constitutive of an internal relationship, but it also presupposes the personal otherness of the agents involved.

What Lévi-Strauss criticizes in Mauss is precisely his failure to grasp the principle-based unity of the three gestures as part of a single structure. Mauss is aware that those three gestures are related; this is even the main lesson of his *The Gift.* But how is it insufficient? Mauss views the fact of *reciprocating* as paradoxical or even contradictory if it constitutes an obligation. This amounts to a de facto acknowledgment that the unity of the three gestures remains incomprehensible. In his definition of this unity as an *exchange,* Lévi-Strauss chooses a term that for him—this is self-evident in *The Elementary Structures of Kinship*—designates above all the *reciprocity of offerings* (as in exogamy, said to be "the rule of giving par excellence"). "But exchange is not something [Mauss] can perceive on the level of the facts. Empirical observation finds no exchange, but only, as Mauss himself says, 'three obligations: giving, receiving, returning.' So the whole theory calls for the existence of a structure, only fragments of which are delivered by experience—just its scattered members, or rather its elements."[50] For Lévi-Strauss the answer is that "the primary, fundamental phenomenon is *exchange* itself, which gets split up into discrete operations in social life."[51] This formulation matches remarkably the difference between dyadic and triadic facts according to Peirce. What Lévi-Strauss calls "exchange" is an inherent structure of reciprocity; the entirety of a relationship must be understood from the outset as integrating the steps and elements that form it: The fact of reciprocating is already entailed in the fact of receiving, which is entailed by giving, constituting the "structure, only fragments of which are delivered by experience." Thus with respect to the avuncular relationship: "We do not need to explain how the maternal uncle emerges in the kinship structure: He does not emerge—he is present initially. Indeed, the presence of the maternal uncle is a necessary precondition for the structure to exist."[52] For Lévi-Strauss this is the symbolic origin of society. The exchange—whether gift exchanges or the matrimonial alliance, which is its optimal expression—does constitute a *structure* in which all the terms are interconnected from the outset, or in Peirce's words a relationship according to a law. This defines an institution. Peirce also explains that every triadic relationship remains relevant in polyadic relationships with *n* parties. This applies to the *postponed reciprocity* exemplified by the *hau* cycle. But there is even more to this, which takes us beyond Peirce (see Chapter 2 above): In the pact that the ceremonial gift constitutes, what is given in and through the thing offered is not a mere thing: It is *oneself*. The good offered is precious because it testifies to the agreement made, by representing or embodying the party who commits himself, either as an individual or in the name of his group. This presents an additional level that reveals a different kind of intentionality inherent to reciprocity: the commitment of the parties *as persons* according to a law. Every pact must be reciprocal; it can exist only through the reply of each party to the other; the ceremonial gift is such a pact. To reply is to accept the alliance, to commit and venture oneself; the thing given testifies to this commitment.

In Conclusion

In Lefort or Descombes the question of reciprocity as discussed and called into question by the philosophers who consider it from the perspective of a phenomenology of givenness does not appear as a problem; both present their views based on entirely different premises. But this does not mean that the problem has been solved.

From the outset Lefort situates his reflection on the gift within the mental landscape of the societies Mauss discusses: agonistic exchange— that is, the alternation of gift and countergift. This exchange is reciprocal by definition. The gift exists only through this reciprocity. This is so obvious that Lefort feels no need to discuss this concept, probably a reasonable choice in a fairly short writing such as his. His main question has a different focus: those societies' relationship to history. Our own reservation has to do with his conception of this question, which carries a strong evolutionistic and teleological presupposition; in those societies supposedly based on "exchange through gifts" he sees an unaccomplished form of humans' relationship to the natural world. For him those humans show an excessive focus on social relationships, aiming at an immediate and intense unanimity. They lack the patience of mediation, the step of retention (Hegel's *Hebung*), reserve for the purpose of another kind of exchange that is more calculus-based and focused on the long term—history—which is nothing else than the commercial exchange. Once again, to call on history as the global movement of societies amounts to associating its emergence as the emergence of capitalism (the "bourgeois" stage Marx explicitly theorizes). But this genealogy becomes fragile or even misleading when the ceremonial gift is understood, rather than as an archaic form of exchanges of goods, as procedures of public recognition among groups (which, contrary to an enduring prejudice, also practice separately useful and profitable exchanges). This is precisely the question on which a discussion on reciprocity becomes crucial since the requirement of public recognition necessarily entails reciprocity. The shift to Modernity is not a shift from exchanges "through gifts" to profitable exchanges (those two forms have always coexisted); it is the fact that the public reciprocal recognition guaranteed by ceremonial exchanges in societies without a state organization is now guaranteed to all by law and expressed in political, legal, and economic institutions—which does not preclude other levels of recognition in everyday life and interpersonal social relationships.

In Descombes's analyses an entirely different problem arises. His sound use of the triad defined by Peirce makes possible a major advance in the understanding of the bond among the giver, the recipient, and the thing given. But the obligation to reciprocate the gift remains to be explained. This concept is once again crucially situated to illuminate the specific character of social relationships. Here again it is important to grasp its logic to understand gift exchanges as a procedure of recognition and alliance among groups, most often through characters that represent those groups. From this perspective we must remember the relevance of Lévi-Strauss's famous example at the beginning of the chapter on reciprocity in his *The Elementary Structures of Kinship*: the gesture of the customers in restaurants who pour the content of their flasks of wine into the glasses of the persons in front of them. In his somewhat ironic comment on this example, Descombes fails to grasp the stakes of this gesture:[53] This is not an exchange in the trivial sense since in physical terms it is a zero-sum gain operation. The purpose sought by those customers brought together by accident and unknown to one another is to enter a relationship of reciprocal acceptance through the thing offered, to affirm the existence of the Other who faces them, and even to obligate themselves to do so. In Japan the custom requires that one wait for another person sitting at one's table to fill one's cup with saké; here again, what we most yearn for we must get through and from Others.

CHAPTER 8

Propositions III:
The Dual Relationship and the Third Party

The gift relationship, as a privileged form of the relationship to others, can obsess or fascinate us. Whether private or socially instituted, it appears to embody certain exemplary dimensions of being-with-others and living-together. A reflection on this type of gesture or procedure, however—the diversity of which we are now aware of—brings to the fore a number of unresolved problems and, for this very reason, occasions a number of mis-understandings. The main difficulty, which we have often mentioned here, has to do with the indeterminacy of the very term, *gift*, too often used with respect to profoundly heterogeneous situations. This indeterminacy encourages a tendency to privilege the sense of the word sanctioned by an age-old religious and moral tradition that, because of its very stability across time, appears based on common sense and tends to be viewed as the standard by which the other forms of gift can be assessed: the unrecipro-cated generous gesture. This oblative quality makes possible an indeter-minate use of the term, with sometimes even a metaphysical formulation: "There is a gift." The gift thus appears as another name of being. But this ontology is of little help when we attempt to answer questions such as the following: Who gives what to whom, under what circumstances, and for

what purpose? This question concerns intersubjective as well as social relationships. It is therefore crucial to clarify the status of the partners involved
and the nature of the "thing" that is offered by one to the other or that
circulates between the two partners. On a formal level it is a dual relationship, but it operates through the mediation of something that is outside of
the partners. There is a third element, which brings about what Peirce calls
a triad—that is, a relationship among three logical subjects—exemplified
by trivalent verbs (discussed in "Propositions I" above and in the previous
chapter). The triad is akin to the model of the symbolic system in the sense
of a pact guaranteed by a *symbolon*. What we encounter here is the essence
of intentional relationships and the genesis of institutional order. We must
therefore accept that, although dual by definition, the relationship of reciprocity cannot be reduced to a one-on-one interaction: It necessarily includes a third element, a thing from the world, which can sometimes be a
mere word, or even—when the institution is already in place—an easily
recognizable gesture.

Yet this is not the figure of the third party to which philosophers of
ethics and theorists of the social relationship usually refer; what they refer
to is a different agent that intervenes in addition to or across our relationship to others. This is the figure of the *socius*. To call it a third party is in
fact a linguistic convention. This collective singular is made up of all the
others. It is somehow expected to represent them. How so? According
to what procedures? This involves at least two different perspectives: the
social relationship beyond the intersubjective relationship, and the ethical relationship beyond the relationship between the self and others. This
third-party agent, however, tells us nothing of the third-party thing that
bonds together the partners in the gift or in any reciprocal exchange. It is
remarkable that the reflections on those two sets of questions—the personal third party on the one hand, and the impersonal third party on the
other—remain separate. Yet it may be that their articulation is crucial and
that, on this point also, the model provided by the relationship of the ceremonial gift can be highly instructive in that our relationship to others is
always mediated by something that is not us: our relationship to the world.
In the same way, our relationship to the world always involves our relationship to others.

The Third Party as a Person—I: Simmel

The reflection Georg Simmel presents on the question of the third party
strikingly exemplifies the originality of his sociological approach as an

attempt at recentering the field of his discipline.[1] He meant for sociology not only to take into consideration the fields that involve a social dimension (running the risk of absorbing within sociology history, politics, religion, the economy, and culture), but also to identify the very process of formation of society: what turns agents into a group, what he calls *Vergesell-schaftung*, literally "sociation" (usually translated as "socialization"). This methodological requirement explains the second remarkable feature of Simmel's approach: the priority he grants to the point of view of the agent. According to him the specific object of sociology must be the study of interaction: *Wechselwirkung* (a term often translated as "reciprocal action," although "interaction" would be more accurate). Simmel thus opened the way to what came to be called microsociology. It is not surprising that one of his earliest focuses was on the question of the size of groups and what he calls their "quantitative determination": He seeks to establish how changes in numerical thresholds modify the structures of groups. To that end he considers the smallest of units: two and three. Let us try to follow his analysis of those determinations before considering whether the phenomenon of *sociation* actually appears more self-evident, and above all what it teaches us about the figure of the third party.

Simmel starts with a trivial observation: The existence of a group requires the interaction of at least two agents (without considering whether or not this implies the emergence of society). This bipolar interaction is obvious in various situations, such as companies with two partners, shared secrets, private pacts based on trust or on a shared fate and, more generally, on the existence of personal intimacy between friends, relatives, or lovers. According to Simmel this type of dual formation is characterized by several features. First, a relationship where one faces a single party constitutes a kind of privilege that is experienced as such. It precludes third parties. Each party receives from the other a particular attention and a unique valorization that enhance his individuality. Furthermore, each party is aware that the disappearance or departure of the other amounts to the end of the grouping. There is therefore in this dual reality a dimension at the same time potentially tragic—the possibility of disappearance—and elegiac—the certainty of irreplaceability. The same thing that makes it strong also makes it fragile.

This relationship—a point Simmel emphasizes—is characterized by this direct relationship between the agents, which confirms the absence of any supra-individual unit. He notes, however, that something surprising occurs in units of this type because of effects potentially generated by institutions where a dual relationship—which Simmel sometimes calls *dyad*—

develops. The exemplary case is marriage: The surprising stability of this union between two persons in spite of often considerable differences has less to do with their individual qualities than with the institution itself. Through the rituals and rules it requires and the representations and values it carries, the institution constitutes a supra-individual entity that does not emerge in informal dual relationships. We might now expect Simmel to scrutinize more precisely this institutional level capable of expressing the dimension of the third party; but he does not do so, probably because from his purely sociological and pragmatic perspective the only conceivable third party must also be an agent, an actual person who intervenes directly in the relationship. This limitation of the conceptual field requires a discussion.

What of this third-party agent? Once again the example of the couple allows Simmel to identify various modalities depending on which the irruption of a third character can change the relationship. The most obvious of those figures is that of the child. Contrary to the commonplace assumption, however, we must recognize that a child can be a divisive as well as a unifying factor. More generally, a third party who immixes in a preexisting dual relationship can take on the figure of an intruder just as well as of a conciliator. In every case, through the intervention of the third party, each agent becomes a potential mediator between the two others. Each of them can either bind or separate. The presence of three agents can potentially pit a majority against a minority. The combinatorial arrangement of the relationships becomes complex and fluctuating. Simmel proposes a kind of typology of those triangulations, based on three main figures: mediator, spectator, and divider. The first is the figure of the impartial judge, an external character uninvolved in the dual relationship he is led to manage (because of his recognized personal charisma, respected public visibility, or required institutional function). History presents innumerable examples of those mediations provided by external characters to conflicting parties. The second figure of the third party is what Simmel calls *Tertius gaudens*: literally, the profiting third party, who, without interfering, benefits from a conflict between two competing individuals or groups. This profiting spectator takes great care to keep at an even distance from the opponents, to display passive neutrality, to show benevolence toward both parties, and to avoid intervention. He is courted by both sides (as in the case of a small political party that reserves the privilege to lean toward one or the other of two larger parties). The final figure of the third party is very different: It is the divider who generates or activates a rivalry between two other agents, to be able to appear as a referee and to best control the situation, as expressed by the classical principle, "Divide and conquer." Simmel reminds us that this was one of the keys to the success of the Venetian Republic, whose diplomacy aimed through various means at creating conflicts between its competitors. He also gives the example of the Inca Empire, which split conquered tribes, subjecting each of them to two leaders and giving one leader a slight hierarchical superiority over the other so that they would be busy with internal quarrels instead of confronting their conqueror.

Simmel provides multiple analyses of such triangulation games, easily demonstrating the decisive social function of the figure of the third party. Yet he missed one of those functions, no less crucial: the *witness*. This character plays a central part in legal procedures, counterbalancing the other triad formed by the two parties involved and the judge. The witness is he who has observed, and who knows. Between the defendant and the plaintiff, he is supposed to be the spokesperson for the facts. He may have misobserved or misheard those facts, and other witnesses may then contradict him. What matters is that, in interpersonal conflicts, physical events and observable facts are granted special consideration. This crucial role of the witness intervenes within the framework of an institutionalized legal system and of complex procedures aiming at establishing the truth. Not only is his function symmetrical to that of the judge, but it is inseparable from it. That Simmel omitted it in his typology is not a trivial fact.[2] It is related to other problems with his approach, which will soon become apparent; let us mention a few of them.

First, what Simmel show us is not exactly the genesis of the social realm, in the sense of a process of *sociation*. His method consists instead of selecting exemplary cases of relationships sampled within existing society. Those cases make the functioning of these relationships explicit on the level of their agents, as in his study on solitude, which can be analyzed only as a phenomenon of isolation or separation within the group. This analysis does not introduce us to the next level, that of the dual relationship of which it discusses various cases; the same can be said of the relationship among three parties since even though Simmel shows how a third party intervenes in an existing binomial and changes its functioning, it does so at the level of events rather than as an intrinsic necessity. Simmel and Charles Sanders Peirce thus conceive of the triad in very different ways. For now let us just note that, contrary to what some have claimed, those two authors do not discuss the same thing. This probably has to do with the difficulty Simmel has of conceiving of a third party who is not an agent—with the status of a person—in the relationship. For him the third party is a character within a triangular interplay of roles; this presupposition precludes a reflection on that which—in the form of a symbol/thing or pact, and more generally of the law—can establish a positive or conflictual bond between two agents or groups. This is a limit of the pragmatic approach itself, which is ill-equipped to account for the institutional dimension of interactions. In addition, it is difficult for Simmel to distinguish intersubjective from specifically social relationships. He constantly shifts from one level to the other, as in his examples, which move without critical distinction from personal relationships to political or collective situations. All these questions will require a more in-depth discussion.

The Third Party as a Person—II: Levinas

In many ways shifting from Simmel to Emmanuel Levinas may seem a surprising or even odd choice. Those two authors do not use language in the same way, and their methodologies are not comparable. Generally, the requirement of sociological objectivity is not commensurable to the normative aim of ethics, all the more so when this normativity is pervaded by the sense of *commandment*. As does Simmel, Levinas explicitly raises the question of the third party in terms of a person. Paradoxically, at least at first glance, his approach gives us a better grasp than does Simmel's of the genesis of the relationship to the group.

It is surprising to observe how steadfastly Simmel resists the specifically institutional dimensions of social problems. In this he shares the intellectual concerns of an age marked by the discoveries of experimental psychology and psychiatry and, more generally, the importance newly given to individual experience. The highest expression of this focus is found in thinkers as diverse as Nietzsche and Bergson; in others it can lead to an empiricism Husserl opposed from the outset, and indefatigably attempted to dispel. If Simmel sometimes appears to give in to this tendency, it is probably because he does not "see" language—that is, he does not clearly see that the attitudes and practices of agents can be caught within formal networks of organization whose expressions they shape or influence. Thus in the case of marriage Simmel acknowledges, as a kind of secondary parameter, that the matrimonial institution guides the spouses' behavior within the dual relationship. He should have shown on the contrary that the existence of the institution changes everything and constitutes the underlying third party that regulates the dual relationship, even before the intervention of the figure of the child. But doing so required understanding and defining an institutional third party that can take on many names: the rule, the law, the symbol, language. The psychological approach acts as an obstacle to this understanding.

Levinas on the contrary belongs to a generation and a tradition well aware of this fundamental hold of the institutional dimension (language, justice, the work), even if he suggests rather than demonstrates it. This is apparent above all in the discreet but omnipresent influence of his reading of Husserl, Hegel, and Heidegger, but also philosophers of language and signs. Unlike Derrida and Ricoeur, Levinas did not write explicitly on those questions, yet they run across his entire work, mark its boundaries, or underlie it much more profoundly than it seems, as shown by his conception of the dimension of the third party—of which we will have to discuss certain limitations or obscurities.

The passages of *Totality and Infinity* and especially *Otherwise than Being* on the question of the third party have generated many debates. There has been less consideration of an earlier article, "The *I* and the Totality" (1953),[3] in which this question is explicitly raised and later developments are heralded; before discussing more recent writings we must reexamine this tightly written article. Levinas begins with the uniqueness of the Self, defined not by what distinguishes it from others within a generic whole, but by the fact that it is posited as unique in reference to itself. In this sense it does not involve a third party. This original self-reference determines the unique character of the relationship between the Self and the other, and prefigures the motif of the face that asserts the radical otherness and exteriority of the other. At this point two modes of being-together can be considered: the intimate society of love and friendship, and the society of others condensed in the figure of the *third party*. What is the difference between those two forms of societies? Levinas's response is not that of a sociologist, but of a moralist. His criterion may seem surprising; it has to do with the difference between offense and harm. In my relationship to the other, I am aware that an offense can be forgiven because it can be attributed to someone. My action remains contained within the relationship to the other; it does not extend into ramifications that escape my control. Compensation can therefore be provided for this action. But when my action generates effects that disseminate beyond my intention, then it belongs to a totality alien to me, and it may cause harm of which I am unaware; injustice is thus inflicted on others. This injustice can arise from the mere fact of my belonging to an intimate society: "Such a society consists of two people, I and thou. We are among ourselves. Third parties are excluded [. . .]. A third party listens, wounded, to the amorous dialogue."[4]

Here Levinas introduces a logic that pertains to the *work* and designates actions whose effects develop within an objectiveness that escapes the will of the agent.[5] Through my work—that is, through what I have done—I am capable of a wrongdoing unrelated to my intentions (these analyses inevitably bring to mind Hegel's discussion of the tragic figure in Chapter 7 of the *Phenomenology of the Spirit*). Once my work has been created it no longer belongs to me: "In this sense, every work is a failed act."[6] We are caught in a drama of which we are not the authors: "The social wrong is committed without my knowledge, with respect to a multiplicity of third parties whom I will never look at directly."[7] The possibility is thus always present of a conflict between the intimate society and the social totality of the third parties: "The intersubjective relation of love is not the beginning of society, but its negation."[8]

For Levinas the challenge consists of avoiding restricting the relationship to the other to the circle of intimacy. How can the face-to-face relationship be the founding moment of the unconditional call that arises from the other without reducing this face-to-face to a private encounter? Levinas aims at overcoming this difficulty through his conception of the human face. To say that the face "rends the sensible," that it escapes intentional aim and moves beyond all cognitive grasp, amounts to saying that it requires us infinitely beyond its own phenomenal existence. But then another difficulty arises: For the face to be the "locus" of the expression of infinity amounts to suspending the relationship to infinity to a sensory experience, even if this experience is immediately transcended. In any given face every face must appear, and the face must be present even when it does not appear. Universality (a term Levinas avoids) must therefore be immediately given not only in this appearance, but also in its possibility alone. The conception of the third party developed in *Totality and Infinity* satisfies this requirement. In *Otherwise than Being*, however, another inflection arises that testifies to a hesitation, or at least to a different way to articulate the connection of the Self to society.

Let us return to the formulation that sums up this articulation in *Totality and Infinity*: "The third party looks at me in the eyes of the Other."[9] This statement should be read along with the following sentence: "Language is Justice. It is not that there first would be the face, and then the being it manifests or expresses would concern himself with justice; the epiphany of the face qua face opens humanity."[10] We may wonder why the question of language unexpectedly intervenes here, and even more so why language is defined as justice. Without getting into the details of a complex demonstration, let us recall that for Levinas language—rather than the senses—is a means of access to the objectivity of the world ("The objectivity of the object and its signification comes from language.");[11] it is the condition of every symbolism ("Language is not one modality of symbolism; every symbolism refers already to language").[12] In language objectivity and truth come together. Such is also the world we share with others as ruled by justice. The infinity revealed in the face of the other radically transcends the realm of equal relationships. And yet there must be justice, and justice requires comparisons; it assesses, attributes, and distributes; it subjects humans to shared standards of evaluation. This is why to say that the third party watches us in the eyes of the other means that in facing every human face we face humankind itself, and above all that the third party is there— always already there—in every human face. Thus do we overcome the aporia that risked making unthinkable the simultaneity of the relationship to the other as a face and to society as a totality. Furthermore, if the third party appears to us in the face of others, then the equality that justice presupposes among us cannot be natural. It does not derive from our shared belonging to our species, but from the fraternity that every face "coming from beyond the world"[13] makes possible.

In *Otherwise than Being* Levinas returns to this relationship to the other and the third party from the perspective of their articulation in the human face. He takes up the question in a radical way, by reopening the tension between other and third party, or between proximity and justice. The intervention of the third party disrupts our relationship to the other; it forces us to a response that involves justice, not only because the third party watches us in the eyes of the other, but also because it is the other of the other ("What then are the other and the third party for one another?"),[14] and because we do not know how to account for the relationship that defines them ("What have they done to one another? Which passes before the other?").[15] We must divest ourselves from proximity, including in relation to the other, enter in the operation of comparison, and accept the logic of the system and even the simple visibility of human faces. The intervention of the third party is the intervention of reason in the relationship, the intervention of a reality principle, the *time* of "the reckoning of possibles, the comparison of incomparables."[16] Levinas states once again that the third party appears to us along with the other as if superimposed on it, or rather as necessarily included in it, and that this inclusion presents us with the possibility or emergence of human society as a fraternal community, but now he goes further: He understands the third party as embodying a different requirement: "In no way is justice a degradation of obsession, a degeneration of the for-the-other [. . .]. [J]ustice remains

justice only in a society where there is no distinction between those close
and those far off, but in which there also remains the impossibility of passing by the closest. The equality of all is borne by my inequality, the surplus
of my duties over my rights."[17]

Levinas praises Buber for asserting that the relationship to other humans—between I and Thou—is incommensurable to the relationship to
the world—between I and It. Between the world and others lies an abyss:
the abyss of infinity revealed by the face of the other. This does not mean
that we should ignore the existence of the world—the realm of immanence:
There is a time for knowledge as an intentional relationship; there is a
realm of need (the economy; the dwelling). The world has not disappeared.
But when we face the gaze of the other, the world remains in the background; ontology comes after ethics. Yet at the same time that we live with
others we also live among things—whether natural or artificial. There is
the third party as person and also the third party that is the world: he/she,
and he/it. How should we understand *it*? Is it the world to be known and
transformed? It certainly is, but this is not all that it is. Levinas seems to
ignore that the things of the world cannot be reduced to objects of knowledge and means of subsistence, but that they are also symbols of relationships. It is on this point that his view is the least convincing. In the alliance
between groups as in any interpersonal relationship, the bond is nurtured
by goods, as the ceremonial gift shows us. It is not enough to say that the
mirror-like face-to-face of lovers is transcended through the subjection to
infinity that the face of the other requires. The relationship between the
self and the other includes the world, invokes it, and is expressed through
it, but it does not do so in the mode of a mediation that in the end gives way
to the terms I-you. The third party as "it" includes more than itself: The
thing *testifies* to the person who commits him/herself; it can represent the
subject; this testimony is called symbol. What we give through the thing
we give is always ourselves. The reciprocal bond always has the structure of
a symbolism. Let us return to the foundational relationship between I and
you, which every language invents in various forms.

The Grammatical Persons—I-You and the Absent Party: A Linguistic Approach to the Third Party with Benveniste and Beyond

Through surprisingly diverse and subtle modalities that involve the use of
appropriate markers, every language deals with and resolves the problem
of the designation of the self by the speaker, at the same time as the designation of the addressee and of any being—whether personal or not—

outside their relationship but implied by it. Language—any language—is always and everywhere capable of taking charge of the dual relationship between the speakers, as well as of the third element (the topic of which they speak), an element present in the linguistic exchange through a variety of markers, even if this element is not explicitly discussed. Languages provide a complex and complete set of evidence to the logic that underlies the speech relationship, inseparable from a realm where other speakers are also speaking and objects or a world in general also exist, which can be discussed and constitute the background or horizon of speech itself. We must understand what language teaches us.

In its chapter on verbs, every grammar book describes three persons—singular and plural—as if they formed a simple and uniform distribution—as if all those grammatical entities had similar statuses. Yet we sense, for example, that a question such as "Who are you?" belongs to an entirely different mode of speech than does a question such as "Who is he?" or "Who is that other one?" Why is there such a considerable difference between those questions? After all, at first glance the only shift involved is from the second to the third person. But this apparently trivial shift has crucial ontological implications; the question, "Who is that other one?" is stated from the position of any curious observer seeking information, or of those people inquisitive by nature—and by occupation—who are judges, scientists, historians, detectives, and other professional investigators. The questioner gives way to what he/she is questioning (even if his/her position is clearly marked by the demonstrative); he/she keeps at a distance from his/her object; he/she aims at creating a truth recognized by and acceptable to peers capable of verifying the validity of the research procedure and of accessing documents available to other investigators. This mode of objectivity and verification belongs to what is designated as the "third person," which some grammarians call "nonperson." The question, "Who are you?," on the contrary, can be asked only by "me." True, anyone can take on the position of the "I" who asks the question. but the problem lies elsewhere. The question, "Who are you?" brings about a breech in language through which *the very existence* of the questioner and of the addressee emerge. A shift has occurred from one level to another and even from one realm to another. This shift is powerful evidence, present explicitly or implicitly in every language; it probably means that the relationship between "I" and "you" exists only in *action*, that it is a relationship of *reciprocity*, and that it commits speaker and addressee through a kind of pact, be it an implicit one. What is the nature of this pact? Only one answer can be given: It is a pact that involves the very fact of an inseparable bond, but a bond *between separate and separable beings*. I am, and therefore you are, but I am not you—or conversely, you are, and therefore I am, but you are not me. Our bond exists only through the decision of an *alliance* included in the relationship between "I" and "you." This face-to-face immediately involves something else: the other, outside both of us, also *is*. What is this other? It encompasses not only all *those* who are neither me nor you, but also everything *that* is not us and among which we exist. Each of us exists for the other because he/she exists through the other outside of us—or rather, *between* us: The other person who watches us or intervenes, or the thing that we are watching or exchanging. Furthermore, we must accept that we have no direct access to each other, but that we can *testify* to our reciprocal commitment in two different ways: first by proclaiming it before the *third-party* agent who can be witness to it, and second through the things that we give each other in the gesture of alliance as tokens of our very being.

What can language teach us on this point? Since childhood—that is, since we have learned to conjugate verbs—we believe that it goes without saying that every language has three types of grammatical persons, of which "I" is the first, "you," the second, and "he/she," the third. We also believe that their distribution is relatively universal in spite of the diversity of the circumstances in which they are used and of the multiplicity of existing languages. We are thus surprised to learn from linguists that this tripartition is an illusion, and that only the first two persons ("I" and "you" in the standard classification) deserve their names, whereas what we—at least we Westerners—usually designate as the "third person" is not actually a person. Arab grammarians apparently had the most accurate sense of this point, and chose to call the first person ("I"), "the speaker," the second, "the addressee," and the third, "the absent"—since the latter position is not situated on the same level as the other two. This is what Émile Benveniste underlines in several seminal articles[18] that can guide our understanding of the linguistic grounding of the relationship of reciprocity.

To better situate the stakes of this distribution, let us attempt to distinguish the ontological status of grammatical subjects from their relational or social status.

Ontological Status: Benveniste notes that in the Western tradition— probably for reasons associated with a metaphysical worldview well-established since classical Greece—a confusion has developed between person and grammatical subject; hence the promotion by grammarians of a "third person," in line with the other two. This assumed continuity is misguided.

Let us consider the "I-you" binomial. The word "I" can be uttered only by someone in the process of speaking: "I" refers to the speaker at the moment when he/she is speaking (whether in ordinary life, reported speech, or fictional writing). "I" is thus *self*-referential: "I" immediately constitutes a proclamation of and attestation to the existence of the speaker. It is also an attestation of subjectivity that signals the speech-act position of the speaker as unique. It is I and no one else who is speaking or acting: "The form of *I* has no linguistic existence except in the act of speaking in which it is uttered," Benveniste writes.[19] "*I* is 'the individual who utters the present instance of discourse containing the linguistic instance *I*.'"[20] In other words, the term "I" is the locus of a coincidence between speech act and existence. This is also true of the word "you," whose definition is conversely "the 'individual spoken to in the present instance of discourse containing the linguistic instance *you*.'"[21] You and no one else are the person I am addressing. Furthermore, the relationship between "I" and "you" is such that the "you" I am addressing is also an "I" for whom I am a "you": Even if the relationship between "I" and "you" is from the outset a relationship of perspective from "I" on "you," it entails as a principle the *reversibility* from "you" into "I" of the person I am addressing and who, by definition, can reply to me. In other words, is called *grammatical person* he/she and only he/she is recognized capable of this proclamation and reply. "I" and "you" can exist only in the speech *act*. Hence the various space and time deictics associated with those pronouns: "here," "now," "yesterday," and "tomorrow," which refer to a speech act, whereas when using the "third person" we will say, "in the same place," "at the same time," "the day before," "the day after." The words "I" and "you" belong exclusively to the *present* of the speech act, and in the view of linguists this is what gives them the status of *persons*. This is the path through which linguistic analysis leads to pragmatics in the form of an analysis of speech acts (*pragmata*).

But the same is not true of "he/she," which is also a grammatical subject, but one that does not constitute a "third person." A "person" exists only through the *self*-referential postulation of existence implied by the speech act. "He/she" is a grammatical subject whose *tertiary position* designates not only any human as absent from the relationship between "I" and "you," but also nonhumans, whether animals or things. This is noticeable in many languages, Benveniste notes, through the absence or presence of a verb ending (such as "s" in English: *I/you do*, but *he/she does*). This is not a depersonalization, but merely the positive marker of that which is not a person in grammatical terms. It involves a process in which the presence of an agent may be identified or not. Thus, in Latin *volat avis* should not be translated as, "the bird is flying," but, literally, as, "it is flying, the bird." Benveniste notes that this tertiary form can contaminate everything that is not "I," and even affect "you," giving it a depersonalized value outside the "I-you" binomial, as when "you" means "one"; this is true of any generalizing statement such as "If you want peace, prepare for war," or "For a dollar you can't get anything anymore." This use of you in the sense of "one" is observed in many languages, and it can be reversed, as in French *Comment va-t-on?* [How is one?], meaning *Comment allez-vous?* [How are you?]. Those variations signal that the position of "you" in the speech act is capable of transpositions that are denied to the first person, whose anchoring function resists every rhetorical manipulation.

Relational Status: Subjectivity and Polarity. The discussion above makes it possible to identify the specificity of the relationship between "I" and "you" and to bring to the fore the referential character—or rather the perspective position—of "I." "I" always signals the speaker, while "you" always signals the addressee. There is a "you" for and only for an "I," signaling and continually proclaiming the *position of subjectivity* par excellence of "I," and therefore its preeminence over "you." Benveniste sums this up as follows: "One could thus define *you* as the *non-subjective person*, in contrast to the *subjective person* that *I* represents; and these two *persons* are together opposed to the *non-person* form (= he)."[22] From this perspective plural forms are interesting: "we" does not designate "I" with added plurality, Benveniste writes, but an "amplified I" (also called "complex I")—that is, a speaker who takes on the position of subjectivity on behalf of a group of persons, whether inclusively—"I and you"—or exclusively—"I and they." The echo of this "amplified I" can be heard in the royal "We" and the rhetorical "we" of authors, or, more rarely, in the statements of communities of persons that form single entities, as in the famous "We the people" of the Declaration of Independence of the United States (let us note that the word "people" is used only in the plural). By the same logic "you" can become a courteous form (so much so that in English this form has prevailed as a substitute for "thou," which has disappeared in ordinary usage).

We still need to examine more in depth the nature of the "I-you" pair and specify its unique relational status. To say that "I" is an act that necessarily entails "you" as addressee means that "I-you" forms an indivisible entity, which Benveniste defines as pertaining to a fundamental *polarity*, condition of any process of communication: "It is a polarity, moreover, very peculiar in itself, as it offers a kind of opposition whose equivalent is found nowhere else outside of language."[23] This polarity does not amount to equality and symmetry, since "I" remains the point of view that gives "you" its position. The two persons are connected in a mode of integral reciprocity, since "you" is inevitably reversed into "I" in the reply, which conversely turns the original "I" into "you." To say "I" is therefore to recognize from the outset this reversibility of subjectivity: "Consciousness of self is only possible if it is experienced by contrast. I use *I* only when I am speaking to someone who will be *you* in my address. It is this condition of dialogue that is constitutive of *person*, for if implies that reciprocally *I* becomes *you* in the address of the one who in his turn designates himself as *I*."[24] Let us add that any strong reciprocity presupposes a relationship of *reply*, an alternation of the positions in the speech act or in action, and therefore an unpredictable successiveness, and thus an open temporality, which is evidence to the freedom of those engaged in communication. This helps us better understand Benveniste's assertion that in the speech act the entirety of language as a system is appropriated by the speaker and *subjectivized as speech* addressed to an addressee: "Language is so organized that it permits each speaker to *appropriate to himself* an entire language by designating himself as *I*."[25]

The Absent, the Third Party, and the Others. Benveniste's analyses are highly productive, and they retain all their relevance. They strangely underplay, however, this "third person" that is not a true person. Clearly, the author's entire theoretical effort aims at the establishment of a linguistics of discourse. His interest is focused on the operators of transformation of the linguistic system into an act of the speaking subject—that which in a statement creates the emergence of the speech act. Without this position of subjectivity, language would simply not be possible: "A language without the expression of person cannot be imagined."[26] This cannot be denied. But we must immediately add that this primordial subjective position, inseparable from its polarity with "you," is also—though in a different way—inseparable from the position of the third party: he or she, or that. It is true that none of the so-called third-person pronouns are reflexive or self-referential. They serve above all as substitutes for various elements of the statement. They are devoid of the speech-act markers specific to discourse. But that is because they fill a very different and essential function: to provide the indices of language as repertory, combinatory, and objective process in the formation of sentences. Benveniste appears to see in them only an ancillary function with a very limited reason for being that must give way to the position of subjectivity. This contempt is surprising, and it has often been noticed. We must reinstate the rights of this almost-excluded third party. Its importance is shown with perfect clarity by the expression par excellence of the position of "I" in the speech act: the acts of language performed by so-called *performative* verbs.

This particular form of speech acts was first described by John Austin,[27] and later explored further by John Searle[28] and many others.[29] They are first-person statements—involving only a certain number of verbs—in which the speech act itself performs the very action it designates. The exemplary case is that of formulations such as, "I swear," "I promise," or "I make the commitment." Those statements display in all its fullness the function of "I," which is to testify to the being of the speaker. *To testify* means to put oneself forth as witness to oneself, as being he or she who is here and now committed to and by what he or she says. Committed to whom? By necessity, committed above all to "you" in the exchange; bound to the being—whether individual or group—who is the addressee of the statement. But is this all there is? At this point the question of the third party arises, which Benveniste deals with only incidentally; we believe, on the contrary, that it is crucial.

In the speech act associated with certain formulations, "I" am committed not only *to* "you," but also *before* others who are witnesses to the oath or promise, situated in the specific position of *third party*, and who must be understood as being both the public and the voice of the objective world. In speech acts the grammatical bond is transcended into a social bond and a bond with the world. Benveniste pays little attention to the social conditions of validity of the speech acts he gives as examples. Yet Austin (in his book's sixth study) clearly underlines the fact that such an act presupposes not only a particular status of the speaker and addressee, but also the public before whom the commitment is made, whether directly or not. It should also be mentioned—and this appears to have been ignored—that the object (or motivation) of the commitment must also be legitimate. To sum up, the speaker must be in the statutory position of having to swear; the other party must have a reason to be involved (whether as direct beneficiary or representative of an institution); and the public must be involved as a community interested in the commitment between the parties (whether marriage, trial, fight, or contract). Finally, the goal—the object of the commitment—must be acceptable to and have an importance recognized by all (one cannot solemnly and legally commit to not be absent-minded, but one can commit to provide a specific benefit in a time and place agreed upon). It is thus clear that performative verbs, in which the position of subjectivity takes on its highest expression and exceptional character, are precisely those that most strongly call on the third-party elements of the witness (the community of "them") and of the theme or object ("that") of the speaker's commitment.

This kind of speech act powerfully exhibits the institutional bond (which can be called political in the sense of the *politeia*), in that the "I-you" binomial appears as a *pact* where language displays its collective structure and society its nature as an implicit convention, an alliance accepted among subjects capable of free choice. The statement "We the People" remains the paradigmatic formulation of this pact. Performative statements bring us to an experiential field where speech act and social action become one. But beyond the assembly of the witnesses capable of testifying to the pact, underlying every linguistic relationship, at the same time invisible and always already there, lies the base of reality that preexists every exchange: the world itself, present as third party in the speakers' commitment, including in their very bodies, voices, and existence. This anchoring that precedes every speech and every exchange is expressed from the outset by the term "there" in "there is." Beyond grammatical persons and nonpersons, we must now explore this figure of the third party.

The Impersonal Third Party—I: Institution, Law, and Symbolism

The linguistic approach, with and beyond Benveniste, has made obvious to us the existence of the third-party element in the form of the grammatical nonperson or, more broadly, of the missing element in the "I-you" relationship. This *absent* element is nevertheless the active subject of a verb, and as a social being it remains a personal third party. On the contrary, the third-party element appears clearly in its impersonal reality through the markers—such as the various deictics (or demonstratives)—that designate the environment of reference of the speech exchange. To presuppose the existence of this environment in an undetermined way, however, is not sufficient: It is not merely the world in general, or the social context already in place. It precedes us and makes us feel its presence in the language whose rules we are using. It is this aspect of a regulated order, which mediates our interpersonal relationships and to which we belong from the outset through words we utter, that we must better understand.

Any relationship of interlocution is established and develops within the element of language; language precedes and carries us in any face-to-face exchange, even a silent one. Only within language can we see, encounter, and recognize one another. Language is within us just as we are within it. We are and remain speaking beings even in our most immediate and sensory life—not because we need words to feel or to recognize one another, but because the differentiating and ordering power of language has constituted us even in the sensory dimension of our beings. We are thus from the outset within the institution: within a system of sign ordering that is the condition that makes it possible for us to communicate and understand one another through those signs. Let us consider the demonstration Edmond Ortigues presents in *Le Discours et le symbole*.[30]

What makes his approach interesting is the way he brings to the fore a specifically symbolic level in the constitution of any language. Since Ferdinand de Saussure, the distinction identified within the sign between signifier and signified has been part of the canonical results of linguistics. More precisely, the sign is constituted by two inseparable *orders of relationships*: sensory-signifier relationships and intelligible-signified relationships. Those are the orders, in the sense of articulated sets, that make it possible for a word to be recognized and understood; its meaning does not exist in isolation. In addition, the association between a sign and the thing (whether physical or nonphysical) of which it is the sign is not necessary (the same can be said of various synonyms and across different languages). Following Ferdinand de Saussure this has been called the "arbitrariness of the sign"—a formulation often misunderstood. It would be better to call it the contingent character of the sign (or its unmotivated character, to use Benveniste's words), or, better yet, its conventional dimension—provided that we understand "convention" not as a conscious decision of the speakers aiming at facilitating exchanges, but as an implicit pact, a system of rules inherent in language as such. Those rules are themselves underlain by networks of differences, such as those that make the phonological recognition of words possible. Saussure compares them to values, in the mode of currency units horizontally equivalent to various amounts of the same level (or to different currencies) and vertically exchangeable for various goods. Ortigues calls this system of differences "symbolic" in the literal sense of the *symbolon*, a pottery shard that, in classical traditions, contracting parties used to break into two, with each party keeping a half that was capable of matching exclusively the other half and thus testifying to the agreement. Every symbolism implicitly amounts to a pact of this nature. Any system that establishes differences—such as the system of phonemes for speakers of the same language—that are constitutive of an order recognizable by a group is a form of symbolism, at the same time instrument of and witness to an agreement. Hence the following definition: "Symbols are distinctive values that can be contrasted with one another and whose potentialities for

meaningful combinations testify to a rule of exchanges or mutual obligations: your law shall be my law."[31] The author expands this as follows:

> In general terms, symbols are the constitutive materials of a linguistic
> convention, a social pact, and a guarantee of mutual recognition among
> free subjects. Symbols are the founding elements of a language, con-
> sidered in their interaction to one another as constitutive of a system
> of communication or alliance, a law of reciprocity among subjects.
> Whereas signs are the union of a signifier and a signified, symbols initi-
> ate a relation between a signifier and other signifiers. Whereas signs
> point to a signified that belongs to an order different from that of the
> signifier, symbols belong to an order of signifying values that presup-
> poses itself in its radical alterity to any given reality.[32]

What is remarkable about this definition is that it is applicable to purely
formal symbols (those of logics or mathematics) as well as traditional symbols. First, with respect to the linguistic elements that belong to the category of symbols—that is, the signifiers: "Every sign is necessarily com-
posed of symbols in the sense that, to become a specific sign that refers
to something outside language, it must first belong to a linguistic system,
be endowed with a value within language such that every element can be
contrasted and combinable with others according to rules."[33] This is why,
according to Ortigues, the *values* Saussure discusses must be understood
as symbols. Thus, "A phoneme is a symbol. . . . We will call symbols the
formative elements of language in the sense that they are constitutive of
the linguistic convention, that is, the possibility to speak to someone."[34]
The recognition of this symbolic dimension internal to the linguistic sign
brings up three sets of considerations.

First, it can be claimed that this symbolic level internal to language,
which constitutes language as a system and involves that which in language
itself can be described as a system of common values, is also what makes
language a *convention*. True, this convention is implicit, but it is nevertheless real in that it makes it possible for every speaker to recognize the
words uttered, grasp their articulations, and correctly apply the rules of expression necessary to form sentences. This symbolic level has no meaning
in and of itself; it is the condition of the emergence and consistency of any
meaning and of the possibility of connecting sentences to form a discourse;
it constitutes a system of differences that form an order. This order *displays
itself*, or, in other words, "Whereas signs express, symbols testify, and they
permanently testify to the structure of language as such."[35] Symbols are

above all operators,[36] and their specific operation consists of making form and meaning inseparable. It is this ability that makes them capable of constituting a convention in a more elaborate sense: an organized set of elements that makes it possible for the members of a group not only to agree on what is said, but also to recognize one another. The ordering that guarantees this agreement occurs spontaneously at the phonetic level. It becomes more complex in the implementation of grammatical rules and the formation of discourse. It forms among speakers the system of linguistic differentiation and the environment of public exchange that underlies their speech, of which it constitutes the law. At the same time common ground and set of norms, it is always already there, as a convention that precedes speech and makes it both possible and recognizable—nothing more, but nothing less. It thus acts as a third party in any linguistic relationship, and it makes it possible.

Second, this symbolic level also constitutes a system of *communication*. As an arrangement of differential elements, it forms a code internal to language that founds the possibility to "speak to someone," the precondition to "speaking about something." This structure of linguistic exchange opens the way to the structure of referential speech; the system of differences gives access to reference. But those two structures are interdependent: The dialogue between the speakers is conceivable only because of that which in language precedes them, calls on them, and positions them as parties in a linguistic exchange.

Finally, this symbolic structure internal to language makes it possible for the Self to return to itself through *reflexivity*. Discourse can perform this return by designating what it states. It is because, on the level of signifiers, the question of meaning is not relevant—forms do not mean, they perform—that on the level of the sentence (and therefore potentially the level of discourse) meaning can emerge as something other than form. Without this formal differentiation internal to signs, first-person speech acts would not be possible. Speech thus includes a third-party element carried by language as a semiotic system; this element is the condition of possibility of speech as a subjective semantic process.

The approach to language as symbolism that Ortigues proposes makes it possible for us to return to Peirce's triad, which we have already encountered twice (in Chapters 2 and 7). Pierce's formulation includes an element that we need to examine: In contrast to the dyad, locus of a causal relationship between two logical subjects (for example, Cain kills Abel), the triad reveals a relationship among three logical subjects (for example, A gives B to C) that forms an inseparable unit: A giver presupposes a recipient and a thing given. This is an internal relationship with an open range of instantiations: A teacher presupposes a student and an object of learning, etc. This first meaning involves a law in the sense of a necessary relationship among the terms involved—that is, a sense similar to the one that applies to the natural world, where the relationship is predictable: One term cannot exist without the two others. In some formulations, however, instead of writing, "according to a law," Peirce writes, "according to *Law*."[37] Furthermore, through the giving of thing B to C, C becomes the *legal* owner of B. This is a clear reference to civil law, which preexists the relationship between the parties and makes the exchange possible by conferring on them a status; furthermore, this law guarantees the personal difference and therefore the ontological otherness between A and C: Thing B has really moved from one owner to another. The triad therefore refers to the law in the dual sense of the word (as Montesquieu reminds us); it expresses both the nature of things and the conventions humans give themselves. The relationship between the agents emerges and is even possible only in the context of this order of the law, presupposed and reactivated every time. Furthermore, to call a relationship of the type "A gives B to C" a triad amounts to granting comparable statuses to those three terms, posited as logical subjects. In a way, each term is for the two others in the position of a third party—even though, obviously, only the agents are endowed with intentionality.

This conception of the triad is very different from that of Simmel, for whom, as for all sociological theorists (such as Goffman),[38] the third party is another agent. Contemporary research on forms of joint attention and triangular cooperation demonstrate the fertility of this figure of the third party in action.[39] These analyses remain within the category of the personal third party. But a reexamination of Benveniste's analysis of the pronouns and the question of symbolism according to Ortigues makes it possible to bring to the fore the impersonal third party and situate its importance. Should we thus separate those two categories of the third party? Is one category conceivable without the other? Are there not situations where those two models obviously intervene at the same time? This could be precisely the case of the procedures of matrimonial alliance observed in traditional societies.

THE CASE OF THE MATRIMONIAL ALLIANCE

Lévi-Strauss is undoubtedly among those who have given the question of alliance the importance it now has in kinship theories. His reexamination of the nature of exogamic relationships allowed him to identify its central operator: the prohibition of incest. Until his own work on this issue—starting with *The Elementary Structures of Kinship*—the question of filiation had dominated the discussion, especially in English-language anthropology, so much so that A. R. Radcliffe-Brown, one of the most famous authors in that field, claimed that the elementary structure of kinship consisted of a husband, his wife, and their children. This model, based on the biological fact of procreation, appeared guided by common sense. Lévi-Strauss calls into question this self-evident conclusion; first, because it can account neither for the universality of exogamic rules nor for the universality of the prohibition of incest. Lévi-Strauss decisively demonstrates that this prohibition is not primarily a negative interdiction on sexuality as such, but a positive requirement for reciprocity that, by obligating fathers to give away their daughters, or brothers their sisters, guarantees that the women of their own group will be available as wives to an allied group, which will reciprocate. This means that any marriage is above all a union between two groups (whether clans, lineages, moieties, etc.) through the wife given by one group and received by the other. Here the wife appears in the position of a third party, akin to position B in Peirce's triad (A gives B to C). True, the wife is a person; her position is nevertheless identical to the position of any being or good that mediates the relationship between two agents. In fact, the model Lévi-Strauss uses to explain the requirement of reciprocity that founds the prohibition of incest, and thus generates exogamic exchanges, is the model of ritual gift exchange as analyzed by Mauss.[40] More precisely, matrimonial alliance is the primordial and most accomplished form of gift exchange relationships as constituting a pact among groups. Lévi-Strauss thus writes that in this procedure the wife is "the supreme gift among those that can only be obtained in the form of reciprocal gifts."[41] The elementary structure of kinship is therefore not Radcliffe-Brown's biological nuclear family; it is defined instead as an *exchange according to a law* between group A and group C through wife B, which Lévi-Strauss formulates as follows: "We reduce the kinship structure to the simplest conceivable element, the atom of kinship, if I may say so, when we have a group consisting of a husband, a woman, a *representative of the group which has given the woman to the man*—since incest prohibitions make it impossible in all societies for the unit of kinship to consist of one family, it must always link two families, two consanguineous groups—and one offspring."[42] This structure involves a dual logic, both institutional and pragmatic. From the perspective of the system the wife is the object of the alliance, its symbol, the third-party element exchanged by the two groups. From this standpoint the wife personally occupies an impersonal position, but from the perspective of the husband and wife as individual agents, the union is interpersonal; it is made possible by the mediating third party: he who gives away the wife—very frequently, the wife's brother, who will become the maternal uncle of the future child. Let us now consider a new perspective: In addition to the relationships between adults committed in the alliance through the mediation of a third party who gives the wife, there is also the triad of the triangular relationship among the child and his/her parents, or among each of them and the maternal uncle. Although the attitudes of the participants are individual and vary based on the moods and specificities of the agents, those attitudes of trust or distance can be predicted depending on positions in the system of relationships. The "atom of kinship" involves both the triadic relationship according to Peirce and the triangular relationship according to Simmel.

To sum up, whether we consider the perspective of the institutions and the constraints of the system or the perspective of the agents, a purely dual relationship can be nothing more than an abstraction created by a theory alien to its object. The third party—understood both as the order of norms and the position of the *socius*—is always already present in any face-to-face. Our concept of the impersonal third party, however, needs to be broadened: It is not only an institutional system and an implicit order of rules, but also that which intervenes more consistently, and by which the exchange necessarily involves something from the world, as well as the world in general, even though the relationship appears at first glance as a face-to-face between the parties.

The Impersonal Third Party—II: The Thing, the Exchange, and the World

How do the things from the world intervene in the relationships among humans? What is their status? Do they have a mediating function? Can they stand for those who give or exchange them? Can they remain irrelevant? Do those things that circulate (gifts and commodities) share a third-party position similar to that of the things viewed above all as objects of knowledge or contemplation?

THE GOODS OFFERED AS SUBSTITUTES OF THE BRIDE

Let us return to the case of the matrimonial alliance. It can be conducted in a direct and simple form: One group gives a wife; at the same time, or soon afterward, the receiving group gives a wife in return. This is the so-called "limited" exchange. The configuration of the so-called "generalized" exchange is very different. Rather than two exogamic groups, it involves several groups on either side. As a reply to the gift of a wife, the husband's group gives a set of precious goods (depending on the society, they can be heads of cattle, manufactured objects, ceremonial weapons, finery, jewelry, or pieces of clothing). Those precious goods are guarantees offered to the giver of the wife; their function is to give him access at a later point, through those very goods, to a wife from one of the exogamic groups in his society. Those goods (which have often been inaccurately defined as the "price of the bride") have a very specific status: They represent at the same time the sister given and the future wife, of which they are the substitutes; they are therefore associated with prohibitions that place them outside any commercial system of exchange or ordinary consumption. As guarantees that a wife can later be obtained, they constitute a promise of life, and they physically represent the presence of the allied group in the receiving group. Lévi-Strauss gives an elegant example: Among the Thonga, a Bantu population from South Africa, between the husband (Ego) and the wife of his wife's brother—called Great Monkōnwana—an extremely respectful or even tense relationship exists. To account for this, observers have proposed various hypotheses, including the idea that the Great Monkōnwana is a presumptive mother-in-law. There is in fact a simple explanation based on the logic of reciprocity. The wife of the brother-in-law has been obtained through goods provided by Ego—cattle called *lobola* and associated with prohibitions; she is therefore in the exact position of Ego's sister. It is as if Ego had obtained his own wife as a countergift in exchange for his symbolic sister, the Great Monkōnwana. The natives call her "of his own flesh and blood"; this is why she is situated for Ego within the domain of the prohibition of incest, as are the products of *lobola* (milk and meat).

This example shows us in a particularly cogent way the relationship that exists between the parties involved in the gift exchange and the things exchanged; those things are always more than mere things. They can be called symbols, but only in the strongest sense of the word. They stand for the future wife. They are tokens of the parties involved, since they carry their very beings, their Selves. They testify to them; better yet, they are their substitutes over time. They ensure continuity between the human world and the broader world.

Within the space of gift exchange, the goods are guarantors of the bond. It is therefore not surprising that they play a crucial part in another form of agonistic exchange: the procedures of compensation that are part of vindicatory justice. A large number of ethnographic inquiries have helped us better understand how justice is exercised in traditional societies, especially those where no central power stands above the lineages or other kinship groups.[43] When a serious offense has been committed, compensation must be provided. In murder cases, justice can be carried out through an equivalent loss of life in the murderer's group. It is remarkable, however, that most societies have invented other forms of compensation—for example, by giving a wife to the victim's group, which will make it possible to engender a child with the value of a substitute of the victim. Very often the compensation offered is a set of goods identical to those given on the occasion of a wedding (demonstrating once again the analogy between gift exchange and vindicatory reparation). Those goods can thus have the value of a life, both by ensuring through the matrimonial alliance the regeneration of the group and by preserving through procedures of justice the equilibrium between the loss of a life and the return of another life.

But as soon as a monetary system emerges, this compensation tends to take the form of units of the circulating currency. A remarkable equivalence occurs between ancient symbolic goods and commercial currency, so much so that, with the development of urban cultures and systems of arbitrational justice, the sanction increasingly takes the form of a financial penalty. This shows a tendency to turn criminal debts into contractual debts, along with a transfer of the symbolic charge. This shift appears to sanction the power of an ever-more important mediation: money. Yet it would be wrong to presuppose a genealogy in which commercial relationships are the heirs to gift relationships. Those two types of exchange have always coexisted, primarily because they have profoundly different purposes. The aim of gift relationships is to generate reciprocal recognition, to create or renew the social bond; the goods thus exchanged have no economic purpose. The aim of commercial relationships, on the contrary, is utility: to ensure subsistence, in the same way that the purpose of the appropriation of goods is consummation and the preservation of physical life. This appears clearly in the circuits of exchange in the Trobriand Islands, already discussed above: The circuit of *kula* goods associated with prestige, honor, and festive prodigality is in no way related to *gimwali* exchanges, which aim at equivalence, private advantage, and ordinary subsistence.

Ceremonial exchanges show that goods can become symbols—tokens and substitutes of ourselves—in our relationships. The aim of the contractual worldview is to suspend this quality within commercial exchanges. Between those two modes of relationships and exchanges, areas of intersection or permutation exist: Precious goods can serve as currency in commercial exchanges, while currency can take on the status of a precious good in rituals.[44] In every case, though in different modes, the function of the impersonal third party is crucial, but this probably has to do also with the fact that, in a more essential and implicit way than in the mediation provided by various goods, the impersonal third party stands out against the background of our inaugural relationship to the world.

THE WORLD AS THIRD PARTY: INTERLOCUTION AND REFERENCE

To say that the world appears in the position of a third party entails pointing out the existence of the world with respect to a dual relationship: interlocution. The presence of the world is revealed in an exemplary way by every deictic form: demonstrative articles and pronouns (this, that, these, those), ostensive spatial and temporal adverbs (here, now). They are markers of reference that make it possible in every discourse to point to what is in question in the situation (or has just been stated). They thus necessarily presuppose a speaker and an addressee (the latter can be implicit or even virtual, as is the future reader of a written discourse, necessarily addressee of the writing). Any statement, no matter how detached it may seem from any situation of speech—when every trace of the speaker has been erased—thus remains engaged in interlocution, precisely because the virtual existence of an addressee cannot be eliminated. After the "I" of the speech act, demonstratives are the most obvious markers of the presence of the speaker in his/her speech; they presuppose a subjective perspective in that they stand out against a designated referent (whether it is the world in general, the environment, or a physical or mental object mentioned in the discussion). From this standpoint it can be said that the world always stands as a third party in interlocution, and that interlocution can take place only in reference to this world as third party. Whether this reference is explicit or not, interlocution is possible only as mediated by that which stands outside the dual relationship as such: There is no "I-you" without "he/she" or "that." This is the other in general, which marks the boundaries of the person; it is also, at the same time, the marker of a universality necessarily presupposed for interlocution to take place, to refer to an object; without this marker, interlocution is reduced to a specular circularity that amounts to madness. We must therefore return to this power of the referent.

As speech-act theories continually remind us against formalist deviations, to speak is to say something to someone about something. There is a speaker, an addressee, a statement, and an object or referent of discourse. To account for this structure, the extralinguistic element has often been called on, but this is an imprecise formulation. The topic of speech can generally be designated by the speakers as a physical or nonphysical element that belongs to the world. This exteriority is inseparable from the objectivity criterion, what makes the world a *common world*, a truth horizon of speech. It is a common world on at least three levels, which represent three degrees of increasing objectivity. First, the world is that which the speakers refer to simultaneously. Every reference is therefore a *coreference* in the dialogic sense of the word.[45] This coreference is marked by the various ostensive terms: Speaker and listeners refer to the same thing. There is shared reference about the situation. Second, it must be underlined that every speech includes an element of *publicity*. In the field of conversation, in the relationship of interlocution, the object referred to is necessarily public in the sense that its designation is subjected to shared rules of statement, accessible in principle to all speakers and identified by all of them as being the same. This public character can already be verified on the level of language, which can be understood only as a shared language. In this sense it can be claimed along with Ludwig Wittgenstein that there is no such thing as a private language; at most there are idiosyncratic uses of a shared language. Finally, we must consider the level where, beyond the world as shared world—the limited world of the situation designated by ostensive terms and object of coreference—reference is implied in its *universality*. It involves what is yet to come, and it extends to possible worlds. We can call "third party" this objective element necessarily present and continually referred to by the relationship of interlocution.[46]

We must recognize that *the third party* is a complex and even paradoxical concept. Although it is not a pronoun, it often takes on the value of a pronoun; it designates the other—whether personal or impersonal—according to a position. It has a reason for being only in relation to the dyad. It is thus not merely "the rest" or "the others." Its function in relation to the dyad is to bring objectivity—the objectivity of the world, of the law, or of an external agent. This objectivity exists on several levels: in the search for truth through deliberation subjected to contradictory arguments; in the choice of the just decision through the arbitration of the judge who decides among the witnesses and seeks to establish the facts; in the social distribution of rights and duties, which makes it possible to establish a balance among all the members of a society. The third party is thus not an impersonal "one"; it is not just anyone. It has a specific function: to situate the speakers and addressees relative to each other, and sometimes to decide among them. It is not a supplement added to a relationship, or even something that emerges from it; it is what makes the relationship possible.

Three Remarks in Conclusion

Oneself as Another. This phrase clearly echoes Ricoeur's work by the same title, which itself recalls Rimbaud's proclamation, "I is another." How should we understand here the term "other"? Probably not in the sense of the other as "you" who face me; in that case it would be easier to say: "Oneself as the other." This would situate us in the problematic of the alter ego, inappropriate to our discussion. In the same way, the statement "I is another" is not equivalent to "I am the other." It designates a broader and more enigmatic kind of otherness, although it does not exclude the other kind. This otherness present in me is the element from the world that can remain alien to me, while it nevertheless constitutes me, making me appear to others as one body among bodies, publicly identifiable and inseparable from the person defined by a civil status, at the same time subjected to obligations and recognized in his/her rights. On an even more physical level, I am a body that is visible and that can be catalogued and studied by the biological and medical sciences: a body as object, dealt with as such by those who observe or treat it. And yet this is the same body that is "my body," inseparable from my existence and identity. As alien as are the elements that constitute it as an object, it still remains mine, made subjective by the certainty that it belongs to me. This element of otherness carried by my body, this strangeness that, through my body, inhabits me, could be called on a first level "the third party within oneself"—present within oneself—bound to any subjectivity as being the presence of the world, not in the mode of a juxtaposition, but integrated to subjectivity itself. This is what Maurice Merleau-Ponty calls *chiasm*—or flesh. This subjective objectivity is also, on a second level, what makes the act of self-designation possible to me: the reflexive return from the element of otherness that allows me to designate myself to myself, and thus to testify to my own existence and freedom. I am thus to myself the third party that testifies that I exist and that I act, but it also testifies to others, within the space of the pact—the third level—to what I am and what I do. The third party in me meets the third party outside me in all three of these modes: the world, the law, and the other as person.

Autre and *autrui*: Whereas most European languages have only one term—other; *altro*; *otro*; *anderer*—the French language has the advantage of having those two terms, *autre* and *autrui*. This advantage has a cost: uncertainty as to the use of *l'autre*—a term that, just as well as another human being, can designate any element external to the speaker. Levinas makes no distinction between *autre* and *autrui*, or rather he alternates those words for merely stylistic reasons; what he designates is always the other human being that faces us. When he deals with the otherness of the world he always does so in a minor mode. *Autrui* (the other human) alone calls on me unconditionally; only he/she embodies the exteriority of *height* and summons me to answer. The world remains in the order of immanence, as object of knowledge, transformed by human labor, but also residence, object of enjoyment. In Levinas there is no becoming of a world of subjectivity. This becoming probably belongs to the Hegelian view; it is even what makes Hegel's thought novel. The spirit exists only by losing itself in its other, the alien object, by confronting the ordeal of the negative that deprives it of its pure inner essence, but in and through this ordeal the spirit gains the wealth of determinations of its opposite. This other is the element of the world, the otherness that calls on the concept of mediation. The assumption and absorption in the self of the otherness of the world makes the spirit emerge and appear in its objectivity as shared world. This is precisely what is missing in the frontal conflict between the consciousness of the Master and the Slave (literally, the "Servant"): Those two figures are in a face-to-face relationship, as subjectivities that view only each other as consciousness, while excluding the world, each of them demanding recognition from the other. Each consciousness lacks the recognition in the other of a third party, which alone opens the possibility of reciprocal recognition. Beyond Hegel the certainty arises that, for the other to be the other, the third party in him/her, which makes him/her flesh and blood, must call on the third party in me to make us enter a shared world. The other is broader than the other person alone. But only the other person, who calls on me in a face-to-face, makes the other appear as a third party, and turns otherness into subjectivity.

The Distributed Third Party: Everyone and Each of Us

As we noted, the third party is a term with an odd status. On the personal level it can designate "the others" in an indeterminate manner, as well as any agent outside the dyadic relationship (whether it involves speakers, parties to a contract, fighters, partners in a game, or couples of every kind). Those are figures of the personal third party. But on a more general level the third party is a position, a topological concept. Its originality lies in that it has relevance only in relation to two terms defined by their polarity. The question of the third party does not arise with respect to a multitude as such. The third party thus emerges only along with the dyad. It would be a mistake, however, to claim that it is generated by the dyad.[47] It is logically prior to the dyad. De facto the third party is always already there. The third-party position is a potentiality within every collectivity or plurality, because every plurality articulates antagonisms, dyads that presuppose a third party. From this perspective, as persons we are always potential third parties. The third party is at the same time *everyone* and *each one*. "Everyone" should not be understood here as "the others," a term close to the anonymous "they" of gossip. "Everyone" does not designate a multitude, but a qualified and countable plurality (as in "everyone agrees" or "everyone came"). In the same way, "each of us" specifically designates in the singular form each member of this plurality, presupposing a unique identity and personal responsibility for his/her actions. *Everyone* and *each one* are therefore the appropriate pronouns to designate the third party—a dual designation that perfectly indicates its status as distributed third party. These terms point to the third party as neutral arbiter (from *ne-utter*: neither one nor the other), an itinerant judge. *Everyone* and *each one* are pronouns lacking all ostensive markers, and thus capable to guarantee the objective distance of *delocution* (speaking about something). But this grammatically marked distance constitutes the external background, the reflexive level that provides the dyadic relationship with the means to assert itself in the speech act through the "I" that subjectivizes language and engages with a "You" by uttering a speech addressed to someone. But it does so with respect to the "something"—the referent—that comes under the jurisdiction of the third party.

As an old French saying states, "*Jamais deux sans trois*" (There is no two without three); this wisdom is more profound than generally believed. The statement can be understood as a logical requirement: The third party never occurs as a supplement or by accident; it does not intervene unexpectedly after a dyad (although its presence can surprise us because we had not realized it was already there); it is what makes the dyad possible. In the social realm dyadic relationships are a subset of the triadic relationships. This is why the bond of reciprocity always involves a witness, even if it is invisible, and develops in relation to something, even if only an idea. A pure dyad either falls into the specular fascination of the imaginary double or becomes a violent rivalry. The third party stands in-between: It is the law, a thing of the world, or an arbiter. It testifies for both parties to what separates and unites them. It makes possible both the face-to-face of recognition or rivalry and the gesture of reciprocity.

Postliminary Directions

At the close of this book we must return to the presuppositions that form the foundation of the approach I propose. Because I applied to the concept of the gift a critical reflection supported mostly on a confrontation with the concept of reciprocity, I may have given readers the impression that I was extolling the latter concept. This was not my aim—although it is true that, because the content of this notion is the object of a very wide-spread suspicion, an effort at reevaluation was required, which led me to a direct exposition of the misunderstandings or misinterpretations found in the works of many thinkers. In this attempt the results provided by social anthropology proved crucial in making it possible to seriously call into question the sometimes very loose way several authors use the relevant concepts. A more in-depth consideration remains to be conducted of the epistemic status of the cross-pollination between philosophy and anthropology that I have continually practiced in this book.

Thought without Concepts: Philosophy and Symbolic Processes

Let us begin with a dual observation on the phenomena we have discussed in relation to traditional gift exchanges: (1) those exchanges are always associated with precise rituals; and (2) they have no direct counterparts in our own societies. It might thus seem reasonable to view them as things of the past, or even vestiges of a bygone world, hence the following question: What theoretical interest can philosophers find in reexamining the materials of those ethnographic inquiries? Should they even consider at any length the effort at reflection developed by anthropologists on this question? If the answer is no, then what should be their attitude toward this legacy? The first temptation we must guard against is to view those practices as testimonies to archaic forms that have subsisted across time in our collective unconscious or in mental representations passed down to us. This kind of consideration is epistemologically weak. It presupposes an imaginary reserve, an exotic past preserved and capable of reemerging in certain occasions associated with intense social emotions. In the societies that practiced or still practice ritual gift procedures, there is nothing exotic about those procedures, no more than there was in the sacrificial procedures that so impress us. It is crucial to understand the function and meaning of those procedures; this leads us to the following questions: Why, in this form, are they today neither observed nor even possible? Can we identify the modern expression of that which situated them at the core of traditional societies? From the perspective of modern societies we must discuss traditional societies in the past tense, but today many populations in the process of entering modernity through new political institutions, market-based forms of production and exchange, rapid technological transformations, and above all education and access to globalized information still remain strongly attached to practices and rituals that have almost disappeared in the West.

Those facts force us to confront a dual question of transformation and transposition. In "Propositions I" we considered the problem in the following terms: Since the ceremonial gift is primarily a procedure of public reciprocal recognition among groups (a procedure of which the exogamic alliance is the most elaborate form), the difficulty lies in determining how this public recognition is expressed in our own societies, organized around a central power we now designate as the state. Our answer has been that on an institutional level this recognition is now provided and guaranteed by the law and the entirety of the political institutions; on a social and personal level, however, it continues to be expressed by all kinds of procedures or attitudes of reciprocity. A transformation (and therefore a displacement) and a transposition (and therefore a translation) has taken place. But to understand this we have had to keep from a pitfall that leads many authors to interpret ritual gift exchanges as a kind of still-awkward ancestor of trade, a benevolent form of transfer of goods profitable to both parties. We had to relinquish the notion of a "gift economy," usually understood in the sense of an archaic economy. It is not even appropriate to view ritual gift exchanges as generous exchanges of useful goods, since the latter exchanges belong to a different type of relationships. Bronislaw Malinowski thus calls "honorable barter" certain friendly forms of trade among neighbors; this barter tends to avoid simple profit and aims primarily at preserving trust. The solemn presents of the *kula* cycle, on the contrary, are not transfers of goods, but testimonies to a continually renewed pact: What is at stake is not commercial activity, however friendly, or even activities motivated by solidarity, but a political gesture of public agreement.

What can philosophy gain from this effort at a reexamination of anthropological data? Three things:

Understanding in a different way the stakes of the political, legal, and economic institutions of our own times (this is what I attempt to demonstrate in "Propositions I" above). In distant times and locations, the requirements of life in common have received and still receive comparable solutions, but in different modes. To grasp the meaning of those solutions it is important to resist the illusion of false resemblances. In the case of gift exchanges those illusions have to do with their apparent similarities with forms of commercial exchanges. In addition, the term "exchange" cannot be presupposed to designate primarily commercial exchange—this presupposition is inaccurate from a merely lexical perspective; it is even more so from the perspective of the history of the practices this term designates.

This reexamination also leads us to accept the fact of those transformations—which have continually occurred and constitute what we call history—without reducing them to directional and predictable evolutions. To keep to a familiar region of civilization—Europe—profound transformations have taken place from the gift practices of the Greeks of Homer's time, the Celts, the Germans, the Scandinavians, or the ancient Romans, to the public forms of social bonds that can be observed today in their descendants. The same can be said of other cultural regions. There is no doubt that the formation of kingdoms and empires, the emergence of cities, writing, new forms of knowledge, and technological evolutions have profoundly transformed the culture of ethnic groups and everywhere given rise to new institutions that share common features. Our Modernity has had to invent new solutions to ancient problems. This does not, however, make the institutions of our predecessors a few centuries or even two or three thousand years ago "archaic." Those institutions are in fact consistent sets of solutions provided under different conditions.

Finally, we must accept that the expressions of public life in traditional societies are primarily ruled by rituals—that is, complex symbolic systems that involve every aspect of life in common; not everything in those societies is ritualized (unless we—mistakenly—call rituals every set of passed-down habits), but the ritual is the most typical form of the institutionalization of social relationships, themselves inseparable from cosmological representations (whether religious or not). Like myths, rituals are intelligent systems that create order through the use of elements selected from the environment for their differential or contrastive value and combined according to implicit rules. Those systems are intelligent both in their internal functioning and in their ability to express the organization of the world perceived and of social relationships. They are systems of thought in action, which makes them highly interesting to philosophers. It is important for philosophers to grasp how forms of thought without concepts can exist. This is the case for all symbolic systems or systems that function as such: Meaning is immanent to the forms themselves and their arrangement; it does not stand out as the content of an utterance. It is not a representation, but a performance. This immanence of meaning to the form still exists for us in the case of works of art, games practiced according to rules, technical systems, logical and mathematical constructions, and computer software. The same can be said of anything that constitutes a work.

The locus of the problem is therefore the discrepancy between this thought in action at play in symbolisms and artifacts, and the thought that examines itself in theoretical discourse. In its most distanced expressions, theoretical discourse considers the world in a naturalistic mode, as organized according to functional rationality. It subjects the world to the universality of measurement and calculus. On the contrary, the data brought to the fore by ethnographic inquiry remains alien to us in the sense that, in those data, forms of thought and institutions are configured through local symbolisms whose logic we must reconstruct and exhibit.

It is precisely this task that is fertile for philosophy. What the traditional thought systems express through those symbolisms does not inform us about what things were "at the beginning." The reason for being of given elements is not locked within a moment in time from which consequences then unfold. Those systems let us see a different expression of a problem we are still confronting in new forms. Their authority does not lie in their anteriority; what gives us food for thought is their difference. This is why it is important to avoid masking this difference behind a resemblance that gives us the illusion we have captured their meaning. The ritual gift does resemble an exchange or transfer of goods, but if we hastily focus on this analogy to develop its interpretation, chances are we will understand nothing about it. The case of sacrifice is just as telling. Because sacrifice appears as a bloody immolation, we are tempted to see it in every murder, execution, or violent destruction—an easy analogy and a very widespread cliché. Every rigorous inquiry on sacrificial practices lead us to the following observation: Sacrifice always involves domestic animals (and some animals rather than others); it is related to domestication and the power over life that domestication expresses. The analysis of sacrificial symbolisms shows that in the agro-pastoral world that comes after the world of hunter-gatherers (where this ritual does not exist), what matters most is at play in a different kind of negotiation with the spirits or deities: Domestication appears primarily as an encroachment on their prerogatives on the reproduction of life. This is why the agro-pastoral world is both indebted to them with respect to life and faced with the necessity to express and confirm a new mastery over the order of things. Sacrifice then becomes a way to signal union and separation, restore the life taken, rebalance a new relationship to the animal world, guarantee access to meat, and at the same time ward off the cannibalistic threat involved in eating an animal that has become close; its immolation makes it other, sending it into the world beyond and making its flesh edible in this world. A reversal of signs occurs along with a transformation of substances. The question is thus to understand the kind of thought the various forms of sacrifice display, the specific form of logic through which their symbolisms work, and the solutions at which they aim. Through displacement and transposition—and not through causal generation—we can then ask how similar questions—relationships to the environment and to life—are expressed and resolved (or attempted to be resolved) in our own conceptual and technological world. This is only one example, whose approach can be generalized, and which leads us to accept that there is no such thing as a repressed archaic element or things hidden since the foundation of the world. There is no teleological continuum; there is time, history, transformations, transposition—that is, continual processes of translation at work in the forms themselves, in response to new conditions that develop in an environment at the same time natural, technological, and social.

To account for rituals and symbolisms is therefore to read on the very level of symbolic systems a thought "without concepts" that is nevertheless a thought to the fullest extent. The same is true of our relationship to any work of art, whether musical piece, painting, sculpture, poem, or narrative. Thought is displayed from the outset in their arrangements, structures, and transformations. This is the type of thought at play in everyday life, which we call a "practice." The task of philosophy is therefore to make things explicit before claiming to explain them; to give a voice to what appears and to what is done.[1] Thus, in the case of the gift, what we must show is not how generous gestures repeat in a more moral and individual form rituals of gift exchange deemed archaic, but how what was at the core of those rituals—the gesture of reciprocal acceptance and alliance—has been transposed into institutions that guarantee the principle-based recognition of every citizen—that is, a status guaranteed by the law and by a legal system that encompasses the new forms of production and exchange of goods.

The Gift from No One

This clarification should encourage us to reexamine the entirety of the studies we have discussed. The dual direction we identified should now appear more clearly. In spite of differences in their relationship to Husserl (less significant in their relationship to Heidegger), in the heirs to phenomenology a kind of fundamental oblativity of the world emerges through the concept of gift and givenness. The phenomenon "gives itself," appearing to shift away from the neutrality of a process of appearance toward something akin to a gesture that refers to an original gift, or presupposes an unnamed generosity of which we are the beneficiaries.

This is the kind of radical oblativity Derrida continually presupposes— without stating it explicitly—when he calls into question the ritual gift as Mauss analyzes it. When Derrida posits that for a gift to truly exist, the giver must be unaware that he is giving and the recipient unaware that he is receiving, he leads us to the following question: Why should there be a gift in the first place? Derrida does not consider this, but he expresses his suspicion in the following recurrent clausule: "Du don, s'il y en a . . ." [Giving, if such a thing exists]. Why call on this indeterminate generality? It is as if another, more specific question—Who gives what, to whom, in what circumstances?—had to be dismissed because it takes us to the presuppositions of metaphysics (substance, causality, and finality). But why should the designation of a specific giver and recipient and of a recognizable gift constitute a suspicious philosophical choice? A gift cleansed of any relationship becomes a negative entity whose ontological status is in limbo since it is assumed to persist beyond the aporia that paralyzes its phenomenality. The only thing left is to proclaim along with Heidegger that there is a gift.[2] If the gift is another name for being, then this is a gift from no one—as well as a gift to no one. It is a pure oblativity that subsists in and of itself: "It gives." It is difficult to see how this approach could make it possible to comprehend the ritual gift of traditional societies, practiced among groups for specific reasons on specific occasions, using goods with a particular symbolic status. To talk of the gift in the singular and in general as if the complex relationships among groups could be reduced to a relationship between random individual subjects already operates an odd distancing from reality. To anthropologists this operation makes no sense; neither should it to philosophers.

It is as if the task of deconstruction finds itself fulfilled by the operation by which deconstruction exposes the metaphysical heritage that persists in the way concepts are used. This is a radical and healthy effort to reexamine discourse, forcing it to exhibit its genealogies and the presuppositions of categories deemed irreducible—healthy to the extent that it is capable to destabilize from within the instruments as well as the objects of knowledge. But while this effort is being conducted—and it needs to be forever taken up again—an effort at understanding must begin and be developed in detail through a rigorous questioning of the data. At best, the deconstruction stage can constitute the skeptical stage necessary to any advance in thought—and only to the extent that we continue the journey, aware of the direction where our movement take us. To proclaim that the gesture of giving can be consistent with the concept of gift (assuming that we know *what* the gift *must* be) only if this gesture escapes the giver and the recipient amounts to confessing that to discuss the gift is pointless. Maybe this confession should have been the starting point. This would have made it possible to discover an entirely different approach. *Es gibt* would then be adequately translated as "there is": Every thing is presented, and no other claim should be made. This self-evidence is surprise itself, the admiration, the childlike fiat of the gaze, the emergence of the world, "the Oh! of things."[3] This can be said of every being in the world as it appears to us, and with respect to which nothing more is needed than the statement Zen wise men make: This is the way things are. And if the presence of a gift is not required, then there is no need to do away with the giver, the recipient, and the given.

The question arises in an entirely different way in the case of Levinas. His thought is not formed through the deconstruction of metaphysical certainties, although it challenges many of those and reformulates others.

It proceeds through a surprising creation of concepts, conferring new meanings on terms that are not specifically philosophical, such as allergy, proximity, diachronicity, obsession, hostage, hemorrhage, and substitution: "gypsy" concepts that come from far away without being invited. His could be called a reconstructionist thought, whose radicality has to do not with aporias as to what can be said or thought, but with the affirmation of a figure that transcends all figuration: the Other, with his/her infinite otherness, as manifested by his/her face; and the gaze as situated beyond its own phenomenality. This makes it possible for Levinas to affirm Good beyond being, and to constitute ethics as first philosophy—thus proclaiming kindness as that which breaks the circle of immanence, understood as the circle of politics, justice, and equivalence, but also as the everyday world where the goods necessary to subsistence are produced and exchanged. In this most trivial of fields the requirement that the face of others makes on us can also be the most exacting, demanding that we give away our own bread and take the place of the persecuted. In Levinas the givers know why they are giving (because they owe it to others) and what they are giving ("the costly gift"); the recipients know who is giving to them, even if gratitude is not required from them. For Levinas the aporia of the gift as Derrida formulates it is nothing more than a dangerous sophism if it leads to the conclusion that in the real world giving is impossible. This is obviously not the case since the aporia calls instead for an absolute lack of self-interest—so absolute, however, that it rejects the requirement that a norm be formulated; hence the following question: Can deconstruction lead to an ethic? There is reason to doubt it because the prior task to identify and disassemble the metaphysical heritage that persists in the very moral concepts would be never-ending. This leaves only one option: to indefinitely postpone the moment of decision-making, as does Descartes, and keep to a "provisional" morality, including with respect to the gift. For Levinas, on the contrary, we live in a state of permanent emergency; when facing the distress of our neighbors no postponement can be tolerated.

Whereas Derrida and Levinas make a limited use of the resources of phenomenology, Marion intends to situate himself as a direct heir to Husserl. More crucially, the horizon of his questions can be traced back to the works of Heidegger. Marion appears to rediscover an intuition Levinas left unexploited: The given refers to a giver. Yet this apparent kinship is an illusion. This reference leads Levinas to claim that others preexist our relationship to the world, and are even the "principle of the phenomena." But he does not claim the existence of an offering. Marion considers the question in a very different way: He views the givenness of phenomena "as the giving of a gift." In Marion, Husserl's givenness, an operation without any oblative connotation, turns into an explicit *gesture* of giving that becomes legitimate at the end of the process of reduction, which removes this gesture from the "exchange" and, as a consequence, from metaphysical presuppositions. Hence, once again, the following question: Who is the giver? Marion's answer is the following: The gift comes from no one—unless the figure of the giver is to be discovered, like the "figure in the carpet."[4] Here again, for phenomenology, formulating an ethic is a struggle. A reflection on the gift appears capable of providing the prolegomena of this endeavor. Its aim would be to show that at the core of Husserl's *Gegebenheit* and, even more so, of Heidegger's *Es gibt*, is a givenness that not only is the form of the appearance of phenomena, but also points to the gesture of a mysterious generosity that presupposes an authority that remains unnamed only because of the duty of self-restraint incumbent on philosophers.

Ricoeur does not give in to this temptation because from the outset he follows Pascal's path: to raise the issues in terms of orders of legitimization. He never doubts that each realm—the development of knowledge; the statement of moral norms; the formulation of legal rules; the formation of the political realm; the expression of religious belief (hence his interest in Michael Walzer's *spheres* and Luc Boltanski and Laurent Thévenot's *cities*)—has its own specific methods and arguments. This is why Ricoeur's interventions in the various fields of research and discussion that he approaches are always specific and based on strong arguments. Nothing in his work suggests that a seamless transition can be established between Husserl's givenness and the generous gift—whether ritual or private. This clear separation among different realms, whose formulation generally remains implicit, makes it possible to understand his positive approach to phenomena of reciprocity, even if in the final analysis the concept of *agapē* alone seems to him capable of meeting a higher requirement of solicitude.

The same caution and pluralism characterize Descombes's approach, although his own inquiries are more focused on the question of the epistemological status of the objects he studies. He raises the issue in an entirely different way: For him the question of the gift as formulated by Mauss is one possible aspect of the relationship to others, itself explored through a set of broader questions on the logic of relationships, the specificity of the collective, the criteria of otherness, the objectivity of thoughts—in other words, what he calls *the institutions of meaning*. Lefort proceeds in a different way: He raises the question of the political realm as capable of running across every other realm, without being total and sufficient. This question is radical and insistent, as shown by his study on the Maussian gift, and self-evident in all of his works, including his reading of Merleau-Ponty. Lefort does not explore the genesis or constitution of the social realm, which must be accepted as a fact; it is for political thinkers to clarify and describe this fact, and to assess its historical forms, of which gift exchanges are for him an exemplary case.

Certain developments of phenomenology show an attempt to transform the description of the appearing of phenomena, understood as "givenness," into a manifestation of a gesture of giving, and thus, through a gradual process of transfer, to shift from the field of knowledge to the realm of an enigmatic oblativity capable of being granted religious as well as moral valence. The position presented in this essay keeps a distance from this kind of amalgamation. By establishing a clear distinction among different orders of the gift that cannot be placed on the same level, it makes it impossible to view the determinations of one of those levels as relevant to an assessment of the others.

The starting point of this essay was a feeling of surprise generated by the observation that so many philosophers favor the most unconditional generosity, going as far as to interpret any expectation of reciprocity as the seeking of selfish interest; to stand back from this highest of standards can only appear petty. Yet it should now be clear that things are not so simple, and that reciprocity involves forms of logic or requirements situated in different fields of questions that should not be confused with one another. We found it healthy and necessary to take on an effort at clarification that led us to a perhaps unusual perspective on a corpus of major works and to a more precise consideration of the concepts in play. It was necessary to present propositions and to engage in a reconstruction.

The question raised at the beginning of this essay still remains relevant: Why has this debate become more intense over the past few years? Circumstantial reasons may be involved, as they were when Seneca wrote his treatise, *De beneficiis*. His passionate call for unconditional giving appeared to him the only possible remedy to the selfishness in which the privileged classes were locking themselves. As for us who, through so many struggles and revolutions, have experienced over the past three centuries the advent of democracies and the legal recognition of social rights, how can we be satisfied with a solution that appears situated primarily on an individual level? Can the gesture of giving make up for the lack of just institutions? Can it be more than a comforting gesture, a mere sign of good will? Yet we must try to grasp and question this sign. Let us consider two plausible although contrary explanations.

The first has to do with what the twentieth century viewed as the failure of the regimes designated as "real socialism." Theirs was a failure in terms of democracy—downgraded as it was to parodies of elections—and, in a more paradoxical way, in terms of social justice—betrayed as it was by the rise of new privileges. But, beyond failure, this was an unspeakable tragedy—awesome enough to rival the Nazi tragedy—in terms of the destruction of millions of human lives. It was mostly in view of the inhumanity of massacres associated with wars, mass executions, camps, informers, and the management of fear that Vasily Grossman affirmed in *Life and Fate* what appears a last resort and an ultimate chance to avoid falling into an absolute despair about our species: compassion for other humans crushed and debased; mere gestures of support, "small kindness," he says: the last thread that bonds us to others. This could be the stake of the generous and most often discrete gesture we commonly call "gift": the first gesture that connects us to life and the last testimony to our humanness. This is what remains after the collapse of the great revolutionary machines, mass ideologies, and grand social constructions. The worldview centered on the gift thus appears, in Mauss's words, as the "bedrock" on which rest the foundations of every community, the support that resists to the end. As Seneca proclaims, the gift is "the chief bond of human society."[5] Here the idea of pure generosity takes on its full meaning—it does not preclude gestures of reciprocity, but neither does it entail them; this is how it generates around itself an emulation that leads others to behave in the same way. After the collapse—into terror and police states—of the most ambitious programs of justice and equality ever attempted in our civilization, we should not be surprised that some twentieth-century thinkers turned to the question of determining *what giving means*. We should ask instead why more of them did not do so.

But this resistance probably found an expression through other paths related to another—just as crucial—phenomenon of our recent Modernity: the triumph, as we are told, of the market economy and, more precisely, of what has prevailed along with it: the tyrannical imperative of profit. Truth be told, the idea of profit is as old as are trade and traders; its legitimacy is as well-established as are the perils it involves. What was new in the shift brought about by political economy—contemporaneous with the shift brought about by financial capitalism since the Industrial Revolution—was the development of an ideology that claims profit as a natural element; this ideology is at the core of the theoretical construction of *homo oeconomicus*, the unquestioned anthropological presupposition that humans are by nature self-interested and even fundamentally selfish beings who spontaneously seek to maximize their advantages. This is even, it is claimed, what makes their behavior predictable and rational. Every generous gesture thus becomes suspicious in theory, especially in the so-called "rational choice" theory whose many variants dominated twentieth-century economic thought. This dogma now appears increasingly untenable even to economists. What shifted the existing positions was thus not the protests of the advocates of a moral or religious view that proclaims the fundamental generosity of human beings, but the consideration of social and economic behaviors (cooperation and trust) that remain incomprehensible within the framework of the canonical hypothesis of primary selfishness. Another difficulty, however, remains in the works of many of the theoreticians who attempt this necessary course correction: the use of a different concept also posited as being part of human nature—altruism. This soon led unreconstructed utilitarians to the following predictable sophism: Being generous can be in the agent's interest.

The worldview centered on *recognition* (*reconnaissance*, *Anerkennung*) opens a different perspective that makes it possible to escape the dilemma between selfishness and altruism and to articulate the relationship between reciprocity and graciousness. The recognition of others is at play on an interpersonal and private as well as an institutional (social, political, and economic) level. It can take the form of a gesture of respect or compassion toward others in distress—a gesture of generosity free of all calculus. But it is also written into law by the promulgation of fundamental rights that publicly guarantee the status of every person as citizen and as human being. Recognition is also at the core of legal procedures and rules of exchange of goods. We saw that it was the very stake of ceremonial gift practices. The requirement of reciprocity is crucial in recognition, not as a prior condition ("recognition is granted if and only if . . ."), but in the sense of a shared respect. It involves at the same time a form of logic and an ethic of relationships among humans. Here "logic" designates the positing of the irreducible otherness of the parties involved, the establishment of rules of communication and collective action and of statuses and forms of authority; this is the realm of the third party. "Ethic" designates respectful attitudes, whether in informal encounters where relationships are improvised, or in public-life situations where norms apply to all. The question of recognition is important to us, not because we presuppose a kind of universal oblativity, but because the various forms of recognition always involve the enigma of our relationship to others. To call it generous is to accept that it pulls us away from our selves and presents and exposes us to one another—through our words, gestures, and works—as unique beings resistant to submission, but also yearning for that which bonds us to one another, and in the end members of an always-uncertain community made possible and livable only by the trust we grant one another and the rules we impose on ourselves. This life lived alongside others preexists and summons us; it attracts us, even though it weighs on us; it remains implausible and risky: to be endlessly constituted, contested, and reinvented. It is a narrative as well as a debate. It opens the stage to the figures of time that deserve to be told and the actions that deserve to be performed. To this entire realm we give a still-misunderstood name: politics.

ACKNOWLEDGMENTS

A few sections of this book were previously published. All were extensively reworked and augmented. I would like to thank the journals and editors who authorized their reprinting. I would also like to thank all those who, through their invitations to conferences they organized, gave me the opportunity to present those papers and engage in fruitful debates.

The content of Chapter 1 on Derrida was published in English in *Derrida and the Time of the Political*, Durham, Duke University Press, 2009, edited by Pheng Cheah and Suzanne Guerlac. It had been previously presented in Italian in October 2006 at Naples' Istituto per gli Studi Filosofici, where I was invited by Domenico Jervolino. It was also published in French in 2010 by *Archivio de Filosofia* 78, no. 1, as part of a book collection of the papers given at the January 2010 Rome Castelli conference on "The Impossible."

The content of Chapter 2 on ceremonial giving was first presented at the November 2005 Paris conference on recognition, organized by Alain Caillé and Christian Lazzeri; they later published it in *La Reconnaissance aujourd'hui* [Recognition Today], Paris, Éditions du CNRS, 2009.

The content of Chapter 3 on Levinas was first presented at the July 18–24, 2006, Cluny conference on "Levinas en héritage" [Levinas's Legacy], organized by Marie-Anne Lescourret and Jean-François Rey; it was published in their *Recherches lévinassiennes*, Louvain, Peters, 2012. This paper was also presented in Italian in October 2006 at Naples's Istituto per gli Studi Filosofici.

The content of Chapter 4 on reciprocity was presented at the October 24–26, 2007 Louvain conference on "Tâches actuelles et enjeux d'une philosophie des normes" [Current Tasks and Stakes of a Philosophy of Norms], organized by Marc Maesschalck; it was published in his *Éthique et gouvernance. Les enjeux actuels d'une philosophie des normes*, [Ethics and Governance: The Current Stakes of a Philosophy of Norms, Hildesheim], (New York: Olms, 2009). This paper was later developed in English on the occasion of a debate organized by Axel Honneth at the University of Frankfurt and presented at Erfurt's Max Weber Institute, headed by Hans Joas, and at the University of Graz, where I was invited by Stephan Moebius for February 21–26, 2010. The Frankfurt debate was published in German in 2010 in the journal *West End* (no. 1), along with articles by Axel Honneth, Dirk Quadflieg, Thomas Bedorf, Robin Celikates, and Stephan Moebius. An earlier English version was published in the journal *Teoria Critica della Regolazione Sociale* (TCRS), Quaderno 2011, edited by Alessio Lo Giudice.

The content of Chapter 6 on Ricoeur was originally published in 2004 in *Cahiers de L'Herne* 81 on Ricoeur, edited by Myriam Revault d'Allonnes and François Azouvi.

The contents of the other chapters were not previously published.

I would like to thank Monique Labrune for originally accepting this project at Éditions du Seuil. I am also grateful to Hugues Jallon for his first reading of the book and his valuable advice, and to Marianne Lagueunière for her meticulous copyediting of the manuscript, after an exemplary re-reading by my friends Daniela Langer and André Sauge, who on this occasion and many others generously contributed the gift of their time.

Marcel Hénaff

I would like to thank Tom Lay for his patient guidance and Edward Batchelder for his precise and thorough copyediting, as well as for his intelligent, thoughtful, and well-informed remarks.

Jean-Louis Morhange

1. To avoid cluttering this historical summary I refer the readers to the detailed presentation I proposed in *The Price of Truth* (Stanford, Calif.: Stanford University Press, 2010), Chapter 1: "Plato and the Sophists' Money," and Chapter 2: "The Figure of the Merchant in Western Tradition."

2. See Moses Finley, *The World of Odysseus* (London: Chatto and Windus, 1956), Chapter 5: "Morals and Values"; and Evelyne Scheid-Tissinier, *Les Usages du don chez Homère* (Nancy: Presses Universitaires de Nancy, 1994); Louis Gernet, "The Mythical Idea of Value in Greece," [1948] in *The Anthropology of Ancient Greece* (Baltimore: Johns Hopkins University Press, 1981).

3. The dates of the life of Siddhartha Gautama, who became the Buddha, are still debated and have tended to be moved back to the end of the fifth century BCE, close to the time of Confucius. As for Lao-Tse, little is known for sure about his biography. Socrates belonged to the following generation. It was his predecessors, Empedocles, Anaximander, Heraclitus, and Parmenides, who were the contemporaries of the great Indian and Chinese figures of wisdom. In any case, the axial age discussed by Jaspers extended over more than three centuries.

4. This unquestionably involves the field of phenomenology: In *Notebooks for an Ethics* [1948] (Chicago: University of Chicago Press, 1992), Sartre approaches explicitly the question of the gift as one of the crucial aspects of the ambiguous relationship of the self to Others: "Freedom exists only in *giving*, it devotes itself to *giving itself*" (282). That ambiguity is confirmed as follows: "The act of gift giving installs my giving freedom in the Other as a subjective limit to the other's freedom. This signifies that the other's freedom will henceforth exist as mortgaged to my own" (376). By generating the Other's reply, the generous gesture turns into reciprocal alienation: "The gift is an ambivalent structure with a perpetual instability: Originally stemming perhaps from a contractual desire between two freedoms, it becomes an attempt at magical enslavement" (376).

5. Claude Bruaire's *L'Être et l'esprit* (Paris: PUF, 1983) is an example of
an examination of the gift developed on a clearly claimed Christian background. Bruaire proposes a series of theses in the great tradition of the
metaphysical construct. At the core of the book—in Chapter 3, titled "L'Être
et l'existant" [Being and Existing]—he develops what he calls an *ontodology*,
literally an articulation of the questions of being and of the gift, with the
following central argument: Personal being cannot be derived from a natural
mechanism: "If the collection of its phenomena forces us to designate it by
the word *gift*, that is because it *is its own essence*, it has its own beginning" (53).
Personal being is spirit and as such being-by-giving. This must be understood
as follows: "What characterizes a being-by-giving is, in strict terms, that it is
everything that it is, and that what it is, is: *what* is given is *nothing* until it is
given, independent of the *fact* of giving" (53). But why should this be called
giving? The author has foreseen this objection; his answer is that giving alone
expresses the fact that personal being is spirit; being as spirit, as opposed to
natural being, is defined by the fact that it is given to itself and to itself alone;
this is what constitutes that being as free and responsible. But precisely, to be
given to oneself does not amount to giving oneself, but to be the addressee of
the gift. Being-by-giving does not grant itself its own foundation. Bruaire's
entire ontodology develops this thesis, while excluding a theological answer.
No matter how careful this method is, it leaves unanswered the question of
the status of the very idea of the gift, and does not examine its philosophical
or anthropological presuppositions.

Michel Henry clearly places himself within the phenomenological
trend. He claims the label even in his last writings, where it is clear that he
belongs to the Christian tradition. It is in those works that the theme of
givenness—or more precisely what he calls self-givenness—is most insistently emphasized. That phrase is the title of a posthumous collection (*Auto-
donation* [Paris: Beauchesne, 2004]), in which only one writing is specifically
dedicated to the concept stated by the title. By choosing that title, the editors
of the book meant to provide a retrospective frame of interpretation for the
philosopher's last publications. In Henry, the concept of self-givenness is
consistent with his enterprise of *Phenomenology of Life* (Paris: PUF, 2004),
whose theses are taken up again in *Auto-donation*: Beyond the intentionality of
the givenness of the world, life must be viewed as self-givenness itself: "The
givenness of givenness, self-givenness, is life." (*Phenomenology*, 127). Life is
not a phenomenon among others, "it is phenomenality itself" (127). "The
self-givenness of life means that what life gives is life itself; what it experiences is itself" (127). It is not surprising that Henry's thought shifts in works
that openly express a Christian commitment, such as *I Am the Truth: Toward
a Philosophy of Christianity* (Stanford, Calif.: Stanford University Press, 2003),

and *Words of Christ* (Grand Rapids, Mich.: William B. Eerdmans, 2012). The latter includes the following statement: "A finite life is a life incapable of giving itself to itself, of bringing itself into the marvelous condition of being a living being. Our life is not grounded in itself. . . . *Left to itself, a finite life is impossible. Precisely because it does not carry in itself the power to live, our life can only live in the infinite Life which does not cease to give it life*" (82–83). Living experiences life as radically antecedent, occurring to it through an original givenness, beyond any possibility of reciprocity. The self receives life from the absolute life that is self-givenness. Henry's perspective becomes openly theological in the foundational argument of the relationship to Others: "Since the self-givenness of absolute life in its Word, in which the transcendental Self that I am is given to itself, is God's life alone, it is in *that* one and the same life that the Self of the other is given to itself in an identical way—in it every possible Self, future, present, or past, has been, is, or will be given to itself so as to be the Self that it is." (*Incarnation* [Evanston, Ill.: Northwestern University Press, 2015], 247). (I would like to thank Benoît Kanabus for pointing out those writings to me.)

6. Paul Ricoeur, *Oneself as Another* (Chicago: University of Chicago Press, 1992), 172.

7. Dominique Janicaud, "The Theological Turn of French Phenomenology," in *Phenomenology and the "Theological Turn"* (New York: Fordham University Press, 2000).

8. Denis Hollier, *The College of Sociology* (Minneapolis: University of Minnesota Press, 1988); Michèle Richman, *Sacred Revolutions: Durkheim and the College of Sociology* (Minneapolis: University of Minnesota Press, 2002); Stephan Moebius, *Die Zauberlehrlinge: Soziologiegeschichte des Collège de Sociologie* (Konstanz: UVK, 2006); Alexander Riley, *Godless Intellectuals: The Intellectual Pursuit of the Sacred Reinvented* (New York: Berghahn Books, 2011).

9. The notion of sumptuary and even destructive expense has a long history. Louis Gernet already identified it in his seminal writing on "The Mythical Idea of Value in Greece." Gernet discusses rituals that express "an intense need for destruction" (88); strikingly, those acts are "not necessarily addressed to any one." They are not offerings to a deity. Émile Benveniste also discusses this notion of expense—*daps*—associated with a generous profusion and its evolution toward *dapánē* and *damnum*: expenditure, damage (*Indo-European Language and Society* [Coral Gables, Fla.: University of Miami Press, 1973], 484–85).

10. This involves only that particular time. The questions that have emerged since the 1980s along with the new inquiries conducted by contemporary ethnography and in the debates developed around the work of Mauss,

in particular in *La Revue du MAUSS* with Alain Caillé, Jacques Godbout, and, more recently, Philippe Chanial, are different. They will be discussed in Chapter 2.

11. This point needed to be made: Whereas the term "exchange" is found in the subtitle and on almost every page of *The Gift*, the very term *reciprocity* is almost absent in the essay, although the idea of reciprocity is omnipresent. That concept, at first implicit, will be explicitly present in Mauss only in later writings. See my article, "Mauss et l'invention de la réciprocité," in *Revue du MAUSS* 36 (Fall 2010).

I. DERRIDA: THE GIFT, THE IMPOSSIBLE, AND THE EXCLUSION OF RECIPROCITY

1. Jacques Derrida, *Given Time I* (Chicago: University of Chicago Press, 1992), 16.

2. Marcel Mauss, *The Gift: The Form and Reason for Exchange in Archaic Societies* [1925] (London: Routledge, 1990).

3. Derrida, *Given Time*, 7.

4. Jacques Derrida, *The Problem of Genesis in Husserl's Philosophy* (Chicago: University of Chicago Press, 2003), 203n89. This work, published fairly late, is in fact Derrida's master's thesis, defended in 1954.

5. Derrida, *Given Time*, 41.

6. Derrida, *Given Time*, 16.

7. Derrida, *Given Time*, 18.

8. Derrida, *Given Time*, 20.

9. Derrida, *Given Time*, 29.

10. Derrida, *Given Time*, 23.

11. This is in fact the choice made by François Fédier, the French translator of *Zeit und Sein* (who supports his choice on the etymology of *geben*, the Latin *habeo* derives from the same Indo-European radical, *ghabh*; this will be discussed more precisely with respect to Marion's "it gives").

12. Derrida, *Given Time*, 37.

13. Mauss, *The Gift*, 72–73.

14. Those are also the four aspects Jean-Luc Marion discusses in the presentation of his approach to Derrida in *Being Given*; the comparison stops here, since Marion's purpose is to assess Derrida's analyses, which call into question the ritual gift by the standard of the phenomenological question of *givenness*; this raises a different kind of problems, as we will see.

15. This is an odd qualifier regarding a 135-page text, first published in 1924 and 1925 in the form of two articles; further along Derrida refers to "those hundreds of pages"; this surprising error of physical appreciation can be interpreted in a positive way as a symptom of admiration for the *monu-*

mental importance of Mauss's essay and its stubborn resistance to Derrida's attempt at "deconstruction."

16. Derrida, *Given Time*, 24.

17. In this type of contract, in Roman law the verb *do* (to give) refers not to giving a present, but to putting forward a good—as in barter—so that the other party will do the same. Let us note that in *The Gift* Mauss does not cite this classic expression of Roman law because his purpose is situated on a different level.

18. Derrida, *Given Time*, 37.

19. This conception of the gift as a loan is not new; it had already been expressed by Franz Boas, the great field investigator of the northwest coast of North America; Mauss makes use of his many works. Boas tried to show to his modern readers the economic seriousness of the populations involved by explaining that the *potlatch*, apparently so wasteful, is in the final analysis only an archaic form of credit; see *Kwakiutl Ethnography*, ed. Helen Codere (Chicago: University of Chicago Press, 1966). Mauss notes the inappropriateness of such views (*The Gift*, 111n133).

20. Derrida, *Given Time*, 27.

21. Derrida, *Given Time*, 137.

22. Derrida, *Given Time*, 13.

23. On this distinction see my book, *The Price of Truth*, Chapter 6: "The Logic of the Debt," 275 *ff.*

24. Derrida, *Given Time*, 23.

25. Derrida, *Given Time*, 23.

26. This is the seasonal ritual exchange of precious goods conducted during sailing expeditions by various groups that inhabit those islands, described by Bruno Malinowski in *Argonauts of the Western Pacific* (London: Routledge & Sons, 1922). This exchange will be discussed below in Chapter 2 and elsewhere.

27. Derrida, *Given Time*, 13.

28. Derrida, *Given Time*, 23.

29. Derrida, *Given Time*, 24.

30. Derrida, *Given Time*, 11 [modified translation—JLM].

31. Marcel Mauss, "A Category of the Human Mind: The Notion of Person, the Notion of 'Self,'" in *Sociology and Psychology* (London: Routledge & Kegan Paul, 1979), 57–94.

32. Mauss, *The Gift*, 20. See also 12 and 14.

33. Mauss, *The Gift*, 12.

34. Derrida, *Given Time*, 24.

35. This is a rather mysterious formulation, and one probably best left to its mystery. The figure of this *circle* that Derrida calls into question is the *kula*

ring discussed by Mauss, who takes up Malinowski's descriptions of the cycles of ceremonial exchanges in the Trobriand Islands of Melanesia (see *Given Time*, 6–7, 25, 30–31). Yet what is remarkable about the *kula ring* is that it is a dual movement (from east to west and back) that does not form a loop; the cycles are always staggered and complex, always taken up again—not because they generate a debt, but because the *challenges* associated with the precious goods given or received must always be taken up again. Let us note that from the moment when the data observed is considered in detail, the overly general categories of philosophical critique turn out to be inoperative, if not harmful; they aim at nonexistent objects. No more than does the suspicion against exchange, the suspicion against the figure of the circle does not make possible a critical and relevant understanding of a social practice, especially one whose procedures have not first been precisely described and adequately assessed.

36. Derrida, *Given Time*, 24.

37. Derrida, *Given Time*, 24.

38. Derrida, *Given Time*, 23.

39. Derrida, *Given Time*, 27.

40. Mauss, *The Gift*, 46.

41. Claude Lévi-Strauss, *The Elementary Structures of Kinship* [1949] (Boston: Beacon, 1969), 481.

42. Émile Benveniste, "Giving, Taking, and Receiving," in *Indo-European Language and Society* (Coral Gables, Fla.: University of Miami Press, 1973).

43. More precisely, in an earlier study (1951) Benveniste remarks: "We shall consider that **dō-* properly means neither 'take' nor 'give' but either the one or the other, depending on the construction. [. . .] **dō-* indicated only the fact of taking hold of something; only the syntax of the utterance differentiated it as 'to take hold of in order to keep' (= take) and 'to take hold of in order to offer' (= give)" (*Problems in General Linguistics* [Coral Gables, Fla.: University of Miami Press, 1971], 272). Benveniste notes that in Middle English *to take* could mean to deliver just as well as to take; the same applies to *nehmen* in old German. With respect to those gestures Benveniste speaks of a *polarity* whose range of application will become clearer (in Chapter 2) when illuminated by Peirce's concept of triad.

44. Derrida, *Given Time*, 82.

45. Derrida, *Given Time*, 55.

46. Derrida, *Given Time*, 13.

47. Jacques Derrida, *Writing and Difference* [1967] (Chicago: University of Chicago Press, 1978), 316n46.

48. Jacques Derrida, *The Gift of Death* (Chicago: University of Chicago Press, 2008), 103 *ff.*

49. Derrida, *The Gift of Death*, 105.

50. Jacques Derrida, *Of Hospitality* (Stanford, Calif.: Stanford University Press, 2000), 75.

51. Derrida, *Of Hospitality*, 77.

52. Derrida, *Of Hospitality*, 79.

53. Derrida, *Of Hospitality*, 79. "This pervertibility is essential, irreducible, necessary too. The perfectibility of laws is at this cost. And therefore their historicity. And vice versa, conditional laws would cease to be laws of hospitality if they were not guided, given inspiration, given aspiration, required, even, by the law of unconditional hospitality. These two regimes of law, of *the* law and the laws, are thus both contradictory, antinomic, *and* inseparable. They both imply and exclude each other, simultaneously" (79).

54. This remark is meant mostly as a greeting in the name of a relationship that always remained cordial; but above all it is an expression of regret for a dialog that never took place. In a letter to Derrida about *Given Time* I tried to clarify the reservations I had already stated in a brief note in *The Price of Truth*. That letter was never sent because of Derrida's illness and passing away; it was read in New York City in the spring of 2005 on the occasion of a tribute to Derrida.

55. Derrida, *The Gift of Death*.

2. PROPOSITIONS I: THE CEREMONIAL GIFT — ALLIANCE AND RECOGNITION

1. On Marcel Mauss's thought, see Bruno Karsenti, *Mauss: L'Homme total* (Paris: PUF, 1997).

2. The following is a chronological listing of a few specifically ethnographic works of the second half of the twentieth century: Andrew Strathern, *The Rope of Moka: Big-Men and Ceremonial Exchange in Mount Hagen New Guinea* (Cambridge: Cambridge University Press, 1971); Marshall Sahlins, *Stone Age Economics* (Chicago: University of Chicago Press, 1974); Paula Rubel and Abraham Rosman, *Your Own Pigs You May Not Eat: A Comparative Study of New Guinea Societies* (Chicago: Chicago University Press, 1978); Pierre Lemonnier, *Guerres et festins. Paix, échanges et compétitions dans les High Lands de Nouvelle-Guinée* (Paris: CNRS Éditions, 1980); André Iteanu, *La Ronde des échanges. De la circulation aux valeurs chez les Orokaiva* (Paris: Maison des Sciences de l'Homme, 1983); Marilyn Strathern, *The Gender of the Gift: Problems with Women and Problems with Society in Melanesia* (Berkeley: University of California Press, 1988); Annette Weiner, *Inalienable Possessions: The Paradox of Keeping-while-Giving* (Berkeley: University of California Press, 1992); Alain Testart, *Les Dons et les Dieux* (Paris: Armand Colin, 1993);

Maurice Godelier, *The Enigma of the Gift* (Chicago: University of Chicago Press, 1999).

3. Marcel Hénaff, *The Price of Truth: Gift, Money, and Philosophy* (Stanford, Calif.: Stanford University Press, 2010).

4. Bronislaw Malinowski, *Argonauts of the Western Pacific* (London: Routledge & Sons, 1922).

5. Homer G. Barnett, "The Nature of the Potlatch," *American Anthropologist* 40 (1938); Helen Codere, *Fighting with Property: A Study of Kwakiutl Potlatching and Warfare 1792–1930* (New York: J. J. Augustin, 1950); Marie Mauzé, "Boas, les Kwakiutl et le *potlatch*: éléments pour une réévaluation," *L'Homme* 26, no. 4 (1986).

6. This point will be discussed in more detail in Chapter 7 below.

7. In *Critiques du don. Études sur la circulation marchande* (Paris: Syllepses, 2007) Alain Testart proposed a reevaluation of the three canonical examples presented by Mauss. In spite of an abundance of considerations in detail, as a whole his approach appears to us misdirected in that it takes it for granted that the concept of exchange designates primarily commercial exchange (even though in Mauss this term applies to agonistic reciprocity) and that gift relationships are transfers of goods. In fact, the ritual gift is not primarily such a transfer—be it disinterested—but a procedure of public recognition through the mediation of those goods.

8. Marcel Mauss, *The Gift: The Form and Reason for Exchange in Archaic Societies* [1925] (London: Routledge, 1990), 11–12.

9. This is reported by Mauss in a long note in *The Gift*, 111n131. He rightly suggests that Boas's terms "debt, payment, reimbursement, and loan" should be replaced by "presents given" and "presents returned."

10. Max Weber, *General Economic History* (New York: Collier Books, 1961).

11. Karl Polanyi, *The Great Transformation* (Boston: Beacon Press, 1944); while this work generally makes an innovative use of ethnographic data, it regrettably presents the system of *kula* exchanges as a vast international network of circulation of commercial goods: "We describe it as trade though no profit is involved, either in money or in kind [. . .], the whole proceedings are entirely regulated by etiquette and magic. Still, it is trade," (50).

12. Georges Davy, *La Foi jurée: Étude sociologique du problème du contrat* (Paris: Alcan, 1922).

13. This point will be discussed in more detail in "Propositions II" with respect to contractual reciprocity.

14. Michael Walzer, *Spheres of Justice: A Defense of Pluralism and Equality* (New York: Basic Books, 1983).

15. Luc Boltanski and Laurent Thévenot, *On Justification: Economies of Worth* (Princeton: Princeton University Press, 2006).

16. See André Sauge, "Homère, Sophocle, Luc: L'étincelle de la grâce," *Revue du MAUSS* 35 (2010): 173–82. According to Sauge, *philia* involves every benevolent behavior not associated with obligatory bonds.

17. Max Weber, *The Sociology of Religion* (Boston: Beacon Press, 1964), 225.

18. This essential difference between symbolic and useful goods appears to us crucial to an understanding of the heterogeneity of the different orders of the gift; greetings and even alliances on the occasion of festive meals involve attitudes entirely different than do offerings of food to preserve Others from famine.

19. This is Alain Caillé's phrase, developed in a series of writings, most of which are reprinted in his *Anthropologie du don* (Paris: Desclée de Brouwer, 2000). The very concept of a paradigm of the gift is important because it makes it possible to situate on a specifically sociological and institutional level a fundamental mode of interhuman relationships that cannot be defined by the purely psychological notion of altruism.

20. Strathern, *The Rope of Moka*, xii.

21. Strathern, *The Rope of Moka*, xii.

22. Jane Goodall, *The Chimpanzees of Gombe: Patterns of Behavior* (Cambridge, Mass.: Harvard University Press, 1986); Frans de Waal, *Peacemaking among Primates* (Cambridge, Mass.: Harvard University Press, 1989), and *Chimpanzee Politics* (Baltimore: Johns Hopkins University Press, 1998); William C. McGrew, Linda F. Marchant, and Toshisada Nishida, eds., *Great Ape Societies* (Cambridge: Cambridge University Press, 1990); William C. McGrew, *Chimpanzee Material Culture. Implications for Human Evolution* (Cambridge: Cambridge University Press, 1992); Frans de Waal, *Primates and Philosophers: How Morality Evolved* (Princeton: Princeton University Press, 2006).

23. This misunderstanding is found in Craig Stanford's "The Ape's Gift," in *Tree of Origin*, ed. Frans de Waal (Cambridge, Mass.: Harvard University Press, 2001).

24. Adam Smith, *An Inquiry into the Nature and Causes of The Wealth of Nations* [1776] (Oxford: Oxford University Press, 1993), Book 1, Chapter 2, 21.

25. Various coalition phenomena have been observed in chimpanzees organizing an attack against another group or an individual (this is different from the coordination found in hunting; the same has also been observed in many other mammals such as wolves, hyenas, and lionesses).

26. This is no more than a model, since the *symbolon* ritual is not in and of itself an exchange of goods.

27. Claude Lévi-Strauss, *The Elementary Structures of Kinship* (Boston: Beacon Press, 1969), 65.

28. Lévi-Strauss, *The Elementary Structures*, 481.

29. Edmond Ortigues, *Le Discours et le Symbole* (Paris: Aubier, 1962), 61.

30. Charles S. Peirce, *Collected Papers* (Cambridge, Mass.: Harvard University Press, 1958), Vol. 7, Book 2, Chapter 8, § 33, 225–26. See also *Peirce on Signs*, ed. James Hoopes (Chapel Hill: University of North Carolina Press, 1991).

31. Vincent Descombes, "Essays on the Gift," in *The Institutions of Meaning* (Cambridge, Mass.: Harvard University Press, 2014), Chapter 18. I will return to this discussion below in more detail (see "Propositions II," as well as the section on Vincent Descombes in Chapter 7).

32. Lucien Tesnière, *Elements of Structural Syntax* (Amsterdam: John Benjamins Publishing Company, 2015), 256–60.

33. See Erving Goffman, *Encounters: Two Studies in the Sociology of Interaction* (Indianapolis, Ind.: Bobbs-Merrill, 1961); Bernard Conein, "Pourquoi dit-on bonjour?," *Les Sens sociaux* (Paris: Economica, 2007).

34. See Raymond Verdier, *La Vengeance* (Paris: Cujas, 1980–86); Mark Anspach, *À Charge de revanche: Figures élémentaires de la réciprocité* (Paris: Seuil, 2002); see also Hénaff, *The Price of Truth*, Chapter 6: "The Logic of Debt"; see Chapter 4 below.

35. See Marcel Mauss, "Gift, Gift," in *Oeuvres* (Paris: Minuit, 1969) 3:46–51.

36. Paul Ricoeur, *The Course of Recognition* (Cambridge, Mass.: Harvard University Press, 2005), 219 *ff.* See the last section of Chapter 6 below.

37. Philippe Chanial proposes a very illuminating general model of the different modes of interhuman relationships (including the gift) along two axes that form four poles: giving/taking associated with generosity vs. violence, and reciprocating/receiving associated with reciprocity vs. power. Chanial makes this model more complex by including subsets of relationships such as those involving grace, vengeance, domination, and role-playing. Gift relationships are thus situated within a broader system that marks their specificity. This model would be even more illuminating if it could incorporate the bond of recognition and the relationship of alliance; see "L'instant fugitif où la société prend: Le don, la partie et le tout," *La Revue du MAUSS* 36 (2nd Semester, 2010): 343–60.

38. Malinowski. *Argonauts*, 95, footnote.

39. Maurice Godelier emphasizes the fact that the public life of traditional societies cannot be reduced to kinship relationships; see *Aux Fondements des sociétés humaines* (Paris: Albin Michel, 2007), Chapter 2.

40. G. W. F. Hegel, *Phenomenology of Spirit* (Oxford: Clarendon Press, 1977), Chapter 7.

41. Marcel Detienne, *The Masters of Truth in Archaic Greece* (New York: Zone Books, 1996), Chapter 5; Pierre Levêque and Pierre Vidal-Naquet, *Cleisthenes the Athenian* [1963] (Atlantic Highlands, N.J., Humanities Press, 1996); Jean-Pierre Vernant, "The Organization of Space," *Myth and Thought among the Greeks* (London: Routledge and Kegan Paul, 1983); Moses Finley, *Early Greece* (New York: Norton, 1970); *The World of Odysseus*, (London: Chatto and Windus, 1956).

42. See André Sauge, *De l'Épopée à l'histoire: Fondement de la notion d'histoire* (Frankfurt on the Main: Peter Lang, 1992). This mediator is called on to authenticate even the word of the king, who has lost his status as "master of truth."

43. Axel Honneth, *The Struggle for Recognition* (Cambridge: Polity Press, 1995).

44. The *agōn* of the ceremonial gift is profoundly different from the Hegelian model of the struggle for recognition. In Kojève's words, Hegel's opponents face each other with nothing else than weapons. They are figures of the individual that belong fully to the space of Modernity. But above all, this subjectivity is the position of reference of self-knowledge and a perspective on action. Hegel's struggle of consciousness has to do primarily with the fact above that each consciousness is advanced based on its own subjectivity; it asks for recognition without ever making a prior offer of recognition of the other.

45. Walzer, *Spheres of Justice*.

46. Boltanski and Thévenot, *De la justification*.

47. See Walzer, *Spheres of Justice*, Chapter 1: "Complex Equality."

48. John Rawls, *A Theory of Justice* (Cambridge, Mass.: Belknap Press of Harvard University Press, 1971).

49. Seneca, *De beneficiis* (Berkeley: University of California Press, 1950).

3. LEVINAS: BEYOND RECIPROCITY— FOR-THE-OTHER AND THE COSTLY GIFT

1. Emmanuel Levinas, *Totality and Infinity* [1961] (Pittsburgh: Duquesne University Press, 1969), 68.

2. Emmanuel Levinas, *Ethics and Infinity* (Pittsburgh: Duquesne University Press, 1985), 98.

3. Emmanuel Levinas, *Existence and Existents* [1947] (The Hague: Martinus Nijhoff, 1978), 95–96.

4. Levinas, *Totality and Infinity*, 64.

5. Although Levinas does not discuss Mauss, he makes several references, on different questions, to the positions of Lévy-Bruhl, whom he knew

and respected—for example, in Emmanuel Levinas, *Entre nous: Thinking-of-the-Other* (New York: Columbia University Press, 1998), 39–51.

6. As on the occasion of the hundredth anniversary of Buber's birth in 1978; see Emmanuel Levinas, *Alterity and Transcendence* [1995] (New York: Columbia University Press, 1999), 91–96.

7. Levinas, *Alterity and Transcendence*, 105–6.

8. Martin Buber, *I and Thou* (New York: Charles Scribner's Sons, 1970); *Ich und Du* [1923] (Heidelberg: Lambert-Schneider Verlag, 1979).

9. Buber, *I and Thou*, 67.

10. In Levinas, "There is" can refer to the neutrality of the phenomenality of the world (as in *Existence and Existents*), but designates primarily the horror of anonymity and indifference. Levinas never abandoned this negative view of "There is." This probably led him to avoid discussing the German equivalent, "*Es gibt*," called on by Heidegger and taken up by some commentators through a literal translation—"It gives"—as we saw with Derrida. We will return to this question.

11. Thus *I and Thou* discusses the question of the tree, which can be viewed as a thing (form, matter, and growth): "But it can also happen, if will and grace are joined, that as I contemplate the tree I am drawn into a relation, and the tree ceases to be an It." Thus arises a *relation* beyond *experience*: "What I encounter is [. . .] the thee itself" (Buber, *I and Thou*, 58–59).

12. Levinas, "Nonintentional Consciousness," in *Entre nous*, 123 [modified translation—JLM]. This debt is reasserted in the last pages of *Otherwise than Being*: "Our analyses claim to be in the spirit of Husserl's philosophy, whose letter has been the recall in our epoch of the permanent phenomenology, restored to its rank of being a method for all philosophy." Emmanuel Levinas, *Otherwise than Being or Beyond Essence* [1978] (The Hague: Martinus Nijhoff, 1981), 183.

13. Edmund Husserl, *Cartesian Meditations* (The Hague: Nijhoff, 1982).

14. Levinas, *Alterity and Transcendence*, 100–1.

15. Levinas, *Totality and Infinity*, 128.

16. Immanuel Kant, *Critique of Pure Reason*, 2nd ed., trans. Norman Kemp Smith (New York: Palgrave-Macmillan, 2006), 233.

17. Kant, *Critique of Pure Reason*, 233.

18. Emmanuel Levinas, "La trace de l'autre," in *En découvrant l'existence avec Husserl et Heidegger* [1949] (Paris: Vrin, 2001), 268.

19. Levinas, *Totality and Infinity*, 68.

20. Emmanuel Levinas, *The Theory of Intuition in Husserl's Phenomenology* [1930] (Evanston, Ill.: Northwestern University Press, 1995).

21. Emmanuel Levinas, *Discovering Existence with Husserl* (Evanston, Ill.: Northwestern University Press, 1998), 47–87.

22. Emmanuel Levinas, "Martin Heidegger et l'ontologie," *En découvrant l'existence avec Husserl et Heidegger* (Paris: J. Vrin, 1949), 77–128.

23. Levinas, *Existence and Existents*, 46.

24. Levinas, *Existence and Existents*, 46.

25. Levinas, *Existence and Existents*, 46.

26. Levinas, *Existence and Existents*, 47.

27. Levinas, *Existence and Existents*, 47.

28. Levinas, *Existence and Existents*, 48.

29. Levinas, *Existence and Existents*, 48.

30. Levinas, *Entre nous*, 139.

31. Levinas, "Nonintentional Consciousness," 123–32.

32. Levinas, "Nonintentional Consciousness," 125–26.

33. In Levinas's work those are not incidental remarks. This views recurs insistently in many other writings. He thus writes in "Diachrony and Representation" [1985]: "It [presence] concretely signifies an ex-position of the other to the *I*, and thus precisely an *offering of the self, a giving of itself, a Gegebenheit.* It is a giving of alterity within presence, not only in the metaphorical sense of the term, but as a giving that signifies within a concrete horizon of a *taking*, already in reference to a 'taking in hands.'" (in *Entre nous*, 160; Levinas's emphasis); and in "The Philosophical Determination of the Idea of Culture" [1985]: "Being in the world, in its exposition to knowledge, in the openness and frankness of presence, is ipso facto a *giving itself* and a *letting-itself-be-taken* to which the com-prehension of truth first responds." (in *Entre nous*, 180).

34. Levinas, *Existence and Existents*, 48.

35. Levinas, *Existence and Existents*, 48.

36. Levinas, *Totality and Infinity*, 92.

37. "Teaching signifies the whole infinity of exteriority." (Levinas, *Totality and Infinity*, 171); "The other [. . .] is [. . .] the first teaching." (Levinas, *Totality and Infinity*, 204).

38. Levinas, *Totality and Infinity*, 92.

39. Levinas, *Totality and Infinity*, 92.

40. Levinas, *En découvrant l'existence avec Husserl et Heidegger.*

41. Benveniste provides a brilliant analysis of the status of the speaking *I* in his/her relationship to the *You* in interlocution; see *Problems in General Linguistics* (Coral Gables, Fla.: University of Miami Press, 1971).

42. Levinas, *Totality and Infinity*, 40.

43. Levinas, *Ethics and Infinity*, 99.

44. On the concept of infinity, see Levinas's explanations in *Alterity and Transcendence*, 53–54. On this question Derrida presents an excellent clarification in "Violence and Metaphysics," in *Writing and Difference* [1967] (Chicago: University of Chicago Press, 1978), 114 *ff.*

45. Maurice Merleau-Ponty, *Phenomenology of Perception* (Abingdon: Routledge, 2012), 410.

46. Merleau-Ponty, *Phenomenology of Perception*, 409. This is one of the very few passages where Merleau-Ponty discusses the face.

47. The most that can be found in Sartre on this question is an analysis of the gaze (*Being and Nothingness* [London: Routledge, 2003], 252–302) supported by detailed descriptions of the relationship between eye movements and the gesture of looking: "If I apprehend the look, I cease to perceive the eyes" (258). To our knowledge Georg Simmel is one of the few authors who have attempted to provide a detailed descriptions of the face as such and as a central element of our relationship to Others, in *Soziologie* [1908] (Berlin: Duncker & Humblot, 1968): "The face, which offers itself as the first object of the gaze between one person and another [. . .]. The face, when viewed as an organ of expression is, as it were, of a completely theoretical nature. [. . .] it never supports the inner or practical behaviour of people, but rather only *tells* others about it." (*Simmel on Culture: Selected Writings*, ed. David Frisby and Mike Featherstone [London: Sage, 1997], 112–13).

48. In "The I and the Totality" (1953), published ten years before *Totality and Infinity*, Levinas states this clearly: "The face is the very identity of a being; it manifests itself in terms of itself, without a concept. The sensible presence of this chaste bit of skin with brow, nose, eyes, and mouth, is neither a sign allowing us to approach a signified, nor a mask hiding it" (*Entre nous*, 33). "The face, then, is not the color of the eyes, the shape of the nose, the ruddiness of the cheeks, etc." ("The Other, Utopia, and Justice," in *Entre nous*, 232).

49. Levinas, *Totality and Infinity*, 198.

50. Analyses on the way the face of Others summons us are found in *Totality and Infinity*, 187–247, as well as in most of Levinas's later publications.

51. Paul Ricoeur, *Oneself as Another* (Chicago: University of Chicago Press, 1992), 336.

52. Such as Ricoeur in *Oneself as Another*, and Jacques Dewitte in "Un beau risque à courir," *Cahiers d'études lévinassiennes* 1 (2002): 55–76.

53. Emmanuel Levinas, *Humanism of the Other* [1972] (Urbana: University of Illinois Press, 2003), 26–27.

54. Paul Ricoeur: "Emmanuel Levinas, penseur du témoignage," in *Répondre d'autrui. Emmanuel Levinas*, ed. Jean-Christophe Aeschlimann (Lausanne: La Baconnière, 1989), 30–39.

55. It is hardly necessary to underline the kinship between Levinas's analysis and Derrida's analysis of reciprocal gestures as embodying the figure of the circle (see Chapter 1 above), at the same time Hegelian cycle of "relief" and loop in the manner of Odysseus's itinerary (both authors discuss this figure).

56. Levinas, *Humanism of the Other*, 26.

57. Levinas, *Humanism of the Other*, 26–27.

58. This phrase constitutes one more example of Levinas's creative appropriation of terms developed in other fields (other examples are exteriority, hypostasis, hemorrhage, constraint, height, and proximity).

59. There is thus nothing in Levinas that resembles Bataille's statements in *The Accursed Share*. The "costly gift" is the polar opposite of sumptuary waste as well as of restraint for the purpose of saving.

60. Levinas, *Humanism of the Other*, 27.

61. Levinas, *Humanism of the Other*, 27.

62. Levinas, *Totality and Infinity*, 261.

63. Levinas, *Totality and Infinity*, 302.

64. Levinas, *Otherwise than Being*, 138.

65. Levinas, *Otherwise than Being*, 138.

66. Levinas, *Otherwise than Being*, 142.

67. Levinas, *Otherwise than Being*, 72.

68. Levinas, *Totality and Infinity*, 134.

69. Levinas, *Totality and Infinity*, 216.

70. This reference recurs unchanged even in Levinas's later writings, such as "Diachrony and Representation" [1985], where he inquires as to whether "for an *I*, the alterity of the other initially signifies a logical alterity; the sort of alterity in which parts of a whole are marked off in opposition to one another, in which, in a purely formal way one, this one, is other to that one, and that one is, by the same token, other to this one. Between the persons included in this reciprocity, language would be but a reciprocal exchange of information or anecdotes, intended and gathered into the statement of each partner" (*Entre nous*, 166).

71. See Jean-Luc Nancy, *Being Singular Plural* (Stanford, Calif.: Stanford University Press, 2000), 1–99.

72. This reminds us of what is called the "network effect": the emergence of a new dimension—or even a different order—through the dynamic combination of the components of a whole; this is designated as self-transcendence, which means, transcendence as the autonomous effect of an immanent process. This is clearly the opposite of the idea of Infinity, the exteriority of the Other and the face, the teaching of/by a speech that nothing precedes or predicts.

73. Levinas, *Totality and Infinity*, 213.

74. Levinas's position on this question will be discussed more precisely below in Chapter 8: "Propositions III: The Dual Relationship and the Third Party."

75. Edmond Ortigues gives a brilliant formulation of this principle at the end of a tight linguistic analysis: "The *I-You* relationship is essentially

defined by its *reversibility*: The addressee is the being who can say *I* in his turn, asserting himself as the real subject of speech by speaking for himself to reply to me. We know that to be grasped in its entirety every relationship must be reversible while moving not backward, but forward through an *oriented progression*. The category of the person thus finds the condition of its integrity in the reversibility of the relationship between speaker and addressee, which constitutes the structure of every communication or exchange. This is a *condition of meaning for every linguistic system*: My speech has meaning only through the possibility of receiving the sanction of a reply from the being in which I must recognize the same personal dignity whose recognition I expect from him for myself." *Le Discours et le Symbole* (Paris: Aubier, 1962), 153 (my emphasis).

4. PROPOSITIONS II: APPROACHES TO RECIPROCITY

1. Alvin Gouldner, "The Norm of Reciprocity," *American Sociological Review* 25, no. 2 (1960): 161–78.

2. Marshall. Sahlins, *Stone Age Economics*, (Chicago: University of Chicago Press, 1974).

3. Gouldner, "The Norm of Reciprocity," 171.

4. "The Prime Principle of Man's Moral Constitution—with the aid of active intellectual powers and the effects of habit, naturally lead to the golden rule: 'As ye would that men should do to you, do ye to them likewise'; and this lies at the foundation of morality," Charles Darwin, *The Descent of Man* [1871] (Princeton: Princeton University Press, 1982).

5. The two commandments listed in Matthew (22) are in fact "You shall love the Lord your God with all your heart and with all your thought, and with all your mind" (22:37) and "You shall love your neighbor as yourself" (22:37) (translator's note).

6. Claude Lévi-Strauss, "The Principle of Reciprocity" in *The Elementary Structures of Kinship* (Boston: Beacon Press, 1969), Chapter 5.

7. As we saw in "Propositions I," this emergence of the convention as the alliance of separate beings is at the core of the political relationship; it even constitutes the pragmatic genesis of the *politeia*.

8. Gouldner, "The Norm of Reciprocity," 167.

9. Bronislaw Malinowski, *Crime and Custom in Savage Society* [1926] (n.l.: Home Farm Book, 2006).

10. Bronislaw Malinowski, *Argonauts of the Western Pacific* (London: Routledge & Sons, 1922).

11. Gouldner, "The Norm of Reciprocity," 171.

12. Sahlins, *Stone Age Economics*.

13. Sahlins, *Stone Age Economics*, 193.

14. Raymond Verdier, *La Vengeance* (Paris: Cujas, 1980–86).

15. Aristotle, *Nicomachean Ethics*, V, 8.

16. Immanuel Kant, "Analytic of Principles," in *Critique of Pure Reason* (Basingstoke: Palgrave Macmillan, 2006), A211; B256.

17. François Rabelais, "How Panurge Praises Debtors and Creditors," in *The Third Book*, in *The Complete Works of François Rabelais* (Berkeley: University of California Press, 1991).

18. "And into that from which existing things come-to-be they also pass away according to necessity; for they suffer punishment and pay retribution to one another for their wrongdoing, in accordance with the ordinance of [*kata tēn tou chronou taxin*]," Anaximander, *Fragment A IX*.

19. "Generalized exchange establishes a system of operations conducted 'on credit' [. . .]. Generalized exchange always contains an element of trust [. . .]. There must be the confidence that the cycle will close again, and that after a period of time a woman will eventually be received in compensation for the woman initially surrendered. The belief is the basis of trust, and confidence opens up credit. [. . .] with generalized exchange the group can live as richly and as complexly as its size, structure and density allow." Claude Lévi-Strauss, *The Elementary Structures of Kinship* (Boston: Beacon, 1969), 265.

20. See "Propositions I" above and Chapter 7 below.

21. The triadic relationship according to Simmel is a different thing; see "Propositions III" below.

22. On this point also see my development of this question in "Vindicatory Justice and Arbitrational Justice," in *The Price of Truth: Gift, Money, and Philosophy* (Stanford, Calif.: Stanford University Press, 2010), 214–25. See also Mark R. Anspach, *À charge de revanche* (Paris: Seuil, 2002). According to Anspach the cycle of vengeful violence can be summed up by the following statement: "Killing the killer"; the cycle can be broken only by the gesture of sacrifice, which amounts to killing "one who has not killed." Although this hypothesis is attractive, we cannot accept it. The justice of traditional societies is vindicatory rather than vengeful: The cycle of *compensation* is strictly ritualized and limited by a procedure whose aim is to bring closure. Occasionally (but rarely) this closure is associated with a sacrificial ritual; the very relevance of the notion of sacrifice is debatable here, since sacrifice emerges only along with the domestication of plants and animals, and its main purpose is to pay a debt owed to the deities for the human hold on life.

23. It may well be, however, that this contractual model has profoundly pervaded the political and social thought of Western democracies, particularly in Northern Europe, where the Reformation arose and developed; this ethic is clearly dominant in the Anglo-American world. This topic is worthy of a complex and fascinating discussion; see my "Religious Ethic, Gift

Exchange and Capitalism," *European Journal of Sociology* 44, no. 3 (2003): 293–324.

24. Paul Ricoeur, *The Course of Recognition* (Cambridge, Mass.: Harvard University Press, 2005), 150 *ff.* See the last section of the study on Ricoeur in Chapter 7 below.

5. MARION: GIFT WITHOUT EXCHANGE—TOWARD PURE GIVENNESS

1. Joan Stambaugh's translation of the epigraph from Heidegger is "We do not say: Being is, time is, but rather: there is Being and there is time." *On Time and Being* (New York: Harper & Row, 1972), 4–5. Jean-Luc Marion's translation is "*Cela donne l'Être; cela donne le Temps*" [It gives Being; it gives Time].

2. This question will be more broadly discussed below in the section, "The Resources of Thought Embodied in Language: The Lexicon of the Gift."

3. *Logical Investigations* (1900); *The Idea of Phenomenology* (1907); *Ideas Pertaining to a Pure Phenomenology and to a Phenomenological Philosophy* (1913); *First Philosophy* (1925); *Cartesian Meditations* (1931).

4. The following cursory summary of the phenomenological project is meant for readers unfamiliar with it; others can skip it and proceed to the next section.

5. As Ricoeur reminds us, "In the final analysis, phenomenology was born from the moment when, leaving aside—either temporarily or permanently—the question of being, the mode of appearing of beings was dealt with as an autonomous problem [. . .]. Isn't Husserl's phenomenology an extraordinary forty-year-long effort at eliminating ontology, in the classical sense inherited from Plato and Aristotle and preserved by Descartes and Kant as well as in the Hegelian and Heideggerian sense? Doesn't this constitute a movement toward a philosophy without absolute?" *À l'école de la phénoménologie* (Paris: Vrin, 1986), 141 and 144 [my translation—JLM].

6. See Edmund Husserl, *Ideas Pertaining to a Pure Phenomenology and to a Phenomenological Philosophy* [1913] (Indianapolis: Hackett Publishing Co., 2014), § 24.

7. Jean-Luc Marion, *Being Given* [1997] (Stanford, Calif.: Stanford University Press, 2002), 5.

8. Marion, *Being Given*, 2.

9. Marion, *Being Given*, 9.

10. Marion, *Being Given*, 9.

11. Marion, *Being Given*, 13.

12. Edmund Husserl, *Idées directrices pour une phénoménologie et une philosophie phénoménologique pure, I* [1913] (Paris: Gallimard, 1950), 52; cited in Marion, *Being Given*, 12.

13. Marion, *Being Given*, 15–16.

14. Marion, *Being Given*, 17.

15. Marion, *Being Given*, 25.

16. Marion, *Being Given*, 27.

17. Marion, *Being Given*, 28.

18. Marion, *Being Given*, 26.

19. Martin Heidegger, *Being and Time*, § 2. Cited in Marion, *Being Given*, 33.

20. François Vézin translates *Es gibt* as *il y a* [there is] (*Être et temps* [Paris: Gallimard, 2004], 30), as does Emmanuel Martineau (http://www.oocities.org/nythamar/etretemps.pdf, 28).

21. Marion, *Being Given*, 34.

22. Heidegger, *On Time and Being*, 18. The first citation is translated by Marion in *Being Given*, 34–35.

23. We will return to this question at the end of this chapter. To be precise, *cela donne* [it gives] translates *das gibt* rather than *es gibt*. *Es gibt* is the equivalent of *es regnet* [it is raining]; "it gives" should thus be understood as meaning "there is giving." In addition, Marion's choice of the demonstrative *cela* establishes a distinction from the outset by pointing to a specific field of reference.

24. Marion, *Being Given*, 36.

25. Marion, *Being Given*, 37.

26. Marion, *Being Given*, 39.

27. Marion, *Being Given*, 53.

28. Marion, *Being Given*, 54.

29. Marion, *Being Given*, 338n99.

30. Marion, *Being Given*, 56.

31. Marion, *Being Given*, 60–61.

32. Marion, *Being Given*, 69.

33. Marion, *Being Given*, 27.

34. [In French,] a *paronymie* is a coincidental resemblance between two words without a shared origin, as between *bailler* and *bâiller*, or *chasse* and *châsse*.

35. Marion, *Being Given*, 74.

36. Jacques Derrida, *Given Time I* (Chicago: University of Chicago Press, 1992), 13.

37. Marion, *Being Given*, 78.

38. Marion, *Being Given*, 79–80.

39. Derrida, *Given Time*, 54.

40. Marion, *Being Given*, 80.

41. Marion, *Being Given*, 81.

42. Marion, *Being Given*, 85.

43. Marion, *Being Given*, 347n40.

44. Marion, *Being Given*, 106.

45. Marion, *Being Given*, 106.

46. Emmanuel Levinas, *Totality and Infinity* [1961] (Pittsburgh: Duquesne University Press, 1969), 134.

47. Marion, *Being Given*, 86.

48. Marion, *Being Given*, 89.

49. Marion, *Being Given*, 113.

50. Marion, *Being Given*, 83.

51. Marion, *Being Given*, 73.

52. Marion, *Being Given*, 75.

53. Marion, *Being Given*, 113.

54. Marion, *Being Given*, 37.

55. Marion, *Being Given*, 69.

56. Dominique Janicaud, *Phenomenology Wide Open* (New York: Fordham University Press, 2005), 35.

57. Janicaud, *Phenomenology Wide Open*, 37.

58. Jocelyn Benoist, "L'écart plutôt que l'excédent," *Philosophie* 78 (2003): 77–78.

59. Benoist, "L'écart plutôt que l'excédent," 82.

60. Benoist, "L'écart plutôt que l'excédent," 82.

61. Heidegger, *On Time and Being*.

62. Marion expresses this vigorously as follows: "It is useless to emphasize here the bottleneck into which one is led by stubbornly refusing to translate 'Es gibt' by 'cela donne' or 'it gives'—unless one adds an unjustifiable gloss, the French and the English become unintelligible while the German remains limpid" (*Being Given*, 335n67).

63. Heidegger, *On Time and Being*, 6.

64. André Sauge, a well-informed philosopher and philologist, notes that *donner* [to give] is a notion that emerged late as a result of a long semantic evolution. In Tocharian the radical means "to take"; in Greek the verb δί-δω-μι [I give] probably originally meant, because of its reduplication (in the present tense): "I act in such a way that someone takes." *To give* must have originally meant: "I act in such a way that someone accepts something and becomes its owner." The act of giving was viewed from the perspective of the recipient rather than the giver. The crucial moment was that of acceptance. Acceptance meant that the recipient accepted the commitment implied— for example, by taking something from a host. A good that was ours, now owned by another, has been taken without being stolen. Germanic languages have preserved as an explicit theme the trace of this ancient meaning in the

form of *two different radicals*, one found in *geben* and the other in *haben*. The presence in German of two different radicals (**hab-/*geb-*) suggests that they originate from two different roots and that **h-* is not a trace of the same phoneme as **g*. In this case the most convincing clue is provided by Latin. As in German, in Latin there are two different families, *hab-e-o* and *cap-i-o*; *hab-e-o* is the counterpart of the German *haben*, and *cap-i-o* of the German *geb-en* (there is a match between voiced and voiceless consonants at the same point of articulation).

Ernout and Meillet explain: "Lat. *habe-* (with a long e, indicating a condition) is to the Irish *gaibim* 'I take' as the old German *habe-* (*haben*, to have) is to the Latin *capio*, Gothic *hafja*," from which *heben* "to raise" (to remove) originates, according to the authors. They thus refer to *capio*, mentioning that this verb must have been formed based on a radical *kep-* (with a long *e*). "This radical competed with another one, closely related, that began with *gh-* and had the same vowel, and (ill-defined) final labial." (Alfred Ernout and Antoine Meillet, *Dictionnaire étymologique de la langue latine: Histoire des mots* [C. Klincksieck: Paris, 1939], *capio* entry). The French verb *happer* [to catch] and the Greek κάπ-τ-ω [I swallow or catch (I appropriate)] seem to preserve a trace of the same radical. All those elements suggest that within one of those languages or across languages there was a crisscrossing between the radicals **kep-* and **gheb-*, whose meanings were close, both involving the idea of taking—in one case in the sense of "grabbing quickly" and "appropriating" (irreversibly, for example, with respect to food), in the other in the sense of "taking" or "holding." Was food the prototypical object of taking, appropriated by swallowing it? Was the shared idea behind those two radicals, "acting in such a way that someone takes something and uses it as his property" or "appropriates it"? We can conclude that on a semantic level *haben* and *geben* were originally close. My own hypothesis is that *haben* meant "to own," while *geben*, through a construction of meaning akin to that of the radical **do-*, originally meant "to act in such a way that someone takes ownership" of something. I have in mind the concrete image "to take in one's hand," but as part of the shift to this meaning there are mediations of which I am unsure. From the idea of giving, the German language seems to have preserved what was originally sensed as its central core: to take something as one's legitimate property. What mattered was not "to give," but to be able to obligate others.

65. This can be clearly observed in the phrase, *Es gibt keine Gabe*, which should be translated as "there is no gift," rather than "it gives no gift," which would verge on nonsense.

66. It is interesting that those resources of European languages have no counterparts in languages from different cultural areas (such as China, Japan,

and Korea). This affects the translation not only of Heidegger's *Es gibt* and *Geben*, but also of Husserl's *Gegebenheit*. In Chinese and Japanese (which are unrelated languages) the lexicon of the gift is strictly circumscribed within the lexical field of presents (which forces translators to use fairly complex formulations to translate "givenness"). On the contrary, the semantic value of *Es gibt* as "there is," without any suggestion of a gift, is fairly easily conveyed by infinitive forms of the verb "to be" or its equivalent (I would like to thank Namiko Haruki and Chunlin Li for their respective explanations about Japanese and Chinese).

67. Heidegger, *On Time and Being*, 18. Let us note once again that *es* is the counterpart of the French pronoun *il* in its neutral sense [it], as in *es regnet* [it is raining], whereas the French *cela* [that] is the counterpart of the German *das* and would be appropriate only to translate *das gibt*.

68. With respect to those technical formulations see, for example, Lucien Tesnière's analyses in *Elements of Structural Syntax* (Amsterdam: Benjamins, 2015), Chapters 102 and 103.

69. This remarkably insistent use of the pronominal construction is not unique to Marion. It is found across all phenomenological writings, where it surrounds concepts with an allegorizing halo that tends to give this kind of philosophical prose a particular dramatic feel and to generate unclassifiable fictional objects.

70. This project becomes clearer in J.-L. Marion's *In Excess: Studies of Saturated Phenomena* (New York: Fordham University Press, 2002).

6. RICOEUR: RECIPROCITY AND MUTUALITY—
FROM THE GOLDEN RULE TO AGAPĒ

1. Paul Ricoeur, *Oneself as Another* (Chicago: University of Chicago Press, 1992).

2. Ricoeur, *Oneself as Another*, 239.

3. Cited in Ricoeur, *Oneself as Another*, 219. [In the Babylonian Talmud the complete text of the sentence quoted is as follows: "What is hateful to you, do not to your neighbor: that is the whole Torah; the rest is commentary; go and learn it."—JLM]

4. Matt. 7:12; the same statement appears in Luke 6:31.

5. Ricoeur notes that Kant rarely quotes the Golden Rule, "and only disdainfully" (*Oneself as Another*, 223).

6. In his dialogue with Jean-Pierre Changeux, Ricoeur also shows his openness to ethological inquiry; after emphasizing the importance of the data provided by primatology to identify the specificity of moral rules, he notes: "Thus one might say, following Darwin, that the golden rule has its origin in moral evolution, which takes over from biological evolution. For 'has its

origin' I would substitute 'searches for its origin.' One searches for what in biological evolution prepares the way for the golden rule [. . .] following the example of humanity's greatest sages." *What Makes Us Think?* (Princeton: Princeton University Press, 2000), 192.

7. Ricoeur, *Oneself as Another*, 172.

8. Aristotle, *Nicomachean Ethics*, IX, 9.

9. Ricoeur, *Oneself as Another*, 187 [my translation—JLM].

10. Ricoeur, *Oneself as Another*, 187.

11. Aristotle, *Nicomachean Ethics*, VIII, 2, 1155b, 25–30 (my italics). For the original Greek, see *Aristotelis Ethica Nicomachea*, edited by Ingram Bywater (Oxford: Oxford Classical Texts, 1986).

12. Aristotle, *Nicomachean Ethics*, VIII, 2, 1155b, 30–35.

13. Aristotle, *Nicomachean Ethics*, 13, 1162b–1163a.

14. Aristotle, *Nicomachean Ethics*, VIII, 14, 1163a–b.

15. Aristotle, *Nicomachean Ethics*, V, 8, 1132b.

16. See Pierre Chantraine, *Dictionnaire étymologique de la langue grecque* (Paris: Klincksieck, 1970).

17. See the important anthropological collection edited by Raymond Verdier, *La Vengeance* (Paris: Cujas, 1980–86).

18. Aristotle, *Nicomachean Ethics*, V, 8, 1133a.

19. In particular René A. Gauthier and Jean-Yves Jolif, who in their critical edition of the *Nicomachean Ethics* (Louvain: Publications Universitaires, 1970), 2:369 *ff.*, confess their discomfort with this passage, which appears to them inconsistent with the rest of the text. From our own point of view the question raised is quite clear.

20. For a precise presentation of this lexicon, see Evelyne Scheid-Tissinier, *Les Usages du don chez Homère* (Nancy: Presses universitaires de Nancy, 1994), Chapter 1: "Les verbes du don et de l'échange."

21. Moses Finley discusses this at length in *The World of Odysseus* (London: Chatto and Windus, 1956).

22. Marcel Mauss, *The Gift: The Form and Reason for Exchange in Archaic Societies* [1925] (London: Routledge, 1990).

23. Ricoeur notes: "The Golden Rule appears to be part of the *endoxa* claimed by Aristotle's ethics, one of those received notions that the philosopher does not have to invent, but to clarify and justify." (*Oneself as Another*, 219).

24. Ricoeur, *Oneself as Another*, 203.

25. Immanuel Kant, *Groundwork of the Metaphysics of Morals*, trans. Mary Gregor (Cambridge: Cambridge University Press, 1997), 7.

26. Kant, *Groundwork of the Metaphysics of Morals*, 31.

27. Kant, *Groundwork of the Metaphysics of Morals*, 38.

28. This concept must be situated precisely within the trinomial *unity of the form* (the law), *plurality of matter or its objects* (the ends), and *totality of its system* (forming a nature), which Kant presents as the categories to be considered to completely determine a realm of ends (see Ricoeur, *Oneself as Another*, 211).

29. Ricoeur, *Oneself as Another*, 224.

30. Ricoeur, *Oneself as Another*, 224.

31. Ricoeur, *Oneself as Another*, 224–25.

32. Immanuel Kant, *The Metaphysics of Morals*, in *Practical Philosophy* (Cambridge: Cambridge University Press, 1996), 570.

33. Kant, *The Metaphysics of Morals*.

34. Kant, *The Metaphysics of Morals*, 579 (Kant's emphasis).

35. Ricoeur, *Oneself as Another*, 331 *ff.* See also "La Cinquième Méditation" in *À l'école de la phénoménologie* (Paris: Vrin, 1986): 197–226.

36. Ricoeur, *Oneself as Another*, 336.

37. Ricoeur, *Oneself as Another*, 338.

38. The concept of *recognition* pervades Ricoeur's entire work from the 1950s (see "Sympathie et respect," in *Revue de Métaphysique et de Morale* 59, 1954) to more recent considerations such as: "The term 'recognition' seems to me much more important than that of 'identity' which is the focus most of the time of the debate on multiculturalism. In the notion of identity there is only the idea of sameness; whereas recognition is a concept that directly integrates otherness and allows a dialectic of the same and the other." See *Critique and Conviction* (New York: Columbia University Press, 1995), 60.

39. Ricoeur, *Oneself as Another*, 212.

40. Ricoeur, *Oneself as Another*, 22.

41. Ricoeur, *Memory, History, Forgetting* (Chicago: University of Chicago Press, 2004); *The Course of Recognition* (Cambridge, Mass.: Harvard University Press, 2005).

42. Paul Ricoeur, "Epilogue: Difficult Forgiveness," in *Memory, History, Forgetting*, 457–506.

43. Ricoeur, "Epilogue: Difficult Forgiveness," 478.

44. Luke 6:32–37 and Matthew 5:44.

45. Ricoeur, *Memory, History, Forgetting*, 483.

46. Ricoeur, *The Course of Recognition*, 232.

47. Marcel Hénaff, *The Price of Truth: Gift, Money, and Philosophy* (Stanford, Calif.: Stanford University Press, 2010), Chapter 4: "The Enigma of Ceremonial Gift Exchange."

48. Ricoeur, *The Course of Recognition*, 221.

49. Ricoeur, *The Course of Recognition*, 223. [Translation altered to reflect Ricoeur's spelling of *agapē* in the original—JLM.]

50. Ricoeur, *The Course of Recognition*, 242.

51. This is the program presented in the Seventh Study of *Oneself as Another*, 169–202.

52. Ricoeur does not preclude the consideration of *capacities* other than the ones he explicitly explores.

7. PHILOSOPHY AND ANTHROPOLOGY: WITH LEFORT AND DESCOMBES

1. On this question, see the excellent collection by Jocelyn Benoist and Bruno Karsenti, eds., *Phénoménologie et sociologie* (Paris: PUF, 2001).

2. This writing is reprinted with this title as Chapter 1 in Claude Lefort, *Les Formes de l'histoire. Essais d'anthropologie politique* (Paris: Gallimard, 1978).

3. Claude Lévi-Strauss, *Introduction to the Work of Marcel Mauss* [1950] (London: Routledge & K. Paul, 1987).

4. Let us note that Lévi-Strauss does not claim that kinship systems constitute the only or even the favored form of organization of those societies: "The kinship system does not have the same importance in all cultures. For some cultures it provides the active principle regulating all or most of the social relationships. In other groups, as in our own society, this function is either absent altogether or greatly reduced." *Structural Anthropology* (New York: Basic Books, 1963), 47.

5. Claude Lefort, "Sociétés sans histoire et historicité," *Cahiers internationaux de sociologie* 12 (1952); reprinted in *Les Formes de l'histoire*, Chapter 2.

6. This somewhat unfair judgment on Durkheim clearly displays the suspicion shared by the authors inspired by phenomenology and Marxism.

7. Marx's term "the total man" designates the reconciliation between man and nature, among men, and between individual and species; this reconciliation is understood as man's reappropriation of the entirety of his historical development in a unity at the same time social, political, ethical, and aesthetic.

8. Lefort, *Les Formes de l'histoire*, 17 [my translation—JLM].

9. In Germany Alfred Schutz, an Austrian economist who became a student of Husserl before moving to the United States, had already set up the foundations of what would later be called a "phenomenological sociology."

10. Marcel Mauss, *The Gift: The Form and Reason for Exchange in Archaic Societies* [1925] (London: Routledge, 1990), 275 (Lefort's emphasis).

11. Lefort, *Les Formes de l'histoire*, 18 [my translation—JLM].

12. Lefort, *Les Formes de l'histoire*, 16.

13. Lefort, *Les Formes de l'histoire*, 17.

14. Lefort, *Les Formes de l'histoire*, 27.

15. Bronislaw Malinowski, *Argonauts of the Western Pacific* (London: Routledge & Sons, 1922).

16. As we saw in Chapter 2 above, this exacerbated form of *potlatch* appeared at a late stage.

17. Claude Lévi-Strauss, *The Elementary Structures of Kinship* (Boston: Beacon Press, 1969), 481.

18. Lefort, *Les Formes de l'histoire*, 21. Lévi-Strauss distinguishes among models of relationships between those immediately observable in the agents' existence, which he calls "mechanical" (as are the parts of a machine) and those brought to the fore by analyses involving large numbers of individuals or cases, which he calls "statistical."

19. No field investigation has ever shown such a feeling of confusion in natives; this confusion is more likely experienced by investigators during their first approaches—above all, it characterizes armchair ethnographers who have never conducted direct research in the populations involved.

20. Lefort, *Les Formes de l'histoire*, 27 (my emphasis).

21. Lefort, *Les Formes de l'histoire*, 19.

22. Lefort, *Les Formes de l'histoire*, 20.

23. Lefort, *Les Formes de l'histoire*, 28.

24. Lefort, *Les Formes de l'histoire*, 28–29.

25. Vincent Descombes, *The Institutions of Meaning* [1996] (Cambridge, Mass.: Harvard University Press, 2014).

26. Lucien Tesnière, *Elements of Structural Syntax* (Amsterdam: John Benjamins Publishing Co., 2015).

27. Descombes, *The Institutions of Meaning*, 237.

28. Bertrand Russell, *An Inquiry into Meaning and Truth* (London: George Allen & Unwin, 1940).

29. Descombes, *The Institutions of Meaning*, 240.

30. Descombes, *The Institutions of Meaning*, 238.

31. Charles Sanders Peirce, *Collected Papers* (Cambridge, Mass.: Harvard University Press, 1958), Vol. 8, Book 8, § 321, 225–26; cited by Descombes in *The Institutions of Meaning*, 241.

32. Descombes, *The Institutions of Meaning*, 242.

33. Descombes, *The Institutions of Meaning*, 246.

34. Ludwig Wittgenstein, *Philosophical Investigations*, § 268, cited in Descombes, *The Institutions of Meaning*, 243.

35. Wittgenstein, *Philosophical Investigations*, § 268, cited in Descombes, *The Institutions of Meaning*, 243.

36. Vincent Descombes, "Relation intersubjective et relation sociale," in *Phénoménologie et sociologie*, ed. Benoist and Karsenti, 127–55; a shorter version of this writing is reprinted in Chapter 38 of Vincent Descombes, *Complément du sujet* (Paris: Gallimard, 2004).

37. Descombes, "Relation intersubjective et relation sociale," in *Phénoménologie et sociologie*, ed. Benoist and Karsenti, 144. Original emphasis.

38. Descombes, "Relation intersubjective et relation sociale," in *Phénoménologie et sociologie*, ed. Benoist and Karsenti, 138.

39. Tesnière proposes to add another list of trivalent verbs that designate telling: to say, tell, state, report, relate, present, explain, teach, demonstrate, prove, etc. (*Elements of Structural Syntax*, 257).

40. Mauss, *The Gift*.

41. Descombes, *The Institutions of Meaning*, 247.

42. Descombes, *The Institutions of Meaning*, 247.

43. Descombes does discuss briefly the concept of reciprocity in a later section (*The Institutions of Meaning*, 267–68)—taking up remarks by Louis Dumont, he criticizes Lévi-Strauss for using this concept too broadly, but to restrict its use without specifying why it is not very useful. A critical assessment of the complexity of the uses and senses of the concept would be preferable; see Chapter 4 above.

44. See Mauss, *The Gift*, 11.

45. Lévi-Strauss, *Introduction to the Work of Marcel Mauss*, 47.

46. Mauss, *The Gift*, 11–13.

47. Dominique Casajus is among the few researchers who considers this point, in "L'énigme de la troisième personne," in *Différences, valeurs, hiérarchie: Textes offerts à Louis Dumont*, ed. J. C. Galey (Paris: EHESS, 1982), 65–77.

48. On Ranaipiri's speech, Mauss comments: "This text . . . is . . . at times astonishingly clear, and presenting only one obscure feature: the intervention of a third person" (*The Gift*, 11).

49. Marcel Mauss, "La cohésion sociale dans les sociétés polysegmentaires," *Oeuvres* (Paris: Minuit, 1969), 3:6–33.

50. Lévi-Strauss, *Introduction to the Work of Marcel Mauss*, 46.

51. Lévi-Strauss, *Introduction to the Work of Marcel Mauss*, 47; my emphasis.

52. Lévi-Strauss, *Structural Anthropology*, 46.

53. See Descombes, *The Institutions of Meaning*, 262.

8. PROPOSITIONS III: THE DUAL RELATIONSHIP AND THE THIRD PARTY

1. "[Die Gesellschaft] da existiert, wo mehrere Individuen in Wechselwirkung treten." Georg Simmel, *Soziologie: Untersuchungen über die Formen der Vergesellschaftung* [1908] (Berlin: Dunker & Humblot, 1958), 4. "[Society] refers to the psychological interaction among individual human beings." *The*

Sociology of Georg Simmel, trans. and ed. Kurt H. Wolf (New York: Free Press, 1964), 9.

2. It is tempting to consider here another figure of the third party: the victim or character excluded from the group. But this pariah is not rejected by two factions; it is instead expelled from the group as a whole, whose tensions he focalizes and whose phobias he condenses. Rather than a third party, he is someone who does not belong. This specific point can remind us of the model of the "scapegoat," provided that we keep in mind that the victim is presented in conflict with the group, and that it symbolizes the figure of the enemy; the relationship is therefore dual. What is missing in this case is precisely the existence of a third-party arbiter capable to establish the facts and return justice.

3. Reprinted in Emmanuel Levinas, *Entre nous: Thinking-of-the-Other* [1991] (New York: Columbia University Press, 1998), 13–38.

4. Levinas, *Entre nous*, 19 and 21.

5. This choice of word seems surprising on the part of a thinker who must have been well aware of the canonical distinction established by Aristotle between action (*praxis*) and work (*poiēsis*); Levinas somehow merges the two concepts.

6. Levinas, *Entre nous*, 29.

7. Levinas, *Entre nous*, 22.

8. Levinas, *Entre nous*, 20.

9. Emmanuel Levinas, *Totality and Infinity* [1961] (Pittsburgh: Duquesne University Press, 1969), 213.

10. Levinas, *Totality and Infinity*.

11. Levinas, *Totality and Infinity*, 96.

12. Levinas, *Totality and Infinity*, 98.

13. Levinas, *Totality and Infinity*, 215.

14. Emmanuel Levinas, *Otherwise than Being or Beyond Essence* [1978] (The Hague: Martinus Nijhoff, 1981), 157.

15. Levinas, *Otherwise than Being*.

16. Levinas, *Otherwise than Being*, 158.

17. Levinas, *Otherwise than Being*, 159.

18. Émile Benveniste, "Relationships of Person in the Verb" [1946]. This reflection is continued in "The Nature of Pronouns" [1956] and in "Subjectivity in Language" [1963]; these articles are reprinted as chapters 18, 20, and 21 respectively in *Problems in General Linguistics* (Coral Gables, Fla.: University of Miami Press, 1971), 195–204.

19. Benveniste, *Problems in General Linguistics*, 218.

20. Benveniste, *Problems in General Linguistics*, 218.

21. Benveniste, *Problems in General Linguistics*, 218.

22. Benveniste, *Problems in General Linguistics*, 201.

23. Benveniste, *Problems in General Linguistics*, 225.

24. Benveniste, *Problems in General Linguistics*, 224–25.

25. Benveniste, *Problems in General Linguistics*, 226.

26. Benveniste, *Problems in General Linguistics*, 225.

27. John L. Austin, *How to Do Things with Words* (Oxford: Clarendon, 1962).

28. John Searle, *Speech Acts: An Essay in the Philosophy of Language* (London: Cambridge University Press, 1969).

29. François Recanati, *Meaning and Force: The Pragmatics of Performative Utterances* (Cambridge: Cambridge University Press, 1987). O. Ducrot, *Dire et ne pas dire*, 2nd printing (Paris: Hermann, 1980).

30. Edmond Ortigues, *Le Discours et le symbole* (Paris: Aubier, 1962).

31. Ortigues, *Le Discours et le Symbole*, 60–61 [my translation—JLM].

32. Ortigues, *Le Discours et le Symbole*, 61.

33. Ortigues, *Le Discours et le Symbole*, 63.

34. Ortigues, *Le Discours et le Symbole*, 64.

35. Ortigues, *Le Discours et le Symbole*, 65.

36. As Sperber explains, "Symbolism conceived in this way is not a means of encoding information, but a means of organising it" (Dan Sperber, *Rethinking Symbolism* [Cambridge: Cambridge University Press, 1975], 70). As a consequence, "Symbols are not signs. They are not paired with their interpretation in a code structure. Their interpretations are not meanings." (Sperber, *Rethinking Symbolism*, 85).

37. Charles S. Peirce, *Collected Papers* (Cambridge: Mass.: Harvard University Press, 1958), Vol. 8, Book 2, Chapter 8, § 33, 225–26.

38. Erving Goffman, *Encounters: Two Studies in the Sociology of Interaction* (Indianapolis, Ind.: Bobbs-Merrill, 1961).

39. An excellent presentation of this question can be found in Bernard Conein, *Les Sens sociaux* (Paris: Economica, 2005), Chapter 9: "Coordination de l'attention et genèse des groupes sociaux." Conein considers these phenomena not only in humans, but also in various types of primates, and he shows the breadth of the ethological investigations in this field. More precisely, just as well as a third-party agent about whom the two parties involved exchange glances, the third party can also be an element of the environment on which they focus their attention.

40. Recent research, such as Laurent Barry's *La Parenté* (Paris: Gallimard, Folio Essais, 2008), tends to show that if the prohibition of incest is indeed a universal phenomenon, its reason for being is not only the obligation of reciprocity, since in many populations—such as Bedouin societies—the favored form of marriage is with the daughter of the paternal uncle, and thus a parallel cousin. In this case the prohibition concerns primarily everything

associated with the mother and her consanguineous relatives, and not the father and his consanguineous relatives; as a result the daughter of the paternal uncle is a possible and even desirable spouse (whereas this type of marriage is considered outright incestuous in most other kinship systems).

41. Claude Lévi-Strauss, *The Elementary Structures of Kinship* (Boston: Beacon Press, 1969), 65.

42. Claude Lévi-Strauss, *Structural Anthropology* (New York: Basic Books, 1963), 72. My emphasis.

43. On negative reciprocity, see Chapter 4 above.

44. Maurice Godelier thus shows that among the Baruya of New Guinea, bars of salt constitute at the same time precious goods used within the group during initiation ceremonies and exchange currency used outside the group to obtain useful goods; see Maurice Godelier, *The Enigma of the Gift* (Chicago: University of Chicago Press, 1999), 139–40.

45. This is the meaning of the term in Francis Jacques's *L'Espace logique de l'interlocution* (Paris: PUF, 1992), 397 *ff.* Gilles Fauconnier presents a different conception in *La Coréférence* (Paris: Seuil, 1974).

46. We can thus say with Michel Serres that in its uncountable multiplicity the world exists as a third party in every form of knowledge: It instructs us by making possible our mutual relationship as a continual intercrossing of the differences among things. Learning is always the learning of otherness, hybridizing among opposites; the intermediate space of the third party is this interbreeding, which gives rise to the new. See Michel Serres, *Le Tiers-instruit* (Paris: Bourrin, 1991).

47. This is Peirce's crucial argument: The triad does not arise from the dyad. The triad brings a different order in which the relationship among the three terms is irreducible to their sum.

POSTLIMINARY DIRECTIONS

1. In this dual requirement two major sources of modern thought emerge: the emergence in the early twentieth century of (1) Husserl's phenomenology, and (2) social anthropology, or in more general terms philosophies of the description of experience (of a Wittgensteinian or pragmatist type) and sociologies of collective practices.

2. In German this would create an oddly redundant statement, *Es gibt Gabe*, comparable, however, to *Die Sprache spricht.*

3. H. Maldiney, *Regard, parole, espace* (Lausanne: L'Âge d'homme, 1973) [my translation—JLM].

4. [The reference is to a short story of the same name by Henry James—JLM.]

5. Seneca, *De beneficiis*, I–IV, 2.

BOOKS AND ARTICLES CITED OR CONSULTED

Anspach, Mark R. *À Charge de revanche: Figures élémentaires de la réciprocité.* Paris: Seuil, 2002.

Austin, John L. *How to Do Things with Words.* Oxford: Clarendon, 1962.

Barnett, Homer G. "The Nature of the Potlatch." *American Anthropologist* 40 (1938): 349–58.

Barry, Laurent. *La Parenté.* Folio Essais. Paris: Gallimard, 2008.

Bataille, Georges. *The Accursed Share.* Translated by Robert Hurley. New York: Zone Books, 1991.

Bedorf, Thomas. *Dimensionen des Dritten.* Munich: Fink, 2003.

Benoist, Jocelyn. "L'écart plutôt que l'excédent." *Philosophie* 78 (2003): 77–93.

———. "Qu'est-ce que le donné." *Archives de Philosophie* 59, no. 4 (December 1996): 45–79.

Benoist, Jocelyn, and Bruno Karsenti, eds. *Phénoménologie et sociologie.* Paris: PUF, 2001.

Benveniste, Émile. *Problems in General Linguistics* [1966]. Coral Gables, Fla.: University of Miami Press, 1971.

Boas, Franz. *Kwakiutl Ethnography*, edited by Helen Codere. Chicago: University of Chicago Press, 1966.

Boltanski, Luc, and Laurent Thévenot. *On Justification: Economies of Worth.* Princeton: Princeton University Press, 2006.

Bruaire, Claude. *L'Être et l'esprit.* Paris: PUF, 1983.

Caillé, Alain. *Anthropologie du don.* Paris: Desclée de Brouwer, 2000.

Caputo, John D. "Apostles of the Impossible: On God and the Gift in Derrida and Marion." In *God, the Gift, and Postmodernism*, edited by John Caputo and Michael Scanlon, 185–222. Bloomington: Indiana University Press, 1999.

Casajus, Dominique. "L'énigme de la troisième personne." In *Différences, valeurs, hiérarchie, Textes offerts à Louis Dumont*, edited by J. C. Galey, 65–77. Paris: EHESS, 1982.

Chalier, Catherine, and Miguel Abensour, eds. *Cahiers de L'Herne* 60. Special Edition: *Levinas* (1991).

Chanial, Philippe, ed. *La Société vue du don*. Paris: La Découverte, 2009.

———. "L'instant fugitif où la société prend: Le don, la partie et le tout." *La Revue du MAUSS* 36 (2nd Semester, 2010): 521–38.

———. "Pour une anthropologie normative de la relation humaine." In *La Sociologie comme philosophie politique*, 254–72. Paris: La Découverte, 2011.

Cheah, Pheng, and Suzanne Guerlac, eds. *Derrida and the Time of the Political*. Durham, N.C.: Duke University Press, 2009.

Codere, Helen. *Fighting with Property: A Study of Kwakiutl Potlatching and Warfare 1792–1930*. New York: J. J. Augustin, 1950.

Conein, Bernard. *Les Sens sociaux*. Paris: Economica, 2005.

Davy, Georges. *La Foi jurée: Étude sociologique du problème du contrat*. Paris: Alcan, 1922.

Derrida, Jacques. *The Gift of Death*. Translated by David Wills. Chicago: University of Chicago Press, 2008.

———. *Given Time*. Translated by Peggy Kamuf. Chicago: University of Chicago Press, 1992.

———. *Of Hospitality*. Translated by Rachel Bowlby. Stanford, Calif.: Stanford University Press, 2000.

———. "Violence and Metaphysics." In *Writing and Difference*. Translated by Alan Bass. Chicago: University of Chicago Press, 1978.

Descola, Philippe. *Beyond Nature and Culture*. Chicago: University of Chicago Press, 2013.

Descombes, Vincent. *The Institutions of Meaning* [1996]. Translated by Stephen Adam Schwartz. Cambridge, Mass.: Harvard University Press, 2014.

———. "Relation intersubjective et relation sociale." In *Phénoménologie et sociologie*, edited by Jocelyn Benoist and Bruno Karsenti, 127–55. Paris, PUF, 2001.

Detienne, Marcel. *The Masters of Truth in Archaic Greece*. Translated by Janet Lloyd. New York: Zone Books, 1996.

Dewitte, Jacques. "Un beau risque à couri." *Cahiers d'études lévinassiennes* 1 (2002): 55–76.

Ducrot, Oswald. *Dire et ne pas dire*. 2nd ed. Paris: Hermann, 1980.

Ernout, Alfred, and Antoine Meillet. *Dictionnaire étymologique de la langue latine: Histoire des mots*. C. Klincksieck: Paris, 1939.

Esprit 323. Special Issue: *La Pensée Ricoeur* (March–April 2006).

Falque, Emmanuel. "Une phénoménologie de l'exceptionnel." *Philosophie* 78 (2003): 53–76.

Fauconnier, Gilles. *La Coréférence*. Paris: Seuil, 1974.

Finley, Moses. *Early Greece*. New York: Norton, 1970.

———. *The World of Odysseus*. London: Chatto and Windus, 1956.

Garapon, Antoine. "Justice et reconnaissance." *Esprit* 323. Special Issue: *La Pensée Ricoeur* (March–April 2006): 231–48.

Gasché, Rodolphe. *Inventions of Difference: On Jacques Derrida*. Cambridge, Mass.: Harvard University Press, 1994.

———. *The Tain of the Mirror: Derrida and the Philosophy of Reflection*. Cambridge, Mass.: Harvard University Press, 1994.

Gernet, Louis. *The Anthropology of Ancient Greece*. Baltimore: Johns Hopkins University Press, 1981.

Godbout, Jacques, with Alain Caillé. *Ce qui circule entre nous*. Paris: Seuil, 2004.

———. *L'Esprit du don*. Paris: La Découverte, 1992.

Godelier, Maurice. *Aux Fondements des sociétés humaines*. Paris: Albin Michel, 2007.

———. *The Enigma of the Gift*. Chicago: University of Chicago Press, 1999.

Goffman, Erving. *Encounters: Two Studies in the Sociology of Interaction*. Indianapolis, Ind.: Bobbs-Merrill, 1961.

Goodall, Jane. *The Chimpanzees of Gombe: Patterns of Behavior*. Cambridge, Mass.: Harvard University Press, 1986.

Gouldner, Alvin. "The Norm of Reciprocity." *American Sociological Review* 25, no. 2 (1960): 161–78.

Greisch, Jean. *Le Buisson ardent*. Paris: Cerf, 2004.

———. *Paul Ricoeur: L'itinérance du sens*. Grenoble: Jérôme Millon, 2001.

Heidegger, Martin. *Being and Time*. Translated by John Macquarrie. New York: Harper, 1962.

———. *On Time and Being*. Translated by Joan Stambaugh. New York: Harper & Row, 1972.

———. *Zeit und Sein* [1962]. *Gesamtausgabe* XIV. Frankfurt-am-Main: Klostermann, 2007.

Hegel, G. W. F. *Phenomenology of Spirit*. Oxford: Clarendon Press, 1977.

Hénaff, Marcel. *The Price of Truth: Gift, Money, and Philosophy*. Translated by Jean-Louis Morhange. Stanford, Calif.: Stanford University Press, 2010.

Henry, Michel. *Auto-donation*. Paris: Beauchesne, 2004.

———. *I Am the Truth: Toward a Philosophy of Christianity*. Stanford, Calif.: Stanford University Press, 2003.

———. *Incarnation*. Evanston, Ill.: Northwestern University Press, 2015.

———. *Phenomenology of Life*. Paris, PUF, 2004.

———. *Words of Christ*. Grand Rapids, Mich.: William B. Eerdmans, 2012.

Hollier, Denis. *The College of Sociology*. Minneapolis: University of Minnesota P, 1988.

———. *Le Collège de sociologie*. Augmented reprint. Paris: Gallimard, 1995.

Honneth, Axel. *The Struggle for Recognition*. Cambridge: Polity Press, 1995.

Husserl, Edmund. *Cartesian Meditations* [1929]. The Hague: M. Nijhoff, 1977.

———. *Ideas Pertaining to a Pure Phenomenology and to a Phenomenological Philosophy* [1913]. Indianapolis, Ind.: Hackett Publishing Co., 2014.

———. *Idées directrices pour une phénoménologie et une philosophie phénoménologique pure, I*. In *Husserliana*, vol. 24, translated by Paul Ricoeur. Paris: Gallimard, 1950.

Iteanu, André. *La Ronde des échanges: De la circulation aux valeurs chez les Orokaiva*. Paris: Maison des Sciences de l'Homme, 1983.

Jacques, Francis. *L'Espace logique de l'interlocution*. Paris: PUF, 1992.

Janicaud, Dominique. *La Phénoménologie dans tous ses états*. Paris: Gallimard Folio, 2009.

———. *Phenomenology and the "Theological Turn."* New York: Fordham University Press, 2000.

———. *Phenomenology Wide Open*. New York: Fordham University Press, 2005.

Kant, Immanuel. *Critique of Pure Reason*. Translated by Norman Kemp Smith. Basingstoke: Palgrave Macmillan, 2006.

Karsenti, Bruno. *Mauss: L'Homme total*. Paris: PUF, 1997.

Lefort, Claude. "L'échange et la lutte des hommes." *Les Formes de l'histoire: Essais d'anthropologie politique*. Paris: Gallimard, 1978.

Lellouche, Raphaël. *Difficile Levinas*. Paris: L'éclat, 2006.

Lemonnier, Pierre. *Guerres et festins. Paix, échanges et compétitions dans les High Lands de Nouvelle-Guinée*. Paris: CNRS Éditions, 1980.

Levêque, Pierre, and Pierre Vidal-Naquet. *Cleisthenes the Athenian* [1963]. Translated by David Ames Curtis. Atlantic Highlands, N.J., Humanities P, 1996.

Lévi-Strauss, Claude. *The Elementary Structures of Kinship*. Boston: Beacon Press, 1969.

———. *Structural Anthropology*. New York: Basic Books, 1963.

Levinas, Emmanuel. *Alterity and Transcendence* [1995]. New York: Columbia University Press, 1999.

———. *Entre nous: Thinking-of-the-Other* [1991]. New York: Columbia University Press, 1998.

———. *Ethics and Infinity* [1982]. Pittsburgh: Duquesne University Press, 1985.

———. *Existence and Existents* [1947]. The Hague: Martinus Nijhoff, 1978.

———. *Humanism of the Other* [1972]. Urbana: University of Illinois Press, 2003.

———. *Otherwise than Being or Beyond Essence* [1978]. The Hague: Martinus Nijhoff, 1981.

———. *Totality and Infinity* [1961]. Pittsburgh: Duquesne University Press, 1969.

Loute, Alain. *La Création sociale des normes: De la socio-économie des conventions à la philosophie de l'action de Paul Ricoeur*. Zurich: Olms, 2009.

Malinowski, Bronislaw. *Argonauts of the Western Pacific*. London: Routledge & Sons, 1922.

———. *Crime and Custom in Savage Society* [1926]. Home Farm Book, 2006.

Mallet, Marie-Louise, and Ginette Michaud, eds. *Cahiers de L'Herne* 83. Special Issue: *Derrida* (2004).

Marion, Jean-Luc. *Being Given* [1997]. Stanford, Calif.: Stanford University Press, 2002.

———. *In Excess: Studies of Saturated Phenomena* [2001]. New York: Fordham University Press, 2002.

———. *Negative Certainties* [2009]. Chicago: University of Chicago Press, 2015.

———. *Reduction and Givenness* [1989]. Evanston, Ill.: Northwestern University Press, 1998.

Mauss, Marcel. *The Gift: The Form and Reason for Exchange in Archaic Societies* [1925]. London: Routledge, 1990.

———. "Gift, Gift." In *Oeuvres*, 3:46–51. Paris: Minuit, 1969.

———. "La cohésion sociale dans les sociétés polysegmentaires" [1931]. In *Oeuvres*, 3:11–26. Paris: Minuit, 1969.

Mauzé, Marie. "Boas, les Kwakiutl et le *potlatch*: Éléments pour une réévaluation." *L'Homme* 26, no. 4 (1986): 21–63.

McGrew, William C. *Chimpanzee Material Culture: Implications for Human Evolution*. Cambridge: Cambridge University Press, 1992.

McGrew, William C., Linda F. Marchant, and Toshisada Nishida, eds. *Great Ape Societies*. Cambridge: Cambridge University Press, 1990.

Merleau-Ponty, Maurice. *Phenomenology of Perception* [1945]. Abingdon: Routledge, 2012.

Moebius, Stephan. *Die Zauberlehrlinge. Soziologiegeschichte des Collège de Sociologie*. Konstanz, Germany: UVK, 2006.

Mongin, Olivier. *Paul Ricoeur*. Paris: Seuil, 1998.

Nancy, Jean-Luc, ed. *Les Fins de l'homme: À partir du travail de Jacques Derrida*. Colloque de Cerisy. Paris: Galilée, 1980.

Nault, François. *Derrida et la théologie*. Paris: Cerf, 2000.

Ortigues, Edmond. *Le Discours et le Symbole*. Paris: Aubier, 1962.

Peirce, Charles S. *Collected Papers*. Cambridge, Mass.: Harvard University Press, 1958.

———. *Peirce on Signs*, edited by James Hoopes. Chapel Hill: University of North Carolina Press, 1991.

Peperzak, Adriaan. *Beyond: The Philosophy of Emmanuel Levinas*. Evanston, Ill.: Northwestern University Press, 1997.

Polanyi, Karl. *The Great Transformation*. Boston: Beacon Press, 1944.

Rabaté, Jean-Michel, and Michael Wetzel, eds. *L'Éthique du don: Jacques Derrida et la pensée du don*. Paris: Métailié, 1992.

Rabelais, François. *Third Book*, in *The Complete Works of François Rabelais*. Berkeley: University of California Press, 1991.

Rawls, John. *A Theory of Justice*. Cambridge, Mass.: Belknap Press of Harvard University Press, 1971.

Recanati, François. *Meaning and Force: The Pragmatics of Performative Utterances*. Cambridge: Cambridge University Press, 1987.

Revault d'Allonnes, Myriam, and François Azouvi, eds. *Cahiers de L'Herne* 81. Special Edition: *Ricoeur* (2004).

Revue du MAUSS 8. Special Edition: *L'obligation de donner*. (1996).

Ricoeur, Paul. *À l'école de la phénoménologie*. Paris: Vrin, 1986.

———. *The Course of Recognition* [2004]. Translated by David Pellauer. Cambridge, Mass.: Harvard University Press, 2005.

———. "Emmanuel Levinas, penseur du témoignage." In *Répondre d'autrui. Emmanuel Levinas*, edited by J. C. Aeschlimann, 30–39. Lausanne: La Baconnière, 1989

———. *Memory, History, Forgetting* [2000]. Translated by Kathleen Blamey and David Pellauer. Chicago: University of Chicago Press, 2004.

———. *Oneself as Another* [1990]. Translated by Kathleen Blamey. Chicago: University of Chicago Press, 1992.

Richman, Michèle H. *Sacred Revolutions: Durkheim and the College of Sociology*. Minneapolis: University of Minnesota Press, 2002.

Riley, Alexander. *Godless Intellectuals: The Intellectual Pursuit of the Sacred Reinvented*. New York: Berghahn Books, 2011.

Rubel, Paula, and Abraham Rosman. *Your Own Pigs You May Not Eat: A Comparative Study of New Guinea Societies*. Chicago: Chicago University Press, 1978.

Sahlins, Marshall. *Stone Age Economics*. Chicago: University of Chicago Press, 1974.

Sartre, Jean-Paul, *Notebooks for an Ethics* [1948]. Chicago: University of Chicago Press, 1992.

Sauge, André. *De l'Épopée à l'histoire: Fondement de la notion d'histoire*. Frankfurt am Main. New York: Peter Lang, 1992.

———. "Homère, Sophocle, Luc: L'étincelle de la grâce." *Revue du MAUSS* 35 (2010): 173–82.

Scheid-Tissinier, Evelyne. *Les Usages du don chez Homère*. Nancy: Presses Universitaires de Nancy, 1994.

Searle, John. *Speech Acts: An Essay in the Philosophy of Language*. London: Cambridge University Press, 1969.

Seneca, *De beneficiis*. Berkeley: University of California Press, 1950.

Serres, Michel. *Le Tiers-instruit*. Paris: Bourrin, 1991.

Simmel, Georg. *Simmel on Culture: Selected Writings*. Edited by David Frisby and Mike Featherstone. London: Sage, 1997.

———. *The Sociology of Georg Simmel*. Translated and edited by Kurt H. Wolf. New York: Free Press, 1964.

———. *Soziologie: Untersuchungen über die Formen der Vergesellschaftung* [1908]. Berlin: Dunker & Humblot, 1958.

Smith, Adam. *An Inquiry into the Nature and Causes of the Wealth of Nations* [1776]. Oxford: Oxford University Press, 1993.

Sperber, Dan. *Rethinking Symbolism*. Cambridge: Cambridge University Press, 1975.

Stanford, Craig. "The Ape's Gift: Meat-Eating, Meat-Sharing, and Human Evolution." In *Tree of Origin*, edited by Frans de Waal, 96–117. Cambridge, Mass.: Harvard University Press, 2001.

Strathern, Andrew. *The Rope of Moka: Big-Men and Ceremonial Exchange in Mount Hagen New Guinea*. Cambridge: Cambridge University Press, 1971.

Strathern, Marilyn. *The Gender of the Gift: Problems with Women and Problems with Society in Melanesia*. Berkeley: University of California Press, 1988.

Tesnière, Lucien. *Elements of Structural Syntax* [1965]. Amsterdam: John Benjamins Publishing Co., 2015.

Testart, Alain. *Critiques du don: Études sur la circulation marchande*. Paris: Syllepses, 2007.

———. *Les Dons et les Dieux*. Paris: Armand Colin, 1993.

Verdier, Raymond. *La Vengeance*. 4 vols. Paris: Cujas, 1980–86.

Vernant, Jean-Pierre. "The Organization of Space." In *Myth and Thought among the Greeks*. Translated by Janet Lloyd and Jeff Fort, 157–262. London: Routledge and Kegan Paul, 1983.

de Waal, Frans. *Chimpanzee Politics*. Baltimore: Johns Hopkins University Press, 1998.

———. *Peacemaking among Primates*. Cambridge, Mass.: Harvard University Press, 1989.

———. *Primates and Philosophers: How Morality Evolved*. Princeton: Princeton University Press, 2006.

Walzer, Michael. "Complex Equality." In *Spheres of Justice: A Defense of Pluralism and Equality*. New York: Basic Books, 1983.

Weber, Max. *General Economic History*. New York: Collier Books, 1961.

———. *The Sociology of Religion*. Boston: Beacon Press, 1964.

Weiner, Annette. *Inalienable Possessions: The Paradox of Keeping-while-Giving.*
    Berkeley: University of California Press, 1992.
Wittgenstein, Ludwig. *Philosophical Investigations.* Translated by G. E. M.
    Anscombe, P. M. S. Hacker, and Joachim Schulte. Oxford: Blackwell,
    1953.

MARCEL HÉNAFF (1942–2018) was Distinguished Research Professor of Literature and Political Science at the University of California, San Diego. His books in English include *Sade: The Invention of the Libertine Body* (Minnesota, 1999), *Claude Lévi-Strauss and the Making of Structural Anthropology* (Minnesota, 2001), and *The Price of Truth: Gift, Money, and Philosophy* (Stanford, 2010).

JEAN-LOUIS MORHANGE is the translator of Pascal Baudry's *French and Americans: The Other Shore* (Les Frenchies, Inc., 2005) and of Marcel Hénaff's *The Price of Truth: Gift, Money, and Philosophy* (Stanford, 2010).